THE ME I WANT *to* BE

Resources by John Ortberg

Everybody's Normal Till You Get to Know Them
(book, ebook, audio)

God Is Closer Than You Think
(book, ebook, audio, curriculum with Stephen and Amanda Sorenson)

*If You Want to Walk on Water,
You've Got to Get Out of the Boat*
(book, ebook, audio, curriculum with Stephen and Amanda Sorenson)

Know Doubt
(book, ebook, previously titled Faith and Doubt)

The Life You've Always Wanted
(book, ebook, audio, curriculum with Stephen and Amanda Sorenson)

Love Beyond Reason

The Me I Want to Be
(book, ebook, audio, curriculum with Scott Rubin)

Soul Keeping
(book, ebook, curriculum with Christine M. Anderson)

When the Game Is Over, It All Goes Back in the Box
(book, ebook, audio, curriculum with Stephen and Amanda Sorenson)

Who Is This Man?
(book, ebook, audio, curriculum with Christine M. Anderson)

JOHN ORTBERG

THE ME
I WANT *to* BE

BECOMING GOD'S BEST VERSION OF YOU

ZONDERVAN

The Me I Want to Be
Copyright © 2010 by John Ortberg

This title is also available as a Zondervan ebook.
Visit www.zondervan.com/ebooks.

This title is also available in a Zondervan audio edition.
Visit www.zondervan.fm.

Requests for information should be addressed to:

Zondervan, 3900 *Sparks Dr. SE, Grand Rapids, Michigan* 49546

This edition: ISBN 978-0-310-34056-0

Library of Congress Cataloging-in-Publication Data

Ortberg, John.
        The me I want to be : becoming God's best version of you / John Ortberg.
            p. cm.
        ISBN 978-0-310-27592-3 (hardcover, jacketed)
            1. Self-actualization (Psychology) — Religious aspects - Christianity. 2. Christian
        life. I. Title.
        BV4598.2O68 2009
        248.4 — dc22   2009040163

Cover photography: Getty Images

First Printing September 2014 / Printed in the United States of America

contents

acknowledgments

Love is eternal. What we achieve and possess may fade, but not love. Books are gifts when they are acts of love. To what extent this book will be a gift only God knows, but I know that it would not have come into existence without much love from people who matter a great deal to me.

It started with a conversation on a golf course, when a few friends talked about a dream of creating a kind of movement for spiritual growth, and I talked about a book I hoped to write, and we wondered if what we hoped to do might intersect. What you hold is what we hope will be the first milepost on a long journey.

I am deeply grateful to Mark Bankord for his ceaseless encouragement and partnering and optimism and prayer. Sherri Bankord has offered wisdom and feedback; Eric Parks has been a fountain of energy and ideas; Nate May and Kevin Small have added enthusiasm and dreams; Elizabeth Maring and the entire Monvee team have been like working with family. Heartland Community Church in Rockford, Illinois, gave me chances to teach on much of this material and get voluminous feedback that sharpened it enormously.

To Menlo Park Presbyterian Church, I am grateful beyond words for love and shepherding and the freedom to write.

Laura (formerly Ortberg) Turner read through the entire manuscript and made hugely helpful suggestions about content, references, and presentation. I am glad you're a "J." Rick Blackmon has made amazingly generous contributions of his time and thoughts on the writing and beyond. Chuck Bergstrom gave both feedback and laughter. Ron Johnson gave wonderful insights on the structure and thoughts of the manuscript, and he cheered me on when I needed it most. My sister, Barbara Harrison, gave me a boost at just the right time.

I am grateful to Lindsay Lang and her team for creating visual illustrations that help illumine content with clarity and flair.

Trudi Barnes was helpful in a thousand ways. John Sloan and David Greene gave twice as much editorial panache as any writer could reasonably expect, and Jim Ruark did his usual excellent job of bringing clarity and life. John Topliff went above and beyond in helping create a unique partnership between a whole team of us involved in this project.

Neil Plantinga was kind enough to offer a long conversation about sin and spirit; I am lucky to get to talk to him. Dallas Willard gave more wisdom than any human being has a right to, as well as more love than I have a right to; his life is one of the reasons I believe.

And to my wife, Nancy — I have never needed you more deeply or loved you more fully than in this season.

PART ONE
finding my identity
»

Chapter 1
Learn Why God Made You

One evening my wife, Nancy, pulled me into our bedroom and said she wanted to talk. She closed the door so that none of the kids could hear, and she took out a list.

I was not happy to see a list. She claims it was an index card, not a list. But it had words written on it, so to me that's a list.

"You know," she said, "when our marriage is at its best, I feel we share responsibilities. We divide our work well and our kids see us do that and I feel valued, and I think that's important for our family. But for some time, because you feel so many demands on your life, this value has been slipping.

"When our marriage is working well, I also feel like we both know each other's lives. You know details about my life and I know details about yours. And I feel like that's been slipping too. Lately I know what's going on with you, but you don't ask me much about what's going on with me." She went on.

"When our marriage is at its best, you also bring a kind of lightness and joy to it." Then she reminded me of a story.

We were on our second date, in the lobby of the Disneyland Hotel waiting to get something to eat, and she had to use the restroom. When she came out, there were scores of people in the lobby, and I was in a goofy mood, so I said loudly enough for them all to hear, "Woman, I can't believe you kept me waiting for *two hours*."

Her immediate response was, "Well, I wouldn't have to if you didn't insist on having your mother live with us so I have to wait on her hand and foot every day." She yelled that, right across the lobby, on only our *second* date, and my first thought was, *I like this woman.*

Nancy told me that story and said, "You know, when our marriage is at its best, you can listen and laugh and be spontaneous. You haven't been doing that for a while. I love that guy and I miss that guy."

I knew what she was talking about.

"I miss that guy too," I told her. "I'd love to feel free like that. But I feel like I'm carrying so many burdens. I have personnel issues and financial challenges at work. I have writing projects and travel commitments. I feel like I'm carrying this weight all the time. I get what you're saying, but I need you to know, I'm doing the best I can."

"No, you're not," she responded immediately.

That was not the response I had anticipated. Everybody is supposed to nod their head sympathetically when you say, "I'm doing the best I can." But Nancy loves truth (and me) too much to do that. So she rang my bell.

"No, you're *not*. You've talked about how it would be good to see a counselor, or an executive coach, or maybe a spiritual director. You've talked about building friendships, but I haven't seen you take steps toward any of that. No, you're not."

As soon as she said that I knew she was right.

But I didn't say that to her immediately because my spiritual gift is pouting, which I exercised beautifully over the next few days. As I did, a question emerged in my mind: *What is it that you really want?*

I began to realize that what I really want isn't any particular outcome on any particular project. Those are all just means to an end. What I really want is to be fully alive inside. What I really want is the inner freedom to live in love and joy.

I want to be that man she described.

I'm a grown man, I thought. *I do not know how many years of life are before me. I cannot wait anymore.* When I was going to school, I was preoccupied with good grades or getting cute girls to like me. As the years went by, I became preoccupied with work and my circumstances because I thought they would make me feel alive. *I can't wait anymore to be that man*, I thought.

I realized this then, and I know it now: I want that life more than I want anything else. Not because I think I'm supposed to, not because it says somewhere that you should. I want it.

There is a me I want to be.

Life is not about any particular achievement or experience. The most important task of your life is not what you do, but who you become.

There is a me you want to be.

Ironically, becoming this person will never happen if my primary focus is on me, just as no one becomes happy if their main goal is to be happy. God made you to flourish, but flourishing never happens by looking out for "number one." It is tied to a grander and nobler vision. The world badly needs wise and flourishing human beings, and we are called to bring God's wisdom and glory to the world. The truth is, those who flourish always bring blessing to others — and they can do so in the most unexpected and humble circumstances.

» One Flourishing Life

Not long ago I boarded an airport shuttle bus to get to the rental car lot. Driving a shuttle bus is usually a thankless job, for the driver is often regarded as the low man on the totem pole. People on the bus are often grumpy from travel and in a hurry to get to their car. No one says much except the name of their rental car company. But not on this bus.

The man who drove the bus was an absolute delight. He was scanning the curbside, looking for anybody who needed a ride. "You know," he told us, "I'm always looking because sometimes people are running late. You can tell it in their eyes. I'm always looking because I never want to miss one. Hey, here's another one!..."

The driver pulled over to pick up a latecomer, and he was so excited about what he was doing that *we* got excited. We were actually cheering him on when he was picking people up. It was like watching Jesus drive a shuttle bus. The man would grab people's luggage before they could lift it, then he would jump back on the bus and say, "Well we're off. I know you're all eager to get there as quickly as possible, so I'm going to get you there as soon as I can."

Jaded commuters put down their papers. He created such a little community of joy on that bus that people wanted to ride around in the terminal a second time just to hang out with the guy. We would say to people who got on after us, "Watch this guy!" He wasn't just our shuttle bus driver—he was our leader; he was our friend. And for a few moments, community flourished. On a shuttle bus for a rental car company—and one person moved toward the best version of himself.

What happened to that shuttle bus driver can happen in you. Sometimes it does. Every once in a while you do something that surprises you and catch a glimpse of the person you were made to be. You say something inspirational at a meeting. You help a homeless man no one else notices. You are patient with a rambunctious three-year-old. You lose yourself in a piece of music. You fall in love. You express compassion. You stand up to a bully. You freely make a sacrificial gift. You fix an engine. You forgive an old hurt. You say something you would normally never say, or you keep from saying something you would normally blurt out.

As you do, you glimpse for a moment why God made you. Only God knows your full potential, and he is guiding you toward that best version of yourself all the time. He has many tools and is never in a hurry. That can be frustrating for us, but even in our frustration, God is at work to produce patience in us. He never gets discouraged by how long it takes, and he delights every time you grow. Only God can see the "best version of you," and he is more concerned with you reaching your full potential than you are.

> For we are God's handiwork, created in Christ Jesus to do good
> works, which God prepared in advance for us to do.

You are not *your* handiwork; your life is not your project. Your life is *God's* project. God thought you up, and he knows what you were intended to be. He has many good works for you to do, but they are not the kind of "to do" lists we give spouses or employees. They are signposts to your true self.

Your "spiritual life" is not limited to certain devotional activities that you engage in. It is receiving power from the Spirit of God to become the person God had in mind when he created you—his handiwork.

» Where Growth Leads

God made you to flourish—to receive life from outside yourself, creating vitality within yourself and producing blessing beyond yourself. Flourishing is God's gift and plan, and when you flourish you are in harmony with God, other people, creation, and yourself. Flourishing is not measured by outward signs such as income, possessions, or attractiveness. It means becoming the person *he* had in mind in creating you.

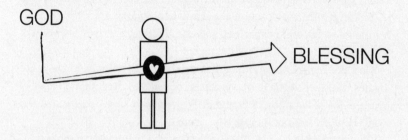

GOD

BLESSING

Flourishing means moving toward God's best version of you.

> "The righteous will flourish like a palm tree.... they will flourish in the courts of our God." (Psalm 92:12–13)

As God helps you grow, you will change, but you will always be you. An acorn can grow into an oak tree, but it cannot become a rose bush. It can be a healthy oak or it can be a stunted oak—but it won't be a shrub. You will always be you—a growing, healthy you or a languishing you—but God did not create you to be anybody else. He pre-wired your temperament. He determined your natural gifts and talents. He made you to feel certain passions and desires. He planned your body and mind. Your uniqueness is God-designed.

Some people think that if they seek to grow spiritually they will have to become someone else. But God won't discard your raw material. He redirects it. Before Paul met Jesus, he was a brilliant, passionate zealot who persecuted people. Afterward, he was a brilliant, passionate zealot who sacrificed himself for people.

Some friends of ours had a daughter named Shauna who was a classic strong-willed child. When she was four years old, she kept trying to go AWOL on her tricycle. Her mom could not rein her in and finally said, "Look, Shauna, there's a tree right here, and there's a driveway right there. You can ride your tricycle on the sidewalk in between the driveway and the tree, but you can't go past that. If you go past that, you will get a spanking. I have to be inside; I've got stuff to do. But I'm going to be watching you. Don't go past either one of those boundaries, or you're going to get a spanking."

Shauna backed up to her mom, pointed to her spanking zone, and said, "Well, you might as well spank me now, because I got places to go."

Would it surprise you to learn that when Shauna grew up, she had formidable leadership capacities and an indomitable drive? She always will have them.

God doesn't make anything and then decide to throw it away. He creates, and then, if there is a problem, he rescues. Redemption always involves the redemption of creation. The psalmist says, "Know that the LORD Himself is God. It is He who made us, and not we ourselves."

Here is the good news: When you flourish, you become more you. You become more that person God had in mind when he thought you up. You don't just become holier. You become you-ier. You will change; God wants you to become a "new creation." But "new" doesn't mean completely different; instead, it's like an old piece of furniture that gets restored to its intended beauty.

I used to have a chair my grandfather helped build seventy years ago. I loved it, but its arms were broken, the wood was chipped, and the upholstery was worn through. I finally gave up on it and sold it for fifty cents at a garage sale. The person who bought it knew about restoration, and a few months later I received a picture of it—repaired, refinished, revarnished, and reupholstered. I wish this was one of those stories where the restorer surprises the clueless owner by giving him back his now-glorious chair. But all I have is this alluring picture. Still, I keep the picture taped inside my desk drawer to remind me that "if anyone is in Christ, the new creation has come. The old is gone! The new is here!"

Redemption always involves the redemption of creation.

God wants to redeem you, not exchange you. If you're a bookish, contemplative type, waiting for God to change you into the kind of person who wears lampshades on your head at parties, good luck on that. Maybe you are a raging extrovert, tired of putting your foot in your mouth all the time. Don't you wish you could become more like those of us who are introverted: wise, calm, and restrained? It's never going to happen.

Too bad—we all wish it could.

It is humbling that I cannot be anything I want. I don't get to create myself. I accept myself as God's gift to me and accept becoming that person as God's task set before me. Inside your soul there is a battle between a flourishing self—the person you were created to be—and a languishing self. This book is all about that battle as it moves from deep inside you to a world waiting for God's redemption.

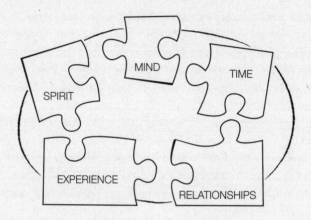

The journey begins with your *spirit*, which becomes empowered by God's Spirit. Every human being has had the sense of receiving ideas or energy from a source beyond ourselves. We speak of being *in-spired*, a Spirit-word that literally means something has been breathed into us. This means that flourishing—being connected with the Spirit of God—is available all the time. When your spirit flourishes, you are most fully alive. You have a purpose for living. You are drawn to put on virtue and put off sin.

Then there is your *mind*. The mental life of your flourishing self is marked by joy and peace. You are curious and love to learn. You do this in your own unique way by reading, talking with people, listening, building, or leading. You ask questions. You are not easily bored. When negative emotions arise, you take them as cues to act.

Your languishing self, on the other hand, feels uneasy and discontent inside. You find yourself drawn to bad habits—watching too much TV, drinking too much alcohol, misusing sex, or excess spending—because they anesthetize pain. In the languishing self, thoughts drift toward fear or anger. Learning does not feel worth the effort. You think about yourself a good deal.

Along with your spirit and mind, when you flourish, your *time* begins to be transformed as well. You have confidence that whatever life throws at you will not overthrow you. When the day dawns, you awake with a sense of expectancy. You have a vibrant sense that *things matter.* You begin to receive each moment as a God-filled gift.

You realize you are never too young to flourish. Mozart was composing brilliant music when he was five. The apostle Paul told Timothy, "Don't let anyone look down on you because you are young." You are also never too old to flourish. Grandma Moses was sixty-nine when she took up painting, and Marc Chagall spent hours a day at his art in his nineties. A few years ago my dad hit seventy, and at seventy years old he started walking three miles a day. (Five years later, we have no idea where to find him.)

Your flourishing self pours blessings into your *relationships.* You find other people to be a source of wonder. They often bring you energy. When you are with them, you listen deeply. You are struck by their dreams. You bless. You are able to disclose your own thoughts and feelings in a way that invites openness in others. You quickly admit your errors, and you freely forgive.

Relationally, your languishing self is often troubled. You are undisciplined in what you say, sometimes reverting to sarcasm, sometimes to gossip, sometimes to flattery. You isolate. You dominate. You attack. You withdraw.

But as God grows you, he wants to use you in his plan to redeem his world, and you find him changing your *experiences.* Your flourishing self works out of a richness and a desire to contribute. You live with a sense of calling. How much money you make does not matter as much as doing what you love and what creates value. You become resilient in suffering. You get better. You grow.

What could you want more than to become the person God created you to be?

» The World God Wants to See

Here is a great secret of the Bible: Your longing to become all you were meant to be is a tiny echo of God's longing to begin the new creation. The rabbis spoke of this as *tikkun olam*—to fix the world. The more concerned you are about your own fulfillment, the less fulfilled you will be. When your life is devoted to yourself, it is as small as a grain of wheat. When your life is given to God, however, it is as if that grain is planted in rich soil, growing into part of a much bigger project.

The picture used at the end of the Bible is that of a wedding, a glimpse of what God has been up to all this time: "I saw the Holy City, the new Jerusalem, coming down out of heaven from God, prepared as a bride beautifully dressed for her husband." One day there will be glorious harmony between God and all that he has made. God wants no one left out. As you flourish, you help in God's re-creation of the world he wants to see.

My niece Courtney got married not long ago, and at the wedding reception they had a dance for married couples in which they would eliminate couples from the dance floor based on the length of their marriage. At the beginning we were all on the floor. Courtney and Patrick were the first to leave, then all the couples married less than one year left, then those married less than five years, and so on. Nancy and I made it to the twenty-five-year cut, and by that time the crowd had thinned out considerably.

Finally, there was only one couple left on the dance floor, and they had been married fifty-three years. Everybody watched them — a tall, courtly, silver-haired man who stood a foot taller than his wife — but they watched only each other. They danced with joy, not in the skill of their dancing, but in the love they radiated for each other. What a contrast between the newlyweds, fresh in the health and beauty of their marriage, and the beauty of another kind of love that shone from the last couple on the floor! Perhaps part of why we appreciate such beauty is that it speaks to us of an inner flourishing not visible to the eye.

When the dancing ended, the master of ceremonies turned to Courtney and Patrick and said to them, "Take a good look at that couple on that dance floor. Your task now is to live and love together in such a way that fifty-three years from now that's you. That dance is your dance. Now it begins."

At that moment we all were struck by the mystery of the brevity of life. When that bride of fifty-three years looked at her husband, she didn't just see an aging grandfather. She saw the young, tanned tennis champion she married five decades earlier. He did not see only a grandmother in her seventies. He saw the lovely, effervescent belle he had loved since she was a teenager. I know, because they are my parents, Courtney's grandparents. And I thought of how, to my mom and dad, their wedding probably seems like yesterday. Time is that way.

Life is that way.

I projected my thoughts to about fifty-three years from now, when Courtney and Patrick will have been married as long as that couple. In fifty-three years my mother and my father will be gone. Nancy will be gone. And I will be 105 years old.

I don't want to miss the dance. I get hung up on so many things in life, worrying about what I will never do or achieve or have. But I don't want to miss the dance. I want to love my wife, care for my kids, and give life to my friends. I want to do the work God made me to do. I want to love God and the world he made. I want to do my part to help it flourish, for my spiritual maturity is not measured by following rules. "The me God made me to be" is measured by my capacity to love. When we live in love, we flourish. That is the dance.

The time to love is now. When we love, we enter into the mystery of eternity. Nothing offered in love is ever lost, for this mortal life is not the whole story. This life is to the next a kind of school, a kind of preparation for the me you were meant to be. That person will go into eternity. What matters most is not what you accomplish; it is who you become.

"The Spirit and the bride say, 'Come!' And let all who hear say, 'Come!'" It is the last, best invitation in the Bible.

Don't miss the wedding, God says. *Save the last dance for me.*

in the flow ≈

"How is your spiritual life going?"

I used to answer this question by looking at the state of my devotional activities: Did I pray and read the Bible enough today? The problem is that by this measure the Pharisees always win. People can be very disciplined, but remain proud and spiteful. How do we measure spiritual growth so that the Pharisees don't win?

I asked a wise man, "How do you assess the well-being of your soul?"

He immediately said, "I ask myself two questions":

≈ Am I growing more easily discouraged these days?
≈ Am I growing more easily irritated these days?

At the core of a flourishing soul are the love of God and the peace of God. If peace is growing in me, I am less easily discouraged. If love is growing, I am less easily irritated. It was a brilliantly helpful diagnostic to assess the health of my soul.

How would you answer those two questions?

Chapter 2
The Me I Don't Want to Be

Henri Nouwen, a priest and teacher who moved in the exalted circles of Harvard and Yale and Notre Dame, came to believe that those settings did not—for him—call forth the person God intended him to be. So this famous writer spent the last decade of his life caring for physically and mentally challenged residents of a small community called L'Arche.

There Henri made friends with a resident named Trevor, who had many mental and emotional challenges. One time when Trevor was sent to a hospital for evaluation, Henri called to arrange a visit. When the authorities found out the famous Henri Nouwen was coming, they asked him if he would meet with some doctors, chaplains, and clergy. He agreed, and when he arrived, there was a lovely luncheon laid out in the Golden Room—but Trevor was not there.

"Where is Trevor?" Henri asked.

"He cannot come to the lunch," they told him. "Patients and staff are not allowed to have lunch together, and no patient has ever had lunch in the Golden Room."

"But the whole purpose of my visit was to have lunch with Trevor,"

Henri said. "If Trevor is not allowed to attend the lunch, then I will not attend either."

A way was found for Trevor to attend the lunch.

The Golden Room was filled with people who were quite excited that the great Henri Nouwen was in their midst. Some angled to be close to him. They thought of how wonderful it would be to tell their friends, "As I was saying to Henri Nouwen the other day...." Some pretended to have read books they had not read and know ideas they did not know. Others were upset that the rule separating patients and staff had been broken.

Trevor, oblivious to all this, sat next to Henri, who was engaged in conversation with the person on his other side. Consequently, Henri did not notice that Trevor had risen to his feet.

"A toast," Trevor said. "I will now offer a toast."

The room grew quiet. *What in the world is this guy going to do?* everyone wondered.

Then Trevor began to sing.

If you're happy and you know it, raise your glass.
If you're happy and you know it, raise your glass.
If you're happy and you know it, if you're happy and you know it,
If you're happy and you know it, raise your glass.

At first people were not sure how to respond, but Trevor was beaming. His face and voice told everyone how glad and proud he was to be there with his friend Henri. Somehow Trevor, in his brokenness and joy, gave a gift no one else in the room could give. People began to sing — softly at first, but then with more enthusiasm — until doctors and priests and PhDs were almost shouting, "If you're happy and you know it...."

All under the direction of Trevor.

No one was preening anymore. No one worried about the rules. No one tried to separate the PhDs from the ADDs. For a few moments, a room full of people moved toward the best version of themselves because a wounded healer named Henri Nouwen lived among the challenged, and because a challenged man named Trevor was living out the best version of himself.

We do not just drift into becoming the best version of ourselves. It can be missed by a genius, and it can be found by Trevor. If I want to become that person I want to be, I will have to come to grips with the counterfeits who elbow in to take his place — the rivals who can keep me from becoming the me I am meant to be.

» The Me I Pretend to Be

God designed you to be you. When your life is over, he will not ask you why you weren't Moses or David or Esther or Henri Nouwen or Trevor. If you don't pursue that life we are talking about, he will ask you why you weren't *you*. God designed us to *delight* in our actual lives. When I am growing toward the me I want to be, I am being freed from the me I pretend to be. I no longer try to convince people I am important while secretly fearing I am not.

A few years ago I had lunch with a man I don't know well. We spent two hours together, and he used the whole time for name-dropping—one name after another of important people he knew, successful people he had impressed, corporate executives he had influenced. What is amazing is not simply that he went on so long, but that he was so clueless. By the end of the lunch I felt drained and depressed. How could someone be so blind, so unaware?

Then I had a horrible thought: *If this man could be that blind, what about other people? What about me? Do I have that same problem and that same blindness?* I decided I had better ask a close friend, so I did the next week during lunchtime.

This woman and I decided that we both had that problem. So we tried an experiment. The next week both of us were attending a gathering with a group of people we regarded as important, and we decided to refrain from saying anything to make us look intelligent or accomplished. I was amazed at how little I had to say.

Sometimes the me I pretend to be leaks out in small acts of vanity. A freshly minted lieutenant wanted to impress the first private to enter his new office, and he pretended to be on the phone with a general so that the private would know he was somebody. "Yes sir, General, you can count on me," he said as he banged the receiver down. Then he asked the private what he wanted. "I'm just here to connect your phone, sir."

Pretending to be someone we're not is hard work, which is why we feel tired after a first date or a job interview or among others we feel we have to project an image for. We are drawn to transparency and long to go where we can just "be ourselves." It is a relief to not have to pretend to pray more than we really do, or know more about the Bible than we really know, or act more humble than we really are.

Inside us is a person without pretense or guile. We never have to pretend with God, and genuine brokenness pleases God more than pretend spirituality. If I am ever going to become the me I want to be, I have to start by being honest about the me I am.

» The Me I Think I *Should* Be

Comparison kills spiritual growth. A mother with three preschool-age children hears her pastor talk about loving God so much that he is up very early every morning to spend an hour of quiet with him. She would love an hour of quiet at any time, but her children simply will not cooperate. What she takes away is that she ought to be doing the same thing, and so she does spirituality by comparison, living under a cloud of guilt. It never occurs to her that the love she expresses to her children might "count" as a spiritual activity. It never occurs to her that perhaps she is serving God more faithfully than the very pastor who may be neglecting his wife and children in the morning so he can have that hour of quiet.

A gregarious, spontaneous husband is married to a woman who loves to be alone. Solitude comes easily for her; she would have to become more extroverted just to be a hermit. He feels he is a failure at prayer because he cannot be alone the way she can. It never occurs to him that his ability to love people "counts," that the way he loves people is shaping his soul and delighting God.

> Henri Nouwen wrote, "Spiritual greatness has nothing to do with being greater than others. It has everything to do with being as great as each of us can be."

Each one of us has a me that we think we *should* be, which is at odds with the me that God *made* us to be. Sometimes letting go of that self may be a relief. Sometimes it will feel like death.

I grew up with a need to think of myself as a leader, as stronger, more popular, more confident than I really was. I ran for class president because grown-up leaders would always say, "Even when I was in high school I was class president." I would think up good slogans and campaign hard—but I always lost. The truth is that I was more introverted, more bookish, and less of the "class president" type than I wanted anyone to think.

As I grew up, my need to be a leader kept me trying to be someone I wasn't. It made me more defensive, pressured, unhappy, and inauthentic in ways I didn't even know. To make matters worse, the person I married is one of those people who ran for school office — and always won. She didn't even have a good slogan: "Don't be fancy, vote for Nancy." (No, I'm not making that up. She actually *won* with that.)

Finally, around the age of forty, I went through six months of deep, internal emptiness and depression like none I had ever experienced. Nancy was involved in work exploding with growth, and I felt as if the trajectory of my life and work was destined to keep arcing downward. It led to a moment I will never forget.

I sat in the basement of our home and said to God, "I give up my need to be a leader." Out of me came a volcano of emotion — wrenching sobs. I felt all my dreams had died. All I knew was that holding onto my need to lead was wrecking my life. So I prayed, "I'll let it go. It's been my dream for so long, I don't know what's left. If I can't become this leader I thought I was supposed to be, I don't know what to do. But I'll try to do the best I can to let it go."

What I was really dying to was a false self, an illusion of misplaced pride, ego, and neediness — the me I thought I was *supposed* to be.

Should is an important word for spiritual growth, but God's plan is not for you to obey him because you *should* even though you don't want to. He made you to *want* his plan for you.

On the other side of death is freedom, and no one is more free than a dead man. Jesus had much to say about death to self, and on the journey to the me you want to be, you will have some dying to do. But that kind of death is always death to a lesser self, a false self, so that a better and nobler self can come to life.

» The Me Other People Want Me to Be

Everyone in your life wants you to change. Your boss wants you to be more productive. Your health club wants you to be more fit. Your credit card company wants you to be in more debt. Networks want you to watch more television, and restaurants want you to eat more food. Your dentist wants you to visit more often. Everybody has an agenda for you. This is the me other people want you to be.

If I spend my life trying to become *that* me, I will never be free. Loving people means being willing to disappoint them sometimes. Jesus loved everyone, but that means at some point he disappointed everyone. Seeking to become the me that other people want me to be is a hollow way to live. Nobody else can tell you exactly how to change because nobody but God knows.

When Nelson Mandela was imprisoned on Robbins Island for his opposition to South Africa's apartheid, he was issued a pair of shorts—not long trousers—because his captors wanted his identity to be that of a *boy* instead of a man. People in power over him wanted him to be a docile accepter of a racist society. Angry people who suffered with him wanted him to be a vengeful hater of their oppressors.

Mandela was neither. During twenty-seven years in prison, he suffered and learned and grew. He called his prison "the University." He became both increasingly committed to justice and opposed to hate, and by the end of his captivity, even his guards were won over by his life. The final official charged to watch him used to cook Mandela gourmet meals. When he went from Prisoner Mandela to President Mandela, he sought to lead the country to peace through the Truth and Reconciliation Commission, established on the biblical principle that "the truth shall make you free."

God didn't make you to be Nelson Mandela. He made you to be you—and no human being in your life gets the final word on who God made you to be.

Even you can't tell yourself how to change, because you didn't create you. To love someone is to desire and work toward their becoming the best version of themselves. The one person in all the universe who can do this perfectly for you is God. He has no other agenda. He has no unmet needs he is hoping you can help him with. And he *knows* what the best version of you looks like. He delighted in the idea of it, and he is already working on it. The apostle Paul said, "We know that in all things God works for the good of those who love him."

Which means God is at work every moment to help you become his best version of you.

» The Me I'm Afraid God Wants

A recent study by the Barna Group found that the number one challenge to helping people grow spiritually is that most people equate spiritual maturity with trying hard to follow the rules in the Bible. No wonder people also said they find themselves unmotivated to pursue spiritual growth. If I think God's aim is to produce rule-followers, spiritual growth will always be an obligation rather than a desire of my heart.

"Rule-keeping does not naturally evolve into living by faith," Paul wrote, "but only perpetuates itself in more and more rule-keeping." In other words, it only results in a rule-keeping, desire-smothering, Bible-reading, emotion-controlling, self-righteous person who is not like *me*. In the end, I cannot follow God if I don't trust that he really has my best interests at heart.

The letter kills, but the Spirit gives life. There is an enormous difference between following rules and following Jesus, because I can follow rules without cultivating the right heart.

A friend of mine recently graduated from one of the service academies where they are very serious about the "clean your room" rule. Sometimes my friend got ink marks on the wall that would not come out, so he would chip the plaster off. The inspectors would give demerits for ink marks, but they figured missing chunks of plaster was a construction problem. The "rules" ended up encouraging the slow demolition of the room.

Jesus did not say, "I have come that you might follow the rules." He said, "I have come that you might have life, and have it with abundance." When we cease to understand spiritual growth as moving toward God's best version of ourselves, the question, *how is your spiritual life going?* frightens us. A nagging sense of guilt and a deficit of grace prompt us to say, "Not too well. Not as good as I should be doing." People often use external behaviors and devotional practices to measure their spiritual health. They measure their spiritual life by how early they are getting up to read the Bible, or how long their quiet times are, or how often they attend church services. But that is not what spiritual formation is about.

» The Me That Fails to Be

We have been overrun by what a friend of mine calls TLAs (three-letter acronyms), and the most memorable one I've ever heard of comes from the field of medicine: FTT.

My wife first introduced me to those initials. Trained to be a nurse, Nancy still loves diagnosing people. She is constantly telling me her private diagnoses of people—even total strangers—based on their skin color. If she gets a long look at your face and the light is good, she can pretty much tell you how long you have to live. But of all the diagnoses I ever heard her discuss, FTT is the one that sticks in my mind. It gets entered into the chart of an infant who, often for unknown reasons, is unable to gain weight or grow.

what is spiritual formation?

There is an outer you — your body — that is being shaped all the time by the way you eat, drink, sleep, exercise, and live. You may do this well or poorly, intentionally or not, but it *will* happen. Then there is an inner you — your thoughts, desires, will, and character. This is being shaped all the time by what you see, read, hear, think, and do. We can call this inner you the spirit.

Spiritual formation is the process by which your inner self and character are shaped.

People sometimes speak as if spiritual formation is an optional activity that some religious people may pursue and others bypass. They think it is reserved for monks, mystics, and missionaries. But that's not true.

Everyone has a spirit. *Everyone's* inner life is being formed — for better or worse.

We flourish when our spirits are rooted in and shaped by the Spirit of God — and God wants to do that in a way that uniquely fits us.

Failure to thrive.

Sometimes, doctors guess, failure to thrive happens when a parent or caregiver is depressed and the depression seems to get passed down. Sometimes something seems to be off in an infant's metabolism for reasons no one can understand, so FTT is one of those mysterious phrases that sounds like an explanation but explains nothing.

Psychologists have begun to speak of what is perhaps the largest mental health problem in our day. It is not depression or anxiety, at least not at clinical levels. It is languishing — a failure to thrive.

Languishing is the condition of someone who may be able to function but has lost a sense of hope and meaning. Languishing is not the presence of mental illness; it is the absence of mental and emotional vitality. In ancient lists of deadly sins it was called *acedia* — weariness of soul and inability to delight in life. We speak of dead marriages and dead-end jobs, and to languish is to feel inner deadness. Languishing is the opposite of flourishing, and it was the fear of Henry David Thoreau that "when I came to die, [I would] discover that I had not lived."

Often people have dreams for their life when they are young, but over time they simply give up. Writer and artist Gordan MacKenzie tells of visiting children in kindergarten and asking them, "Who is an artist?" Every hand shoots up. This decreases to half the class by third grade. By the time the students are twelve years old, only a few hands go up. Over time many find that becoming the me they were meant to be is too hard or that it takes too long. When we give up on our growth and life's purpose, we languish.

But there is a person inside of you waiting to come alive.

» The Me I Am Meant to Be

God showed the prophet Ezekiel a vision of languishing: a valley full of dry bones. It was the image of a failure to thrive. God asked Ezekiel, "Can these bones live?" and Ezekiel answered, "You alone know." God did know, and he made them come alive.

I know a man named Tim who was an addict, lost his family, lost everything, found God, gave up his addiction, and got his life back again. I know a man named Peter who was a tormented slave to sexual impulses, and God got ahold of him and that changed. I know of a woman who hated confrontation so badly she once drove on an extended road trip with her best friend for three days in silence to avoid confrontation. Today she confronts recreationally.

God wants you to grow! He created the very idea of growth. The Talmud says that every blade of grass has an angel bending over it, whispering, "Grow, grow." Paul said that in Christ the whole redeemed community "grows and builds itself up in love."

Your flourishing is never just about you. It is a "so that" kind of condition. God designed you to flourish "so that" you could be part of his redemptive project in ways that you otherwise could not. He wants you to flourish "so that" people can be encouraged, gardens can be planted,

have life

Jesus said, "I have come that they may have life, and have it to the full." We may have heard that without understanding what Jesus offers. When he says he has come to "give life," what *exactly* does he mean?

We all feel that we know what life is when we see it, but life turns out to be surprisingly tricky to define. So we might start here: *Life is the inner power to make something happen.*

Throw a rock, and it soon stops moving. But put a seed in the ground, and something happens — it sends out a root, takes in nourishment, and grows up to be fruitful. To be spiritually alive means to receive power from God to have a positive impact on your world.

What are some ways God gives life and vitality to you? How can you build these into your life and schedule?

- Nature
- Spiritual friendships
- Worship
- Solitude
- Serving
- Study
- Leading
- Art
- Rest
- Celebration
- Scripture
- Recreation
- Exercise
- Family
- Long talks
- Laughter
- Leading a cause
- Retreat
- Small group
- Other

Saint Irenaeus wrote, "The glory of God is a human being fully alive; and to be alive consists in beholding God."

music can be written, sick people can be helped, or companies can thrive in ways they otherwise would not. When you fail to become the person God designed, all the rest of us miss out on the gift you were made to give.

Jesus once said that with God, all things are possible, and the great thing about life with God is that your next step is always possible. That step toward God is always waiting, no matter what you have done or how you have messed up your life. Jesus was hanging on a cross with a thief hanging next to him, and Jesus turned to him and said, "Today you will be with me in paradise."

There is always a next step.

So I propose a toast: "Here's to Trevor. And to Henri. And to the me you want to be."

PART TWO
flowing with the spirit
»

Chapter 3

Discover the Flow

A flourishing life *is* possible.

After the conversation with my wife about "the list," I kept thinking about how I don't want to wait for circumstances to change in order to live the way I was meant to live. I just have to want it more than I want anything else. I usually allow myself to be preoccupied or pulled in multiple directions because I think I have to devote little chunks of my mind to worrying about how I will solve some problem or finish some project, as if success with them will make me happy and free.

The truth is, a life of freedom and joy is available right now. My main job is to remain connected to God. When my primary focus is being present with him, everything else has a way of falling into place. When my primary focus becomes anything else, my inner vitality suffers, and I become a lesser version of myself.

On vacation one summer, my wife—a veteran water-skier—was teaching our family to water ski. I had only water-skied once or twice before, so it took several trips to feel any confidence at all. I decided I wanted to try using only one ski, but the boat could not generate enough power for me to get up out of the water.

Back in the boat, I noticed a button labeled "power-tilt." I know nothing about boats or engines, but it seemed like a promising button, so we gave it a shot. I heard a whirring sound, which I later learned was the propeller being driven much deeper under the water.

I got back behind the boat, balanced precariously on one ski, and yelled to Nancy, "Hit it!"

The bow of the boat lifted out of the water at a 45-degree angle and moved as if it had been shot out of a cannon. Adequate power to get my body up out of the water was not a problem. Survival was. I gestured wildly for the boat to slow down. However, we had not prearranged signals, and my kids interpreted my waving as a desire to go faster, so they revved the boat full throttle. I was not just up, but was bouncing through the air between landings like a rock skipping across a smooth lake. It did not occur to me to let go of the rope. I eventually came down on my face.

For six months I could not smile with the right side of my mouth.

But I did find out I could ski. I just needed power.

Trying to become the person you were made to be through your own effort is like trying to ski behind a rowboat. We need a "power-tilt" for the soul. Where do we look?

Jesus made staggering promises about his ability to transform human lives:

> "Let anyone who is thirsty come to me and drink. Whoever believes
> in me, as Scripture has said, streams of living water will flow from
> within them." By this he meant the Spirit, whom those who believed
> in him were later to receive.

The King James Bible states it this way: "Out of his belly will flow rivers of living water." The belly is the deepest place inside you — the place where you get anxious or afraid, where you feel hollow or empty when you are disappointed. The Greek word is *koilia*, and we speak of getting *colitis* when rivers of stress run in our belly. Scientists say we have a reptile brain — a "brain in the gut" — that is, neurons in the digestive system that produce feelings of well-being or threat deeper than we can put into words. It is in that very deepest place that Jesus says he will produce vitality.

This life is not something we produce; it exists independently of us. It is the Spirit of God. If we turn to any book in the New Testament, we see a picture of amazing life offered by Jesus through the Spirit.

> "You will receive power when the Holy Spirit comes on you."

Though you have not seen him [Jesus], you love him … and are filled with an inexpressible and glorious joy.

"Take my yoke upon you and learn from me, for I am gentle and humble in heart, and you will find rest for your souls."

Would you say this describes you? Are you filled with inexpressible joy? Do other people comment from time to time that your belly is flowing with rivers of living water and that you have more or less mastered humility?

I will tell you what I think happens. I think that often people are moved by the vision of Jesus, they are overwhelmed by the hope and beauty of his promise, and they say yes to it. For a time, there is a kind of spiritual honeymoon period. They are filled with love for God, and they are drawn to the Bible. They want to tell other people about their faith. They love to worship. And some things change. Maybe coarse language gets cleaned up. Maybe certain habits get overcome.

But over time this sense of progress stalls out. Instead of life flowing with rivers of living water, I yell at my children whom I love. I worry too much about money or my job. I grow jealous. I use deception to get out of trouble or to get what I want. I pass judgment on people easily, casually, arrogantly. My prayer life is up and down. I am stuck in a gap.

God's plan is for you to become the best version of you, but right now there are two versions of you. There is the you God made you to be — and there is the you that currently exists.

What do you do with the gap?

» Gap Management

Our problem is that we think we have to close the gap through our own ingenuity. Some people think if they just try harder, they can close the gap between the me God made them to be and the me that currently exists. They think they are simply not being heroic enough in their spiritual effort. "I'll read another book. I'll listen to another talk. I'll learn some new disciplines. I'll serve more. I'll work harder. I'll try to be nicer to the people in my life."

You hear about someone who gets up at four o'clock in the morning to pray, and you feel guilty because you think you don't pray enough. So you resolve to do that too, even though you are not a "morning person" — at four o'clock you are dazed and confused and groggy and grumpy, and no one wants to be around you at that time of the morning. Even Jesus doesn't want to be around you at four in the morning. But you think, *Well, this is exhausting and miserable—I certainly don't like doing it—so it must be God's will for my life. It must be spiritual.* You keep it up for several days or weeks or months, but not forever. Eventually you stop. Then you feel guilty. After enough guilt, you start doing something else.

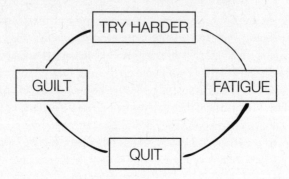

Sometimes we manage the gap by pretending. We learn to fake it. We speak as if we had had deeper spiritual experiences than we really have, as though our sin bothers us more than it really does. We pray as though our voice is throbbing with an emotion that we really have to generate ourselves. Sometimes we play spiritual musical chairs, always searching for a different church or tradition or spirituality that has the magic key. Some people flit from one spiritual experience to another, continually rededicating their lives to God and then falling away, hoping to recapture the emotions they felt when they first met God. Some people quietly, secretly give up. They still hope they will go to heaven when they die, but between now and then they have been disappointed too often to expect change any more. They have gotten used to languishing.

At the beginning of our life with God, we are aware of a gap between God and us, separation from God because of sin.

We come to understand that we cannot bridge this gap by our efforts or good behavior. We cannot earn God's love and forgiveness; it comes only by God's grace. Salvation is given by the grace of God,

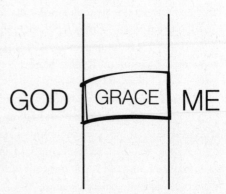

achieved through the power of God, offered through the Spirit of God, and made secure by the promise of God. And so we commit our life to God.

But there is still a gap.

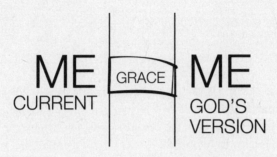

Now the gap is between the me I am right now and the me I'm meant to be—"current me" and "sanctified me." But here's the problem: People think it is our job to bridge that gap by our effort. But we can't. This gap, too, can only be bridged by grace. Self-improvement is no more God's plan than self-salvation. God's plan is not just for us to be *saved* by grace—it is for us to *live* by grace. God's plan is for my daily life to be given, guided, guarded, and energized by the grace of God. To live in grace is to flow in the Spirit.

We have now reached the foundational idea of this book: *The only way to become the person God made you to be is to live with the Spirit of God flowing through you like a river of living water.* The rest of this chapter will gives us a clear picture of what it looks like to live from one moment to the next in flow with the

> God's plan is not just for us to be saved by grace — it is for us to live by grace.

Spirit—not in following rules or trying harder—so that you receive the power to flourish as the me God made you to be.

» Flowing with Life

Experiencing the flow of the Spirit, spiritually speaking, is what makes us come alive, and the picture Jesus uses for life in the Spirit in the book of John is a river. Rivers are mentioned 150 times in Scripture, often as a picture of spiritual life, and for good reason. Israel was a desert, so a river is grace. A river is life. We don't know much about the Garden of Eden, but we do know this — a river ran through it.

> A river watering the garden flowed from Eden.
> (Genesis 2:10)

If a river flows, life flourishes. If a river dries up, life dies. So it is with you and the Spirit. The first human being was just a lump of clay until God breathed into him the "breath of life." (In Hebrew the word for *breath* is the same word used for *spirit*.) One of the signs that you are in the flow of the Spirit is a sense of God-given vitality and joyful aliveness overflowing in you.

When our son was three years old, he wanted to pour his own glass of milk out of a very full carton. Nancy was reluctant; we had three small children and spills were a way of life. But our son was so set on it that she couldn't say no, although she did warn him to be careful. His little hands picked up the heavy gallon container, and the milk went gushing into the glass — but wonder of wonders, it stopped just in time. The glass wasn't just full; the milk crowned the top of it. Not a drop was spilled. *Gloria in excelsis.*

But then Johnny was so excited that he grabbed the glass and swung it exuberantly from the counter to the table. The spillover was tremendous.

When someone bumps into me, what spills out of me reveals what is inside of me. That is the idea behind one of Paul's favorite words — *perisseuein* — to "overflow" or "abound" with life. He spoke of people being "full of the Spirit," and the spillover effect was tremendous. Jesus told his followers that when the Spirit arrived, they would receive power. When the Spirit flows in you, you are given power to become the person God designed.

You become you-ier.

» Flowing with Soul Satisfaction

As the deer pants for streams of water, so my soul pants for you, my God.

This psalm got made into a song, and sometimes when people sing it they think it means they are *supposed* to long for God or like church services and church songs. But this psalm is much bigger than that. It means that God is my life-giver and therefore my desire for life cannot be satisfied apart from him.

This is not a picture of Bambi wondering through a leafy-green, stream-laden forest with a slightly parched throat. This is desert country. No rivers, just wadis—gullies that would contain water only in the rainy season. Now the wadis are dried up, and the deer is going to die if it doesn't find water. That is us. We were made for soul satisfaction and simply die without it.

If you want life, you want God. You want him the way a deer dying of thirst wants water. You want God more than you know.

In Jesus' day the Jews celebrated God's gift of water and life at the Feast of the Tabernacles. The chief priest would dip a golden pitcher into the pool of Siloam and lead a parade up to the temple. This was the most joyful moment in the life of Israel. It was said that whoever had not seen the Feast of the Tabernacles did not know joy.

The priest would shout to the crowd, "With joy you shall draw water from the well of salvation!" Then he would pour the water out onto the ground. In the desert land of Israel, where drought was a constant fear, no one poured good water onto the ground. It was a kind of acted-out parable that God would one day satisfy his thirsty people with more water—more life—than they could handle. It was at that feast—maybe at that moment—when a rabbi stood up and cried out in a loud voice, *"Whoever is thirsty, let them come to me and drink...."*

When I am in the flow of the Spirit, sin looks bad and God looks good. When I experience gratitude, contentment, and satisfaction deep in my soul, there is a good chance it is the Spirit flowing within.

» Flowing with the Fruit of the Spirit

There is a river at the beginning of the Bible, and there is a river at the end:

> Then the angel showed me the river of the water of life, as clear as crystal, flowing from the throne of God and of the Lamb down the middle of the great street of the city. On each side of the river stood the tree of life, bearing twelve crops of fruit, yielding its fruit every month. And the leaves of the tree are for the healing of the nations.

Even here in California we don't have trees that yield their fruit *every* month. This scene is a picture of supreme flourishing, for the water flows from God, the source of life. In particular, when we are in the flow of the Spirit, we become increasingly full of the fruit of the Spirit: "love, joy, peace, patience, kindness, goodness, faithfulness, gentleness and self-control." The best indicator that I am living in the flow is the growth of the fruit.

A woman sees a father shopping with a fussy two-year-old in his grocery cart. "Be patient, Billy," he whispers. "You can handle this, Billy. It's okay, Billy."

The woman said to him, "I don't mean to interrupt your shopping, but I just had to tell you how wonderfully loving and patient you are with little Billy."

The man replied, "Actually, my son's name is Patrick. *My* name is Billy."

The Spirit is available to whisper to us thoughts of love and joy and peace and patience every moment of our life. *Right now.* All we have to do is stop, ask, and listen.

I can't make myself loving or joyful. A tree's job is not to try to bear fruit; the tree's job is to abide near the river. And the fruit does not ripen overnight.

When I am in the flow of the Spirit, I am moved toward greater love and more joy. And the blessing does not stop with me. The apostle John says the tree bears twelve crops, which calls to mind the twelve tribes of Israel and the twelve disciples of Jesus. In other words, God is giving life to his people.

Then comes the line in the Bible that takes your breath away: "And the leaves of the tree are for the healing of the nations." This is good news, but not just for Israel. Not just for the insiders. It is good news for the world. You and I—the leaves—are to flourish for the healing of the nations. For the healing of the Gaza strip. For the healing of Darfur. For the AIDS ward in the Sisters of Mercy hospital in Addis Ababa. For the apartment building full of loneliness. For the expensive home in the suburbs ripped by a divorce. For the lonely worker at an office party. For the forgotten woman at a homeless shelter.

The Spirit never just flows *in* us; he always flows *through* us so that others might flourish as well.

Anytime you see life flourishing, it is receiving nourishment from beyond itself. This is true of a tree, it is true of you, but it is also true of the world around you. The river can flow in you. The river can flow through you.

When you are in the flow of the Spirit, there is going to be some spill-over that blesses someone else.

» In Flow with the Presence of God

What if God really is at work in every moment, in every place? What if your job is just to jump into the river? What if your job is to figure out, from one moment to the next, how to stay in the flow? How to keep yourself aware and submitted to God's Spirit so that rivers of living water flow through your belly, through the core of your being?

The apostle Paul gives a simple command, which in a sense is all we need to do: "Do not quench the Spirit." The Spirit is already at work in you. Jesus says if you have come to him, if you are a follower of his, the Spirit is there. He is bigger than you; he is stronger than you; he is more patient with your failures and your gaps and your inadequacies and your pretending than you are. He is committed to helping you 24/7. So Paul says, in a sense, your only job is not getting in his way. Just *don't quench the Spirit.*

As we go about life, either we do things that open ourselves to the Spirit's influence in our lives — which Paul talks about in terms of "walking in the Spirit," "keeping in step with the Spirit," or "sowing to the Spirit" — or we do things that close ourselves off to the Spirit. For instance, Paul wrote, "Since we live by the Spirit, let us keep in step with the Spirit. Let us not become conceited, provoking and envying each other."

Here is a simple example of what I mean by closing ourselves off to the Spirit. Nancy and I had dinner with two other couples, some of our best friends, which we always do between Christmas and New Year's Eve. We look back on the past year and talk about high points and valleys, what we have learned and how we have changed. It's an annual highlight.

At one point I was talking about me, and Nancy gave my hand a little squeeze. No one else could see it. Just me. It was a little signal: *You're talking too much. Give someone else a turn.* The old squeeze play. We hadn't worked out the signal before; it was spontaneous. My immediate thought was, *I don't like the squeeze play. I think what I was saying about me was really interesting. I think Nancy is being overly directive.*

Here was the biggest problem: After dinner was over, I didn't say anything to her. I just thought to myself, *It's not a big deal. We don't need to talk about it.* I decided I would rather avoid a potentially unpleasant conversation than honor our relationship, learn more about myself, and wrestle with being honest. (Have you never done such a thing? Am I the only one?) In that decision I cut myself off just a bit from the flow of God's Spirit. In that one small area I quenched the Spirit's leading in my life.

The next day I spent time with another good friend. We talked about our families and marriages, and that incident from the previous night came up. Immediately I knew I had to talk to my wife about the squeeze thing, sooner or later. (Honey, if you're reading this, stop squeezing my hand.)

There was a lag between the time when she first squeezed my hand and the time when I finally talked with her about it. The lag lasted about twenty-four hours during which I resisted the flow of truth in my life. Yet one of the goals of spiritual life is to reduce the lag time of being out of the flow of the Spirit.

Nancy and I had a good talk that night about what the squeeze play meant, about the kind of person I want to be, the kind of person she wants to be, and what kind of marriage we want to have. And in that moment, I was back in the flow.

» Just Plunge In!

The Holy Spirit is always ready to guide you toward God's best version of yourself. Of course, many times I don't want to be guided! I want to blow up at someone, or be greedy, or lie to get out of trouble. I want to quench the Spirit. The more my habits are formed around resentment or anxiety or greed or superiority, the more often I will quench the Spirit. It will take time and wisdom for habits to get re-formed. But the Spirit of God is tenacious. All that is needed in any moment is a sincere desire to be submitted to the Spirit's leading. We need not worry about God's response; a sincere heart never needs to fear that God is upset.

I was traveling on obscure back roads in a part of the country I had never been to before. When I obtained a rental car, the man at the counter said to me, "Along with this car, if you want, you can also get a little box, a guidance system." Have you ever seen one of these? You plug it in and punch in your destination, and a voice will tell you how to get to wherever it is that you are going.

"Do you want to add this to the car?" he asked.

My immediate response was, "No. I'm not going to pay for that. I can find where I'm going without that."

But when I went out to the parking lot, I could not find my car. I could not remember what stall it was in. I had to go back to the counter and tell the man I had gotten lost before I found my car.

I decided to get the box.

There was a voice coming out of the box. You don't even have to look at a screen or follow a map. Someone talks to you. It is a British voice, because people who talk with a British accent always sound smarter. You're just inclined to do what they say. And it was a woman's voice, because ... same thing.

You can get the box. You can have the lady's voice in the car, but that doesn't mean you trust her. If you trust her, what do you do? You do what she says. You go where she tells you to go. If she says, "Turn left," you turn left. If she says, "Turn left," and in your heart you think, *Oh, but I want to turn right*, you remember that verse, "There is a way that seemeth right unto a man, but the end thereof are the ways of death."

To live in the flow of the Spirit means doing what Jesus says. I will mess up a lot. I am going to need his power. I know that, but I form the intention. I say to him, "God, with your help, as best I can, I will do what you say. I will give you my life, my time, my obedience." If that is not my settled intent, then it is best to be honest about it.

There is something else you need to know. At one point when I was driving in the unfamiliar territory, I was quite sure the lady in the guidance system was wrong. She said to go left, and I didn't go left. I went right because I knew she was wrong. Then, in a fascinating response, she said, "Recalculating route. When safe to do so, execute a U-turn." I knew she still was wrong ... so I unplugged her. That is the beauty of that little box — you can unplug her.

And — would you believe it? — I got lost as a goose, which my wife enjoyed immensely. So we plugged that lady back in, and you know what she said?

"I told you so, you little idiot. You think I'm going to help you now? You rejected me. There is no way. You just find your way home by yourself."

No, of course she didn't say those things. She said, "Recalculating route. When safe to do so, execute a U-turn."

That is grace.

God will say to you, "Here is the way home. Execute a U-turn." As soon as you are ready to listen, as soon as you are ready to surrender, that is repentance.

He will say, "I will bring you home." That is grace.

Jesus is the only one with authoritative wisdom about how to live. He is the only one to bring about the possibility of forgiveness for your sin and mine. He is the only one to give any kind of realistic hope of conquering death. To all who approach him, he is the thirst-quencher, the life-giver, the Spirit-bringer. No matter how wrongly you have erred in the past, if you are sincerely ready to listen to and obey God, *you do not have to worry about God being mad at you.*

He is not that kind of God.

Chapter 4
Find Out How *You* Grow

When a young shepherd boy named David was preparing for battle against Goliath, King Saul stepped in to help. But he made the mistake we so often make in other battles: He figured that whatever would be helpful to *him* would also be helpful to *David*. So King Saul—who stood "head and shoulders" above every man in Israel—dressed up David in his own tunic and armor, crowned him with his helmet, and armed him with his sword. David "tried walking around" in them, the Bible says, but it was no use. Saul was a size 52 long and David was a 36 regular. Saul was a warrior; David was a shepherd. Saul was a man; David was a teenager. The very things that would help Saul in a battle would only hinder David. Saul's tunic did not fit. His helmet was too big, his sword was too heavy, and his armor would only slow David down.

Fortunately, David had enough self-awareness and courage to name the problem. "I cannot go in these," David said, "because I am not used to them." David had to set aside Saul's equipment and use what would help *him*—a sling, some stones, and nimble feet—and Saul ended up sending David with the best help he could give: "Go, and the LORD be with you."

The greatest battle of life is spiritual. It is the struggles with resentment and anger and greed and superiority that keep me from living in the flow with God. How often in spiritual life do we get burdened because we try to wield weapons that have helped someone else in the battle? We hear about how someone else prays, or reads Scripture to start or end their day, or worships, or studies, or serves—and we feel guilty if we don't do the same. We get frustrated because what works for someone else is not helpful to us. We are like David, trying to walk around in Saul's armor.

The apostle Paul said to "put on the full armor of God," which includes truth and peace and prayer and faith. Have no doubt, it will fit you. If David had gone into battle using Saul's armor, he would have lost. God knew what Saul needed. God knew what David needed. And God knows what you need.

> For we are God's masterpiece. He has created us anew in Christ Jesus, so that we can do the good things he planned for us long ago. (Ephesians 2:10 NLT)

The Bible does not say you are God's *appliance*; it says you are his masterpiece. Appliances get mass-produced. Masterpieces get handcrafted. God did not make you exactly like anyone else. Therefore his plan for shaping you will not look like his plan for shaping anyone else. If you try to follow a generic plan for spiritual growth, it will only frustrate you. Paul said, "Where the Spirit of the Lord is, there is freedom."

It is time for you to stop walking around in Saul's armor. It is time to get free.

» The Freedom Way

Many approaches to spiritual growth assume that the same methods will produce the same growth in different people—but they don't. Because you have been created by God as a unique person, his plan to grow you will not look the same as his plan to grow anyone else. What would grow an orchid would drown a cactus. What would feed a mouse would starve an elephant. All of those entities need light, food, air, and water—but in different amounts and conditions. The key is not treating every creature alike; it is finding the unique conditions that help each creature grow.

Imagine a doctor's office where every patient is told, "Take two aspirin and call me in the morning." If I have a headache, that is great advice, but if my appendix has just burst, I will be dead before morning. Imagine a store that sells only one kind of shirt—one color, style, fabric, and size—and makes the same deal on pants. There are no "one-size-fits-all" stores, because God made people in different sizes. Imagine a parent who thinks, *No matter how many kids I have, I will treat them each exactly the same way. Each kid will be a blank slate for me to write on, pliable clay for me to mold. They will all be motivated by the same rewards, impacted by punishment the same way, and attracted by the same activities.*

What obliterates these ideas?

Reality, such as actually having children and becoming quickly aware that every human being is different. If we really want to help someone grow, we will have to help them in a way that fits their wiring.

Our great model for this is God himself, for he always knows just what each person needs.

He had Abraham take a walk, Elijah take a nap, Joshua take a lap, and Adam take the rap.

He gave Moses a forty-year time out, he gave David a harp and a dance, and he gave Paul a pen and a scroll.

He wrestled with Jacob, argued with Job, whispered to Elijah, warned Cain, and comforted Hagar.

He gave Aaron an altar, Miriam a song, Gideon a fleece, Peter a name, and Elisha a mantle.

Jesus was stern with the rich young ruler, tender with the woman caught in adultery, patient with the disciples, blistering with the scribes, gentle with the children, and gracious with the thief on the cross.

God never grows two people the same way. God is a hand-crafter, not a mass-producer.

Now it is your turn.

God has existed from eternity—but he has never had a relationship with you before. He wants to do a new thing with you. The problem many people face when it comes to spiritual growth is that they listen to someone they think of as the expert—maybe the pastor of their church—talk about what he does, and think that is what they are supposed to do. When it doesn't work for them—because they are a different person!—they feel guilty and inadequate; they often give up.

God has a plan for the me he wants me to be. It will not look exactly like his plan for anyone else, which means it will take freedom and exploration for me to learn how God wants to grow me. *Spiritual growth is hand-crafted, not mass-produced. God does not do "one-size-fits-all."*

Take the practice of writing in a journal, for example. When I mentioned journaling one time while speaking at a conference on spiritual life, I heard groans. I asked, "How many people do not like to journal?" What amazed me was not just how many hands were raised (the vast majority), but the speed and vehemence with which they were thrust into the air. It was as if people were admitting a secret shame they had been hiding for years. I have repeated this question on numerous occasions, always with the same results—once even at a workshop on journaling!

Spiritual growth is hand-crafted, not mass-produced. God does not do "one-size-fits-all."

If you don't like to keep a journal, here is a thought you might like: *Jesus never journaled.* Neither did Abraham or Moses or Ruth. Throughout most of the history of the human race, people loved God without ever picking up a paper and pencil. In fact, in those days most didn't have supplies to journal. Yet people still grew spiritually, examined their souls, fought sin, and learned obedience. "Journal" was not a verb back then; it wasn't even a noun. C. S. Lewis, one of the most influential Christians of the twentieth century, said that he kept a journal until he was converted. Then when he became a Christian, he realized that it was making him preoccupied with himself. So he stopped journaling.

Does this mean that keeping a journal is a bad idea? Not at all! As a matter of full disclosure, I often find it very helpful myself, especially in times of stress or pain. Writing my thoughts in those times helps prevent my self-examination and prayers from slipping into spirals of negativity. You may find that a journal helps you become more aware of God's presence in your life or aids you in praying. If it does, do it.

But you are free. Disciples are handcrafted, not mass-produced. No wonder we get frustrated when we think that everyone is supposed to look like the pastor or the author or whoever is teaching us at the moment about spiritual growth. We learn differently, struggle with different sins, and relate to God in different ways.

When Jesus prayed for his disciples, he did not pray, "May they all have identical devotional practices." He prayed, "Father, may they be one with you." The main measure of your devotion to God is not your devotional life. It is simply your life.

Trying to grow spiritually without taking who you are into account is like trying to raise children on an assembly line. If you train an 80-pound gymnast and a 300-pound linebacker exactly the same, you will end up with two useless 190-pound people.

> The main measure of your devotion to God is not your devotional life. It is simply your life. ✗

A frequent problem in the way we talk about spiritual growth is that there is not much spirit in it — God's Holy Spirit, that is. Only God makes things grow, and that growth is not always predictable. Like a tree beginning to bud, growth always has surprise attached to it.

What, then, do I need to know to learn how God wants to help me grow?

» What Brings Me Life?

If you are looking for a conversation stopper, try asking people this question: *How are your spiritual disciplines going?* Most people think of a very short list of activities that fall in the "I ought to do this, but I don't do it as much as I should, so it makes me feel guilty just thinking about it" category. So here is an alternative question: *What do you do that makes you feel fully alive?*

Everyone knows what it's like to feel fully alive, and everyone longs for that. Maybe you feel alive when taking a long walk at sunset. Maybe it is reading a great book and taking time to savor its thoughts and language. Maybe it is having a talk with lots of laughter in front of a bonfire with a few close friends. Maybe it is watching a movie or a play that causes you to say yes to life. Maybe it is taking a long drive. Maybe you love to play an instrument. Maybe you come alive when you are pursuing a hobby.

A spiritual discipline is simply an activity you engage in to be made more fully alive by the Spirit of Life.

Of course, that is not the same as "doing whatever feels good in the moment." Too much alcohol or too much food or compulsive sexual activity may feel good for the moment, but these activities do not lead us toward life. Eventually they lead to guilt, addiction, or regret.

The things that bring us life are also not simply "what feels comfortable." Giving away money or confessing sin may feel scary in the moment—but so does a good roller coaster ride, which leaves no doubt that I am alive and kicking.

> ✳ A spiritual discipline is simply an activity you engage in to be made more fully alive by the Spirit of Life.

We often assess how "spiritual" we are by how much we are pursuing our distorted list of "what counts" toward spiritual growth instead of by our fullness of life. Working with joy, tipping generously, listening to someone patiently, eating gratefully, reading quietly, playing happily—it all counts! *Every* moment is a chance to live in the flow of the Spirit.

No relationship can last if it is built purely on "should"—not even with my dental hygienist. My wife, my kids—even my dog—don't want me to be with them only because I think I *should*. Because they love me, they give me freedom, and in that freedom desire grows.

Likewise, where the Spirit is, there is freedom. It may seem strange, but when I think of God giving me freedom from the staleness of too many "shoulds," I find that my love and admiration for him grows. I want to be around a God like that!

Sustainable spiritual growth happens when I actually *want* to do what I *ought* to do. This means I have to change how I think about what "counts" as spiritual, for what makes an activity spiritual is not the activity itself. It is whether or not I do it with and through the Spirit. It is the quality of the presence and interaction with the Spirit while I am doing the activity.

»What Is My Temperament?

One of the most common temperament scales—the Myers-Briggs—looks at whether you are introverted or extroverted, whether you prefer data or intuition, whether you are a thinker or a feeler, and whether you like things orderly or open-ended. Each category gets expressed by a letter, so on the Myers-Briggs scale I come out an INFP. I am somewhat introverted, I am intuitive, I am a feeler, and I prefer spontaneity.

Every human being has a temperament, which means certain practices will come more naturally for you than others. Different temperaments are not better or worse, they simply are (although I personally am pretty sure Jesus was an INFP). Everyone needs some time in solitude, but if your personality is marked by being introverted, you have a greater capacity to withdraw from noise and people and tasks to be alone and quiet.

Because I am an introvert, the idea of going off to be alone almost always sounds appealing to me. However, solitude rarely happens by default. Circumstances in my life never conspire to produce a day with no activities or events. I have to choose solitude, and the simplest way is to take my calendar, find a day in the future when I have no commitments, and block it off to go some place I would love to be—out in nature or at a retreat center.

People often wonder how long they should be in solitude. You can experiment, because spiritual practices are about freedom. At first I found that about an hour was all I could handle. Eventually I came to love a day of solitude and found myself feeling free of other people's expectations and demands. When I am alone with God, I remember that all the people in my life are temporary and that their opinions of me don't really matter much.

If you are an extrovert, the notion of a day in solitude may sound like a nightmare. Try it for an hour. Remember, however, that this is not about the time; it's about the Spirit. If you are an introvert and love solitude, it does not mean that you are more spiritual than your extroverted spouse or friend, for whom community and fellowship probably come more naturally. They may have a head start on the very ability to love people that you are hoping God will grow in you when you are alone with him.

One man I know is both an extrovert and a deep feeler. He is in the flow of the Spirit best when he is neck-deep in the soul struggles of another human being. Ironically, even though he is trying to help someone else, it is in those moments when his own soul is healed. He found he needs to schedule several one-on-ones like that every week.

Some people have temperaments that crave regularity, order, and closure. If this is you, then having set times for prayer and lists of whom and what you are praying for may keep you connected to God. I know a woman who could show years of lists of prayers and years of lists of answers, and those lists are priceless to her. But if you have a temperament that craves spontaneity and change, your prayer life is never going to look like that. You may have tried and then given up on the lists, feeling guilty. But that is not because you don't love God; it is because you're just not a list-maker.

God desires to fill you with life, and you cannot get filled up when you are engaged too much in an activity that drains you. It does not mean that you will be less connected to God. Spontaneous people are capable of as much love as well-organized people — they're just messier. A man I know walks regularly and turns his walks into times of prayer. For him, there is something about the act of walking itself that provides enough change in what he is looking at to help his mind stay focused.

» What Is My Pathway?

Author Gary Thomas has written about how we all have what he calls sacred pathways — ways that we find naturally help us experience the presence of God. For instance, because one of my pathways is intellectual, I may find myself drawn deeply to God by a book that might put my wife to sleep. Because one of her pathways is activism, she may find herself intensely aware of God's presence neck-deep in a project that would make me want to take a nap. Often we will recognize our pathways because we find ourselves being changed or making key decisions when we are doing a particular activity. Some people connect to God best through nature. Some are activists, finding God naturally when they are charging into a cause. Intellectuals find their hearts filled with the Spirit when their minds are filled with great thoughts. Some people find the Spirit most alive in them when they are serving. Some connect most naturally with God in solitary contemplation. Others feel closest to God when they are having fellowship with friends. Some sense him nearest in worship.

It is good to be familiar with each pathway, but you will find that one or two are the most gripping for you. When you do identify which ones you resonate with most, you will also find that they are the most sustainable for you, because your desire for them will be highest.

sacred pathways

Naturalist — finds God in nature

Ascetic — is drawn to disciplines

Traditionalist — loves historical liturgies

Activist — comes alive spiritually in a great cause

Caregiver — meets God in serving

Sensate — senses God through five senses

Enthusiast — loves to grow through people

Contemplative — is drawn to solitary reflection and prayer

Intellectual — loves God by learning

(For more information on these categories, read Gary Thomas's book *Sacred Pathways* [Grand Rapids: Zondervan].)

» What Is My Learning Style?

Thankfully, spiritual growth is not restricted to people who like school, for God also wired us to learn in different ways. One man is quite bright and devoted to God, but he hates to read. Consequently, approaches to spiritual growth that require much reading are not going to help him. He has a huge capacity for growth and functions at a high level; he's just not a reader. He learns by listening. He learns from conversations, tapes, and talks.

Others learn mainly by doing. For example, if I try to assemble something, I will read the instructions seven times before trying to put tab A into slot B. But my friend Sam is a hands-on guy. He would try to build a nuclear power plant without looking at directions first. Trial-and-error is the way he learns best, which is great as long as he is not packing my parachute. For Sam, sitting in a church listening to a talk will never be his primary path to growth. An hour of doing is worth ten hours of listening.

Another friend of mine, Lee, learns best when her emotions are deeply engaged. She will be impacted most profoundly by information wrapped up in imagination, art, and other people. Her husband, Wendell, on the other hand, only has an emotion about once a decade. Deep emotion actually interferes with his learning.

You have a natural love of learning. But you have a natural style for learning as well. If someone reads the Bible more than you do, it does not necessarily mean they love God more than you do—they may just love reading more than you do. Try different styles of learning to see which fit you best.

---

learning styles

Visual — learn best by seeing

Auditory — learn best by hearing

Tactile — learn best by doing

Oral — learn best by saying

Social — learn best in groups

Logical — learn best in linear process

Imaginative — learn best through art, story, and image

» What Is My Signature Sin?

Precisely because you are uniquely you, you also wrestle with a unique set of temptations. No one sins exactly like you! As we will see in a later chapter, the sins that are most troubling for you are actually connected to your greatest gifts and interests. People who are great at leading are often tempted to use others; people who are gifted at peace-making can be tempted by avoidance; people with a gift for spontaneity are often tempted by their impulses. Knowing your sin patterns can help remove barriers to living in the flow of the Spirit.

Much of my own signature sin has to do with the need to look better than I really am. This often leads me to want to hide. I was sitting in front of my computer at home not long ago when someone in the family asked if I had a certain phone number. The truth is, I didn't know. I thought perhaps I had it in my cell phone, but I didn't want to take ten seconds to walk to the counter where my cell phone was, see if the number was there, and say it slowly enough for it to get copied down. I was busy. At my computer. Writing a chapter for a book about living in the flow of the Spirit.

But I didn't want to admit any of this. I didn't want the other person to think of me as a time-hog unwilling to serve.

So I just said, "No. Sorry. Can't help you."

Then the tiniest little voice whispered in my mind, *You little pastor scumbag.*

I had to stop, look the other person in the eye, and tell them, "I didn't tell you truth. I lied."

The other person did not respond by saying, "You scumbag." She understood and, unlike that tiniest little voice inside me, was much more gracious. She knew I am capable of much worse than that, and she forgave me. Even in the embarrassment of that moment, I became known more fully and loved more deeply.

Saint Benedict led a community of faith and wrote one of the most famous guidebooks for spiritual growth ever produced, *The Rule of Benedict*. But he built flexibility into it. He speaks of how the abbot must treat each soul differently: "One he must coax, another scold, another persuade, according to each one's character and understanding. Thus he must adjust and adapt himself to all...."

Freedom is the *goal* of growth. A great pianist is free to play notes without worrying about them. A great friend is free to be spontaneous. Spiritual practices are always about freedom.

Also, freedom is needed for the *path* to growth. One pianist might need to practice lots of scales. Another might do better improvising. Another might be helped by sight-reading. The same is true for spiritual growth: You are free to find the path that helps you best.

However, freedom is not the same as self-indulgence. I am not free to become a great pianist by watching TV and eating potato chips all day. I cannot grow in the Spirit if, as Paul says, I use my freedom to "indulge the sinful nature."

When I am aware of my signature sins, I am less vulnerable to them. Knowing where the land mines lie is the first requirement of a safe journey.

» What Is My Season of Life?

How you grow also depends on the season of your spiritual life. When a plant is very young, it often needs external support to help it grow. Tomato plants or young trees, for example, get tied to stakes; vines may need a lattice. But as they grow, the framework that was needed in their early days may actually inhibit growth later on. In spiritual life, structure is often most important when a person's faith is young. You have so much to learn. Worship, prayer, the Bible are all new to you. But as the years pass, what helps in one season may not help in another.

One woman I know loved to study the Scriptures, and she did it regularly for many years. Then her husband died, and she found that in her grief, reading the Bible was not helpful to her. This was not because she was resistant. In her great pain, for many months, it was like dust. So she had to live on what she had already fed her mind. Her hunger for Scripture did return eventually, but for a season of grief she had to receive grace in other ways.

Maybe you have been attending church for years out of a sense of obligation. You show up week after week out of habit, or because someone expects you to, but it is actually increasing the distance between you and God. So here is an idea: Stop going to church. Wait until you want to go again. Find out why you want to go. Trust that if you truly seek, God will bring the desire back to you.

Sometimes people think that because the Bible says "don't give up meeting together," you can never take a Sunday off. But God himself sometimes sent people (including Elijah, Moses, and Jesus) off for more than a month where they weren't around anybody! God's goal is not a perfect attendance record; it is a community of people who actually want to be in community.

Your path to growth will not be quite like anyone else's. It will be unique. It will be you-ier. It won't always be easy. But there is one decision that is always possible—that will always help you grow—and we turn to that now.

Chapter 5

Surrender: The One Decision That Always Helps

There is a God. It is not you.

This is the beginning of wisdom. At first, it looks like bad news because I would like to run the world. I would like to gratify my desires. I would like to have my own way. But once we think about it, this idea turns out to be very good news.

It means that someone far wiser and more competent is running the show. It is his job to be God; it is my job to learn to let him be who he is. The Bible says, "The fool has said in his heart, 'There is no God.'" I suppose the even bigger fool, looking in the mirror, has said, *"There is a god!"* for the oldest temptation is that we "will be like God." Real life, however, begins when I die to the false god that is me.

Jesus said that out of our bellies can flow rivers of living water. The one decision needed for that in any moment is the decision to surrender myself to God. Even when I am not sure what to do, I can place my life in God's hands. John Calvin said that the only haven of safety is "to have no other will, no other wisdom, than to follow the Lord wherever He leads. Let this, then, be the first step, to abandon ourselves, and devote the whole energy of our minds to the service of God." To do this, we will have to face our greatest fear.

» Who Will Drive Your Life?

It is a scary day when parents place their newborn child in a car seat for that child's first day out in the world. As they head down the road, the fragility of life becomes very real. Do you know when the next scary day with your child and the car is?

Sixteen years later. Now you are handing over the keys. They are moving from the passenger's seat to the driver's seat. Up until then, you have been driving. You choose the destination, route, and speed. The person behind the wheel is the one in control.

We live in a neighborhood with circuitous streets, and wherever I am going, even if it's three blocks away, whatever route I take, someone in my family will critique it. "Why are you going this way? This is the long way! You should have gone the other way." I have to tell them, this car is *my car*. These keys are *my keys*. This way is *my way*.

I live in a family where everybody wants to drive.

Many people find Jesus pretty handy to have in the passenger's seat when they require his services.

Jesus, I have a health problem, and I need your help.
Something hard is going on at work, and I'd like it to be different.
I'm feeling anxious, and I want you to give me peace of mind.
I'm feeling sad, and I'd like a little hope.
I'm facing death, and I want to make sure I'm going to heaven.

But these people are not so sure they want Jesus driving, because if Jesus is behind the wheel, they are not in control anymore. If he is driving, they are not in charge of their wallet anymore. They no longer can simply say, "I'll give sometimes when I feel generous, but I reserve the right to keep what I want." Now it is Jesus' money.

When I let Jesus drive, I am no longer in charge of my ego. I no longer have the right to satisfy every self-centered ambition. Now it is his life. I am not in charge of my mouth anymore. I don't get to gossip, flatter, cajole, condemn, lie, curse, rage, cheat, intimidate, manipulate, exaggerate, or prevaricate anymore. Now it is not my mouth—it is his mouth.

I get out of the driver's seat. I hand over the keys to Jesus. I am fully engaged. In fact, I am more alive than ever before. But it is not my life anymore. It is his life.

Have I invited Jesus along for the ride, or is he driving? Who is behind the wheel? Jesus is very clear on this point: *There is no way for a human being to come to God that does not involve surrender.*

> "Whoever finds their life will lose it, and whoever loses their life for my sake will find it." (Matthew 10:39)
>
> "I tell you the truth, unless a kernel of wheat falls to the ground and dies, it remains only a single seed. But if it dies, it produces many seeds." (John 12:24)
>
> "Whoever wants to be my disciple must deny themselves and take up their cross and follow me." (Matthew 16:24)

Surrender is not the same thing as passivity. God's will for your life involves exercising creativity, making choices, and taking initiative. Surrender does not mean being a doormat. It does not mean you accept circumstances fatalistically. Often it means you will have to fight to challenge the status quo. It doesn't mean that you stop using your mind, stop asking questions, or stop thinking critically. Surrender is not a crutch for weak people who cannot handle life.

 There is no way for a human being to come to God that does not involve surrender.

Instead, surrender is the glad and voluntary acknowledgment that there is a God and it is not me. His purposes are often wiser and better than our desires. Jesus does not come to rearrange the outside of our life the way we want. He comes to rearrange the inside of our life the way God wants.

In surrender, I let go of my life. It is a Copernican revolution of the soul in which I take myself out of the center of the universe and place God there. I yield to Him. I offer obedience. I do what he says. I am not driving anymore.

When spirituality gets discussed in our culture, there are some messages from the Bible that everybody likes hearing:

"No matter how much you mess up, God still loves you." Everyone likes that one.

"You are so busy and exhausted—God wants you to be rested and refreshed." That sounds good too.

But what about these?

> Jesus does not come to rearrange the outside of our life the way we want. He comes to rearrange the inside of our life the way God wants.

"You need to surrender. You are sinful, stubborn, and stiff-necked. You are self-centered and self-promoting, your own desires are very often self-serving, your ability to perceive your own sin is blinded by self-deception, you need to bend the knee, you need to submit your heart, you need to confess your sin, you need to *surrender*."

Surrender is a hard word.

I will name one person who I know for sure doesn't like to hear that: *Me*.

» Why Surrender?

When someone throws a winning touchdown pass, when somebody hits the game-winning home run, when a doctor says he has good news, or when someone wins the lottery, we all have a reflexive response with our bodies. We raise them high. During such times we are hardwired to stretch our hands toward heaven. We all want the posture of victory and celebration.

There is another posture, however, that expresses surrender. When we are contrite, when we are submitting, we kneel, expressing with our bodies what is in our hearts. When a subject comes before his king, what does he do to humble himself? He kneels to acknowledge that he is in the presence of his master. When a believer in any religion comes to pray to his God, what does he do? He kneels to acknowledge that he is in the presence of his master. When a man asks a woman to become his wife, what does he do? He gets down on one knee to acknowledge ... well, you get the idea.

Exalted high in victory. Bent low in surrender. The two postures seem opposite, but Jesus understood that if you want to experience victory, you must start in surrender. Surrender brings power, and the need to surrender is deeply tied to Jesus' offer of living in the flow of the Spirit. You receive power through the act of surrender that you cannot obtain any other way; you receive freedom through submission that you will otherwise never know.

The Twelve Steps followed by recovery groups lay out a way of life that is the single greatest path to freedom for addicts the world has ever known. But at the core of the steps lies a great paradox: In which of the twelve steps does it say "now *try really hard* to not drink"? In which of the twelve steps does it even say "now *decide* not to drink"? Amazingly enough, the most powerful tool against the most powerful addiction in the world never asks people to decide to stop doing what is destroying their lives. Instead of mobilizing the will, its followers surrender their will. Try to overcome the problem by your will, and it will beat you. Surrender your will, and sobriety becomes possible. Surrender, which we think means defeat, turns out to be the only way to victory. This is not just the case with alcohol. It is also true with other addictions, with habits, with brokenness—and with sin in general.

Why does the will fail? In *The Big Book* of Alcoholics Anonymous, the writer says that when it comes to drinking, we say and feel "*never again*." But we do it again. *Why?*

> We are unable, at certain times, to bring into our consciousness with
> sufficient force the memory of the suffering and humiliation of even
> a week ago.... the certain consequences that follow taking a drink
> do not crowd into the mind to deter us. If these thoughts occur, they
> are hazy and readily replaced by the old threadbare idea that this
> time we can handle it ourselves.

It is possible to receive power to become the person I want to be. But to do so, I have to hand over the keys.

Another gift of surrender is peace. If I live in the illusion that I am god, I will drive myself and everybody else crazy with my need for control. When I surrender, I don't just let go of my will. I also give up the idea that I am in charge of *outcomes*.

When my children started driving, I would sit in the passenger seat to coach them. I tried to look relaxed, but if I thought they were taking too

"the nature of the will"

In a series of brilliant experiments, psychologist Roy Baumeister has studied the nature and limits of will-power. One key question was, Once you exercise your willpower — say, by resisting temptation for five minutes — does that make your willpower stronger, weaker, or unchanged for the next few minutes?

Baumeister had certain subjects exert willpower by resisting the temptation to eat delicious, fresh, warm, gooey chocolate chip cookies — eating only radishes instead. Another set of subjects did not have to resist eating cookies. Then all the subjects were assigned complex math problems to solve — problems that were actually *impossible* to solve — in order to measure how long people will exercise willpower to persevere in frustration.

The people who had to resist eating chocolate chip cookies gave up on problem-solving much more quickly than the other subjects. In other words, our willpower is easily fatigued. We can use our wills to override our habits for a few moments, but our habits will always beat willpower alone in the long run.

The will is good at big simple choices: getting married, or taking a job, or joining AA. But the will is *very bad* at trying to overcome habits or attitudes that have become embedded in our bodies. Deep change takes more than willpower. It requires God renewing our minds. It requires surrender.

long to hit the brakes, my feet would start pressing into the floor on some imaginary brake on my side. My jaws would clench and my shoulders would hunch, as if my body believed that it could help slow the car by tensing up.

What a relief it is to believe there is someone more competent than me behind the wheel, so that I *do not have to control the outcomes* of my life. I love my children the best I can, but I am not in charge of their destiny. I work the best I can, but I am not in control of the results. I try to make wise choices to save for retirement, but I am not running the stock market. I find that every moment I worry is a chance to practice letting go of the need to control outcomes.

There is a God. It is not me.

» Surrender as a Continual Experience

Surrender is not something we do once and get over. Paul used a striking image in his letter to Rome when he wrote, "Offer your bodies as a living sacrifice...." During a Jewish sacrifice an animal would be killed, then its body would be placed on the altar to be consumed. So what happens if you put a live creature on the altar and say, "Stay there until you're consumed," then light the fire? The creature will jump right off that altar! But Paul encourages us, of our own volition, to crawl back onto the altar. We are called to surrender day by day, moment by moment. In the moment it feels like death, but it is really the only way to life.

For example, suppose someone in the workplace does something to me that really makes me angry. The situation is complicated, so I am not yet even sure of the right way to respond. Without even trying, my mind fills with all kinds of bad thoughts. In the moment, I do not know what I should do. But thoughts come—I know from God—about what not to do:

No murder. *Okay, I won't kill them.*

No violence. *Okay ... I won't have them beaten up.*

No gossip. *But if I agree to no murder or violence, couldn't we leave gossip on the table?*

Surrender means that I will seek to handle the problem facing me in a way that honors God. The options that look attractive to me—avoiding, evading, gossiping, blasting—I relinquish to God. If my hurt runs deep, it will be about five minutes before the revenge fantasies start raging back. I will have to surrender all over again. But I can recognize those fantasies a little quicker and yield a little sooner.

In my life and in your life there is always the question before us, *who is driving?* I can have a rebellious heart, telling God to stay out of my car altogether, that I will go where I want when I want with my life. Or

I can have a divided heart, keeping Jesus in the car, but driving myself, saying to him, "I will keep this area, this pattern, this relationship under my own control. I will hang onto this grudge. I will enjoy the pleasure I get from this habit. I know you want full surrender, but I don't trust you."

The problem is, living with a divided heart makes us miserable. Sometimes we can keep the guilt vague and fuzzy. Sometimes it will be vivid. But if our heart is sensitive toward God and we keep him out of the driver's seat, the guilt will gnaw at us. Only one thing will bring ultimate peace: a surrendered heart.

> I have been crucified with Christ and I no longer live, but Christ lives in me. (Galatians 2:20)

I turn my life and will over to God. I seek to obey the best I can. You lose a life, but you gain a life—a life much better than the one you lost. In the end, it turns out that nothing you lost was really worth keeping anyway.

» The Action of Surrender

Because surrender is so closely connected to our wills, often a price is attached. Sometimes I can *feel* devoted to God, but when it comes time to act, I find that my surrender is only skin deep.

Anticipating this, Jesus often identified the particular area where surrender was needed in a person's life. To a woman caught in adultery he said, "I don't condemn you. Go and sin no more." We need to surrender our sexuality to God. Many times surrender will involve money, because money is all about trust and control. Often surrender will involve an act of self-disclosure about a grudge, attitude, habit, or sin. Sometimes when I am with a friend, I am prompted to talk about a matter in which I have struggled or have failed. My immediate response is generally, *no way*. At other times I may be with someone and feel the need to confront them about something that would make me uncomfortable. My immediate response again is generally, *no way*.

Then I have to decide: *Will I surrender when surrender means doing something uncomfortable?* If it is comfortable, it wouldn't be surrender.

But here again we are never on our own. The Spirit is always available. One of the most amazing teachings of the Scriptures is that in Jesus,

tasks that require the will

≈ Making decisions (which is why a long menu wears us out)
≈ Self-presentation (projecting an image)
≈ Resisting temptation
≈ Persisting in a difficult task
≈ Breaking a habit (smoking, overeating, etc.)
≈ Surrender

Amazingly, the one act of the will that *produces* energy rather than *depletes* energy is surrender. Surrender actually replenishes our vitality. So try praying a prayer of surrender as you think of it through the day. Something like this:

"Father, today I gladly place my life in your hands ..."

≈ When I wake up
≈ When I face a decision
≈ When I am in relational conflict
≈ When I am tempted
≈ When I want to give up
≈ When bad habits reappear

God himself knows the pain of surrender. Jesus knelt in a garden and prayed, "Let this cup pass from me. Nevertheless, not my will, but yours be done." And just as surrender led to resurrection for Jesus, so it does for his followers. The apostle Paul wrote, "For you died, and your life is now hidden with Christ in God. When Christ, who is your life, appears, then you also will appear with him in glory."

What does it mean that you will appear with him "in glory"? It means the day is coming when it will be a glorious thing to be you. One of the noblest thoughts about God ever recorded by a human being came from Moses' encounter on Mount Sinai. Moses asked, "Now show me your glory." We might expect special effects—thunder and lighting and earthquakes and power. But instead God said, "I will cause all my goodness to pass before you."

The most glorious thing about God is how good he is. One day you will share in that goodness. Everything that is small or petty in you will be gone. To glorify God means to be the kind of person people will look at and say, "What a great God God must be to have thought up such a creature!"

That will be you. "In glory." Glorious.

The only way to glory is through humility. The only way to freedom is through submission. The only way to victory is through surrender.

Nancy and I recently decided to take dancing lessons. I grew up Swedish and Baptist, and we were not a dancing people. I also attended a college where it was against the law to dance. But I have been married for twenty-five years, so I guess dancing would be legal now.

We have a terrific dance instructor who, before we began, pulled us aside. "I have a very important question," this instructor said. "You are going to dance now. Who leads?"

There was silence.

I knew the answer, but I wanted to hear my wife say it. A few more seconds of silence, and then through gritted teeth she said, "He leads."

"And who follows?"

Silence. Then, "I follow."

It was hard for Nancy to follow for two reasons. One is that when you aren't leading, you aren't in control. It is hard not to be in control. The other is that when it comes to dancing, I am a thoroughly incompetent leader.

Jesus, however, is a thoroughly competent leader. When you wake up in the morning, you can feel completely confident in saying, "Okay, Jesus, today you lead, and I will follow. Whatever I have to do in my relationships, my body, my health, and my finances are in your hands. I won't try to figure out the rest of my life. I won't try to solve every day. Just today. You lead. I'll follow."

You don't want to miss the dance. It is why you were born. And God leads it, not just for today, but into eternity.

There is a God. It is not you.

Save the last dance....

Chapter 6
Try Softer

Not long ago I went with my wife to a yoga class for the first time in my life. Immediately it became clear to me why yoga will never catch on: They don't keep score. You can't tell who's winning.

Mostly we just stretched, and I am not good at stretching. On a good day I can touch my knees. What made it worse is that most of the other people in the class were clearly double-jointed. There was a middle-aged woman who didn't look particularly fit — I thought I would definitely beat her at whatever you compete at in yoga — but she was a dancer. At one point she did the splits with her legs, bent forward with her torso completely flat on the ground, then tied both her legs around the back of her head. If they had been keeping score, I would have lost at that point on the mercy rule. Afterward, I did ask the instructor if the woman could be tested for performance-enhancing drugs.

As you might imagine, the class was a lot of work and good for my body. But I was struck afterward by a phrase I never heard: *Try harder.* The instructor never said, "Try harder to stretch. Try harder to be flexible. Try harder to contort your body like a fourteen-year-old female Russian gymnast."

When you stretch, you don't make it happen simply by trying harder. You must let go and let gravity do its work. You give permission, opening yourself to another, greater force.

This is not just true when it comes to stretching. As a general rule, the harder you work to control things, the more you lose control. The harder you try to hit a fast serve in tennis, the more your muscles tense up. The harder you try to impress someone on a date or while making a sale, the more you force the conversation and come across as pushy. The harder you cling to people, the more apt they are to push you away.

Sometimes trying harder helps. It can help me clean my room, push through phone calls I need to make, or run another lap. But for deeper change, I need a greater power than simply "trying harder" can provide. Imagine someone advising you, "Try harder to relax. Try harder to go to sleep. Try harder to be graceful. Try harder to not worry. Try harder to be joyful."

There are limits on what trying harder can accomplish.

Often the people in the Gospels who got into the most trouble with Jesus were the ones who thought they were working hardest on their spiritual life. They were trying so hard to be good that they could not stop thinking about how hard they were trying. That got in the way of their loving other people.

The problem when I try harder is that I get fixated on my own heroic efforts. I grow judgmental. I can't let this endure forever. So instead of making vows about how my spiritual life will be perfectly well organized until I die, I seek to surrender my will for just this day. I look for small graces. I try to engage in little acts of service. I pray briefly to accommodate my limited attention span. I look for ways of being with God that I already enjoy. I try to go for half an hour without complaining. I try to say something encouraging to three people in a row. I put twenty dollars in my pocket that I will give away sometime during the day. I take a five-minute break to read a page of great thoughts.

If trying harder is producing growth in your spiritual life, keep it up. But if it is not, here is an alternative:

Try softer.
Try better.
Try different.

A river of living water is now available, but the river is the Spirit. It is not you.

The contemplative Franciscan priest Richard Rohr puts it like this: "Faith does not need to push the river because faith is able to trust that *there is a river*. The river is flowing. We are in it."

Don't push the river.

Trying softer means focusing more on God's goodness than our efforts. It means being more relaxed and less self-conscious. Less pressured. When I try softer, I am less defensive, more open to feedback. I learn better. I stay patient if things don't turn out the way I expected. It means less self-congratulation when I do well and less self-flagellation when I fall down. It means asking God for help.

When I am trying too hard, I cannot stop thinking how nobly I'm behaving. When I take even one step toward growth, my very next thought will often be pride at my goodness — which of course moves me two steps back. True growth always goes in the opposite direction of self-righteousness.

This is the point of one of Jesus' most unusual little stories, sometimes called the "Parable of the Unworthy Servants." Perhaps a better name would be the "Parable of Trying Softer."

Suppose one of you had a servant plowing or looking after the sheep. Would he say to the servant when he comes in from the field, "Come along now and sit down to eat"? Would he not rather say, "Prepare my supper, get yourself ready and wait on me while I eat and drink; after that you may eat and drink"? Would he thank the servant because he did what he was told to do? So you also, when you have done everything you were told to do, should say, "We are unworthy servants; we have only done our duty."

This seems like a strange parable, especially coming from Jesus, Mr. Servanthood. Why shouldn't the master fix dinner for the servants? But this isn't a story about labor relations. Jesus is addressing our tendency to be over-impressed with how hard we are trying, and he is pointing toward the highest stage of spiritual growth. We might think of our growth — and our perception of our growth — in four quadrants.

Incompetent and unaware. In this stage, not only am I incapable of doing something, but I don't even know how incapable I am. I can't sing, and I don't know how bad I sound. The first cost of incompetence is always the inability to perceive incompetence. In a room where one person is drunk and everyone else is sober, the drunk person is least aware of his intoxication. In the spiritual realm, this is the prodigal son who was wasting his father's money and was not even aware of his own spiritual peril.

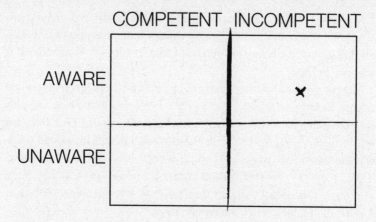

The danger in this stage is living in continued ignorance, and the need is for pain, because pain brings awareness. When the prodigal ran out of money and a famine hit the land, he longed to eat pig slop and "came to his senses." Pain is what we experience when reality crashes into us.

I had a conversation with a lifelong friend awhile back, and he said to me, "You seem so busy that I often feel like I should not contact you. I feel as if I'm usually the one who makes contact if we have contact at all. I'm often afraid that if I call you I'll be one more intrusion on your schedule. It makes me concerned for your life." It was a very painful conversation, but it changed the trajectory of our relationship. Once I was aware of what I was doing, change became possible. This leads to the second stage of growth.

Incompetent and self-conscious. Now I am still incompetent, but I have become aware—or self-conscious—of my incompetence. This is the person who always thought being a parent is easy, that controlling children is just a matter of common sense and setting boundaries—and then one day has a child and actually becomes a parent. This is the person who thought skiing looked easy until she put on a pair of skis. This is the prodigal son "when he comes to his senses." Now he realizes what a miserable failure his approach to life has actually been, and he decides to return home. But he does not think he can come back as a son. The best that he can hope for is to return as a servant.

The danger of this stage is that I will despair over my incompetence and give up. I compare myself to the old-timer who is said to have spent three hours a day on his knees in prayer, and I become so discouraged over my prayerlessness that I give up altogether. I see a family where everyone looks happy, healthy, and overachieving and think my own fathering is hopelessly inadequate. I compare my insides with other people's outsides and decide my insides are too unhealthy to be redeemed. The need in this stage is for hope.

Competent and aware. This is the person who has just received her license to drive, but must monitor where the car is in the lane and plan through every turn. This is the piano player who has to keep thinking which finger goes where. This is the alcoholic on the first day of sobriety, for whom each moment of not drinking seems worthy of applause. These people are constantly thinking about themselves and their efforts at growth. Often they compare themselves to other people, as the elder brother did in the story of the prodigal son.

The danger here is pride. William Lang, who was Archbishop of Canterbury in the first half of the twentieth century, had a painting done of himself that he did not like. He asked the Bishop of Durham what he thought of it, saying that it seemed to portray him as "proud, arrogant, and worldly." The bishop asked him, "To which of those three does Your Grace take exception?"

Stage three lostness can be the worst of all, because it carries its own blindness. People see therapists and pastors every day for anger or anxiety or addiction problems, but rarely does anyone seek help for their pride problem. There are no Betty Ford Treatment Centers for the Insufferably Arrogant, but not because we don't need them.

In another parable about trying harder, Jesus talked about a Pharisee who thanked God that he was not like a sordid little tax collector. Many contemporary Christians read this story and think, *That Pharisee thought he had to earn his way into God's favor, but I'm smarter than he was. My theology is right. Thank God I'm better than that guy who thought he was better than everybody else.*

The need here is for humility. Sometimes it takes a crisis in the area of our greatest pride — reputation, family, spirituality — for our own smugness to be punctured.

Competent and unself-conscious. This is the skier who is flying down the slopes, no longer having to think of herself, free to enjoy the thrill of skiing. This is the father welcoming home his son. In this stage, competence no longer looks heroic — just sane. This is the recovering alcoholic who has been sober twenty years. Sobriety now means not having to think about sobriety all the time, but being free to think of more interesting things.

There was a remarkable village in southeastern France called La Chambon, in which the people risked their lives to protect Jews during World War II. In later years documentaries were made about them; a wonderful book entitled *Lest Innocent Blood Be Shed* was written about them by Philip P. Hallie. But the villagers tended to be irritated by questions that made their risks sound noble or praiseworthy. "What else would you do?" they responded. "You do what needs to be done."

This is the point of Jesus' story. When we truly grow, then obeying God no longer looks like something that requires an appreciation banquet. It just looks like what should come naturally, like something that needs to be done.

Of course, we do not progress through these quadrants strictly in a linear, sequential fashion in our daily lives. We can go back and forth all the time. They can vary from one habit to another. I might be in quadrant four when it comes to alcohol and quadrant one when it comes to anxiety. But they help me remember the goal. The best version of myself lives in quadrant four, where the skier effortlessly glides down the slopes, where the father graciously welcomes his son, where the servant joyfully delights his Master.

There is an old story of an ambitious young person approaching a master and saying, "I want to be your student, your best student. How long must I study?"

"Ten years."

"But ten years is too long. What if I study twice as hard as all your other students?"

"Then it will take twenty years."

There is a river of life all around. But you can't push it.

Try softer.

PART THREE
renewing my mind

»

Chapter 7
Let Your Desires Lead You to God

Two very athletic nine-year-olds start taking swimming lessons. One begins because he has seen the Olympic Games and wants more than anything in the world to win a gold medal when he grows up. He pictures himself on the podium; he surrounds himself with Olympic pictures; he listens to the national anthem every day. The other kid starts lessons to please his father. Which one is likely to make it to the Olympics?

The one who is swimming for his dream.

Two twenty-year-olds have a goal to save ten thousand dollars. One of them has a dream to buy a used sports car that he loves, that he has wanted since he was sixteen, that will mean a new independence. The other twenty-year-old is saving because he thinks he should. Who do you think will reach ten thousand dollars first, willing to keep track of his expenses, eat cheaply, and forego new clothes?

The one who is saving for his dream.

In Genesis we learn that Jacob fell in love with Rachel so deeply that he agreed to work for seven years to pay her dowry. "So Jacob served seven years to get Rachel, but they seemed like only a few days to him because of his love for her." Who would regard seven years of work as a couple of days?

The one who is working for his dream.

There is no power in life like the power of "got-to-have" desire.

When Jesus described life with God, he told stories about "got-to-have" desire. He said it is like a man who found a treasure buried in the field and joyfully sold everything he owned because he had to have it. It is like a merchant who found a pearl he had been dreaming of his whole life.

Periodically when people listened to Jesus, some of them had this desire awakened in them. They saw how Jesus lived his life. They were drawn to his peace, his courage, or his wisdom. Sooner or later the thought would go off in their brain, *I must have what he has.*

Maybe you already have that burning passion. If so, you can skip this chapter. But too often we are told that we *should* desire God above all things without being told *how.* We cannot conjure up desire on command. So if your spiritual want-to factor wobbles now and then, keep reading.

» You and Your Like-o-Meter

Spiritual growth requires that our life with God move from the "should" category to the "want-to" category, and the most basic assessment we have for any experience or event is what psychologist Jonathan Haidt calls our "like-o-meter." Your like-o-meter was running the day you were born. Taste receptors in babies are pretty well developed, so for them the like-o-meter usually involves what goes into their mouths: "like it — gotta have more" or "hate it — get it out of here." As you continue to grow up, everything registers on your like-o-meter without you having to think about it. Every sound you hear, every conversation you are a part of, every bite you eat either rates positively or negatively on your scale.

Because of this, people also register somewhere on *your* like-o-meter. In the briefest of conversations you will find yourself leaning toward some people. Something in your spirit says, "I like this person. I'm enjoying this conversation." Other people will register negatively on your scale — and at the same time you're doing this, everyone around is rating you on their own like-o-meters. Rarely will we insinuate, "Right now you're about a negative seven on my scale, and if you keep talking you'll sink lower." But it's always going on. So here is a thought to consider:

Do you like God?

That may sound like a strange question, and I don't mean to be glib about God. But if I do not like being with God, I simply will not be with him much. It is good to be honest about this because if you don't like God, there's no use trying to fake him out. The point of this is not to make you feel guilty that you *should* want God more.

"Should" simply does not have the power to get you there.

» The Little Auxiliary Engine That "Should"

"Should" is a kind of auxiliary engine. It is necessary to have this, and sometimes I must do things simply because I should. But if I am running in a marathon, it doesn't matter at mile marker twenty-three whether I think I *should* finish. I will finish because I *want* to finish. "Want" will eventually wear down "should."

Likewise, spiritual growth doesn't mean a life of doing what I *should* do instead of what I *want* to do. It means coming to want to do what I should do. Jesus' point in these stories about desiring the kingdom of God is that when people come to understand how good God is, they *want* him. They don't just love him. They *like* him.

We might look at it this way: When we tell people they ought to do something, we can take that "ought" in two ways — the ought of obligation and the ought of opportunity. The first kind is our duty. You *ought* to pay your taxes. You *ought* to keep your dog on a leash. You *ought* to take your drivers' test. The second kind gives us life. You *ought* to take a break. You *ought* to see the world. You *ought* to taste this cake.

The "ought" of Jesus' message is mainly an ought of opportunity.

When we become aware of this, we feel guilty because our desire for God does not run deep enough — but we cannot make ourselves desire God more by telling ourselves that we should. God is so gracious and patient, wanting us to want him, that he is willing to work with this kind of honesty. That is why we are invited to "taste and see that the LORD is good."

Taste is an experimental word. It is an invitation from a confident chef. You don't have to commit to eating the whole thing; just try a sample — *taste*. If you don't like it, you can skip the rest. But the chef is convinced that if he can get you to take one bite, you are going to want the whole enchilada.

» Use Your Authentic Desires to "Taste and See the LORD is Good"

God made you with desires, and he wants you to desire him most of all — but not only to desire him. Part of trying softer is allowing what we naturally desire around us to lead us back to God. There is a pattern to your desires — certain activities, sensations, people, and thoughts that wake up the "got-to-have" response in you. Those desires are God's gift to you. They are part of the you God wants you to be.

When people enjoy what God has created, his heart is pleased. However, many people think, *If I want to be spiritual, I have to avoid sin, and the best way to avoid sin would be to just do away with desire altogether. If I just didn't want sex or money or food or success, I would be really spiritual because then I wouldn't sin.* But then you wouldn't be human, either. A slab of cement doesn't have to worry about weeds — but it will also never be a garden.

> Lewis Smedes wrote, "God is so great that he does not need to be our only joy. There is an earthly joy, a joy of the outer as well as the inner self, the joy of dancing as well as kneeling, the joy of playing as well as praying."

Uncorrupted by sin, desire is fabulous — fabulous because it is part of God's design. The psalmist says to God,

You open your hand and satisfy the desires of every living thing.
The LORD is righteous in all his ways and loving toward all he has
made. . . . He fulfills the desires of those who fear him.

God is a desire-creating, desire-satisfying God. He made birds with the impulse to fly — they want to do it because God made them to do it. Dolphins swim because God made them with an instinct to swim. God doesn't plant wrong desires in his creatures.

How did Adam know he was supposed to become "one flesh" with Eve? Do you think God put it on his to-do list? "Okay, Adam, name the animals, take out the trash . . . and, oh, by the way, don't forget to become one flesh with Eve."

No. Adam looked at Eve, and he discovered he had desire. Where did that desire come from? It came from God.

A beautiful prayer from the *Book of Common Prayer* begins, "Most Holy God, the source of all good desires...." God created desire, and it is God's delight to fulfill desire. I know that my desires are distorted by sin and need to be cleansed, purified, and retrained. This is what Jesus refers to when he says, "Whoever wants to be my disciple must deny themselves and take up their cross and follow me." We must say no to any desires that would keep us from living in the flow of the Spirit. We must always be ready to sacrifice a lesser desire for the sake of living a greater life.

On the other hand, nothing makes a human being more vulnerable to temptation than a joyless life. God's plan is that every time we experience an authentic desire — a God-implanted desire in us — we come to understand more deeply what a good God he is. We learn how God has wired us and what he wants us to do. As a result, we find ourselves loving this great God more and more. This is how we "taste and see" that the Lord is good, and our desire can be part of this river of life that flows in us with power and energy.

James speaks of the fulfillment of desire when he says, "Every good and perfect gift comes from above, from the Father of all lights who satisfies the desires of those who fear him...."

The writer of Proverbs says, "Hope deferred makes the heart sick, but a longing fulfilled is a tree of life." A desire fulfilled is sweet to the soul.

» Desires in Four Flavors

I would like you to walk through four categories of desires and assess yourself. As you do, be honest, because these categories on the surface might not look spiritual. Maybe you have always thought of them as having nothing to do with God, but if you let them, they can become part of living in the flow of the Spirit. The reality — the *spiritual* reality — is that each one of them has a God-designed foundation in our life.

Material Desires

We all have *material desires* — desires attached to money and clothes and cars and houses. If we could purge away all our sin, we would still desire material things because God created that stuff. All stuff, ultimately, is part of God's creation, and therefore it is all good. And therefore it is desirable.

Do you like money? In Acts 16 we read about Lydia, a businesswoman dealing in textiles, who was the first convert to Christianity in Europe. She had an eye for design and a flair for making money. Imagine the passion and drive it would take for a woman to succeed in business in the ancient world. She was good enough at it that she owned her own home, and it was large enough that it became part of her ministry. Lydia's house became the first meeting place of the first church in the history of Europe. Of all the churches built over all the centuries — Notre Dame, Westminster Abbey, and the Sistine Chapel — the very first one in Europe was the home of this Philippian businesswoman named Lydia.

Maybe you have a flair for money. You enjoy it. You don't admit it to anyone at church, but you do. You love being surrounded by beauty, design, and color. That in itself is not a bad thing. God created beauty. God loves beauty.

If these desires choke your generosity, cause you to live in debt, or create chronic dissatisfaction, then it is time to say no. But it is a good thing to put beauty in your environment that speaks to your soul. When you see that beauty, embrace that God-given joy and thank him that he is such a good God.

In that moment, you can experience the flow of the Spirit in your life.

As the Spirit flows in you, maybe God will give you creative, new ideas about how to share what you have, just as he did with Lydia.

Is it a bad thing to like fast cars? That is a material desire. Maybe God placed a desire for fast cars within you so you could be a policeman, so that you could drive really fast and it would be legal. (My nephew is training with the California Highway Patrol, and it sounds like fun.) Or maybe you drive fast so policemen can have something to do.

If you love engines, if you love to work with your hands, remember that you were made in the image of a creative God who engineered this unbelievable, cosmic machine with forces and energies so transcendently mind-boggling that people devote brilliant scientific careers trying to understand just a tiny bit of it. If you are fascinated with engines, that too is spiritual, a direct reflection of the fact that you are made in the image of this God who is the most creative engineer ever. It counts!

Now, if your desire for cars blocks good stewardship or puts you in debt, it is time to say no. If not, is it possible that enjoying a car might be something you could do with God? And when you are driving, you might say, "God, I invite you to be with me in this moment."

The Spirit could be flowing with you right there—*j-u-s-t* under the speed limit.

Achievement Desires

There have been few people in history more motivated by achievement than the apostle Paul. He was constantly moving, teaching, building, and motivating. He described his life with metaphors such as "I have fought the good fight. I have finished the race." God did not take away Paul's desire to achieve; rather, he harnessed it so that Paul could serve others.

We all have desires to achieve things, because God created us to have dominion. That is why the writer of Ecclesiastes says, "Whatever your hand finds to do, do it with all your might." It is a good thing to want to achieve.

Maybe you have a strong drive in your career. Maybe you are highly motivated by the opportunity to learn. Maybe you just love to accomplish. If your achievement desires are leading you to workaholism, to worshiping status, to neglecting prayer, or to using people, then your work needs redirection. But if that is not the case—if you find yourself growing in God and there's an inner fire in you to achieve—go ahead and achieve. Revel in the joy of exercising godly dominion.

Use your ability to accomplish good for others. And when you are doing it—when you are contributing to a meeting, adding value to a team, or formulating ideas—you will know it is more than just you. As you have relational skills that enable you to bond with clients, you can simultaneously pray for them and bless them. Every now and then stop and thank God that you get to do this, for as you achieve and feel joy in doing so, you are exercising dominion and opening yourself up to the flow of the Spirit.

Relational Desires

In the Old Testament we read about the friendship between Jonathan and David. Even though Jonathan was heir to the throne, he voluntarily gave up power because he knew his friend David was God's choice to be king. Jonathan wanted to be friend more than he wanted to be king. That is unusual in circles of power. Jonathan did not become David's friend because he was pursuing the discipline of spiritual friendship. He simply liked David, and that friendship produced generosity and humility in Jonathan that changed the course of Israel. There have been countless kings whom nobody remembers—but Jonathan's friendship with David has inspired the human race for thousands of years.

We all have relational desires, and maybe you hunger for deep relationships but never really pursue them. You get too busy. If deep relationships don't just fall into your lap, you give up. Deep relationships, however, don't just fall into our lap. Jonathan had to overcome unbelievable barriers to build his friendship with David—and there is a good chance that you will, too, to build a friendship.

My friend Chuck has the spiritual gift of breakfast. He meets people at a southern franchise called the Waffle House. The waitress loves to wait on him because he tips well and makes everybody laugh. He is both really funny and utterly unguarded about his own brokenness, which makes people open up to him like tulips in the sun. And although he often ponders doubts when he is alone, he feels God's presence most powerfully when he sits in the Waffle House and is allowed to see someone's soul. It is not coffee that brings people to him; it is the rivers of living water flowing out of him.

If you have a gift for hospitality, throw parties on a regular basis. The joy you feel when people are gathering and talk is flowing and laughter is resounding and new friendships are being forged comes from God. Your living room can become an outpost of the fellowship of the Spirit.

Physical Desires

Because your body was made by God, you also have appetites for things to eat, drink, touch, and see—*physical* desires. The Old Testament is filled with commands for God's people to feast, eat, drink, celebrate, sing, dance, shout, and make music—all things we do with our bodies. These appetites, desires, and delights can then become a way of remembering how good our God is and can lead us to become more joy-filled people.

You learn to connect the gift—which you already love—with the Giver, whom you want to love more. You start with what you already like and work your way back to its source, to God. You taste and see that the Lord is good.

God loves it when you enjoy stretching or training your body in new skills, or when you enjoy what your eyes see, your ears hear, your mouth tastes, and your skin feels. The physical is not separate from the spiritual; it is the Spirit who makes our bodies come to life.

How do you "connect the dots," learning to connect the gift with the Giver?

≈ Take a moment at the beginning of the day to invite God to be with you.

≈ Consciously say "thank you" to him in the midst of your enjoyment.

≈ Meet with other people who share your joys, so that you add community to your delight.

≈ Reflect on how much sadder the world would be without these gifts, which helps you not to take them for granted.

≈ Put pictures on your screensaver or desk of what enjoyably reminds you of God's goodness throughout your day.

≈ Use a "breath prayer" such as "thank you for my body" or "taste and see" to help you share your experience with him. A breath prayer is a simple, one-sentence prayer (I can say it in one breath) that energizes my soul the way oxygen energizes my body.

≈ Reflect on passages in the Bible that show God delighting in bodies and creatures and fulfilling desires. (Psalms 102 and 103 are excellent in this regard.)

Have you ever had the desire to be physically attractive? (I will ask that once in a while at churches, but no one ever raises their hand.) This needs to be kept in proper perspective, of course, for the writer of Proverbs did warn, "Like a gold ring in a pig's snout is a beautiful woman who shows no discretion." Beauty of character is a greater good than exterior beauty — but God *did* create our bodies. So can we get real? God made us with a love of beauty.

Some stylists I know once started what they called a "hairdressers ministry." At first it sounded odd to me. The only hairstylist I could think of in the Bible was Delilah, and that didn't turn out so well. But serving people by cutting their hair is a good thing, and people will sometimes tell things to the person cutting their hair that they don't tell anyone else.

This group began giving complimentary haircuts to physically challenged and mentally challenged folks, and then they traveled to Costa Rica to serve young women trying to escape a life of prostitution. The stylists cared for bodies without wanting anything in return. They honored and freely served bodies that had not been honored or served for a long time, bodies that had been turned into objects. What they did touches our hearts deeply because our bodies were made by God — they are precious to him.

It is a good thing to eat food you love to eat, wear clothes you love to wear, listen to music that makes you feel glad, and then to thank God that he gave you your body so you can see and hear and touch and laugh and dance. As you open yourself to the flow of the Spirit in your physical desires, you begin to love God more and more, not because you should or because it's commanded, but because when you get to know him, you just can't help it. What else could you do?

Hardly anything gives me more joy than when I get to give to one of my kids. When I do and their face lights up because I have satisfied a deep desire in them, that is the best. Of course, I don't want them to become selfish, and so I often try to monitor their character to know when denial is required. But all of that is remedial stuff. It is not my ultimate goal. I just love it when I can give and they light up.

That is the best.

Chapter 8
Think Great Thoughts

One Saturday night our house was assaulted by an odor so indescribably noxious we had to evacuate. We figured it was a gas leak and called both the gas company and the fire department. As it turned out, a skunk had gotten very close to our house.

I made a few phone calls, but no exterminator would come to look for a skunk, so we figured the problem would go away on its own. Most of the odor faded away, and what lingered we got used to. It didn't bother us—until a visitor would enter and say, "It smells like a *skunk* around here."

A week later I was on the road when my family called to say the skunk had struck again. I had to find someone who specialized in the ways of the skunk—a "skunk whisperer." The man discovered that we had two live skunks and one dead one permanently residing in the crawl space under our house. It cost a lot to get the skunks removed. But it was worth it.

You cannot get rid of the skunk odor without getting rid of the skunk.

Our sense of smell has a unique power to evoke emotion, and in our inner lives, our feelings are like aromas. Our positive feelings—joy, pleasure, gratitude—thrill us like the scent of freshly baked bread. Negative feelings—sadness, worry, anger—can make us want to evacuate our lives. When they hit, your mood dips, you lose energy, God seems distant, prayer seems pointless, sin looks tempting, and life looks bleak.

But our feelings never descend on us at random. As a general rule, our emotions flow out of our thoughts. Discouraged people tend to think discouraging thoughts. Worried people tend to think anxious thoughts. These thoughts become so automatic that, like the lingering skunk odor, after a while we don't even notice we are thinking them. We get used to what is sometimes called "stinking thinking."

This can happen to anyone. The prophet Elijah had reached a high point of his life when he defeated the prophets of Baal. Then one event—the opposition of Jezebel—plunged him into fear. Look at his thoughts: he felt worthless ("I am no better than my ancestors"), hopeless ("he ran for his life"), isolated ("I am the only one left"), and unable to cope ("I have had enough"). He actually wanted to die ("Take my life, LORD").

But God is the great healer. He had Elijah take a nap and eat a snack, then he did a little divine cognitive therapy to replace each of these life-killing thoughts. He gave Elijah an epiphany ("the LORD is about to pass by"), filled his future with hope because God would accompany him ("go back the way you came"), revealed that he was not isolated ("yet I reserve seven thousand in Israel"), and infused his life full of meaning because God had a mission for him.

Elijah thought his problem was Jezebel, but there will always be a Jezebel in our lives. The real challenge is between our ears.

The way we live will inevitably be a reflection of the way we think. True change always begins in our mind. The good news is that if God can change Elijah's thinking, he can change ours. What makes people the way they are—what makes you *you*—is mainly the way they think.

> Let God transform you into a new person by changing the way you think. (Romans 12:2 NLT)

Becoming the best version of yourself, then, rests on one simple directive: *Think great thoughts!* People who live great lives are people who habitually think great thoughts. Their thoughts incline them toward confidence, love, and joy. Trying to change your emotions by willpower without allowing the stream of your thoughts to be changed by the flow of the Spirit is like fumigating the house of the skunk smell while the skunks continue to live in your crawl space. But God can change the way we think, and in this chapter we will look at two ways we can open ourselves up to his work: learning to monitor what happens in our minds, and then resetting our minds to a better frequency.

It is time to go after the skunks.

» Learn to Monitor Your Mind

Our thought patterns become as habitual as brushing our teeth. After a while we don't even think about them. We get so used to bitter thoughts or anxious thoughts or selfish thoughts that we don't even notice what we are thinking about.

One of the great barriers to a flourishing mind is sometimes called mindlessness. My body is at the breakfast table with my family, but my mind isn't. It is ruminating over my problems—a repetitive, anxious, dull, low-grade obsession with tasks and problems. I am *absentminded*; my mind has gone AWOL. Other people can tell I am not fully present because my face is less alive and responsive. I talk less, and when I do say something, it is superficial and terse. I don't do this on purpose. It simply becomes a habit of my mind.

The spiritual life begins with paying attention to our thoughts, which is why the psalmist prayed, "Search me, God, and know my heart; test me and know my anxious thoughts." God knows our thoughts better than we do, and he will help us learn what is going on in our mind from one moment to the next.

As I monitor my mind, I will encounter many thoughts that are unwelcome visitors: I get anxious. I catastrophize. I envy. But I will also begin to recognize what kind of thoughts the Spirit flows in. The apostle Paul gives us a great framework for understanding which are the thoughts and attitudes that come from the Spirit. He writes, "The mind controlled by the sinful nature is death, but the mind controlled by the Spirit is life and peace."

Take any thought, especially thoughts that feel weighty or that you find yourself turning over and over in your mind, and ask, *What direction do those thoughts lead me in? Are they leading me toward life—toward God's best version of me? Or in the other direction?*

LIFE & PEACE (spirit) THOUGHTS (sinful) DEATH

I received a letter a while ago containing a criticism of me. When I read it, I could feel a twinge in my belly, that core Jesus talks about. I thought, *Someone sees junk in me. I'm embarrassed and ashamed. It will never change. Lots of people see it.* I was tempted to feel sorry for myself, because there was truth to my thoughts. But they did not lead to life.

Then I had another set of thoughts, in which my negativity was turned not toward me but toward the writer of the letter: *He has bigger problems than I do. I'm a pastor. Who is he to criticize me?* Then I became defensive and withdrawn, and again I went into a downward spiral.

But there is an alternative. I could say, "Holy Spirit, would you help me? Would you give me the right thoughts?"

When I do that, thoughts like these come: *Yes, what you're feeling is hurt, and part of that hurt is nothing more than wounded vanity. We can deal with that. I still love you with all your junk. Your well-being with me is not at risk. The man who wrote this may see a flaw in you, but nobody really thinks you're perfect anyway, except your mother. It will actually be better for you not to have to pretend. Here's a chance for you to grow.*

This is grace. Even though there are elements of pain in these thoughts, they do not paralyze me. They bring energy. They are true, and they give me ground to stand on. I realize that if I can keep my mind centered on these thoughts, right feelings and actions are likely to flow out of them. The prophet Isaiah said that we will be kept in perfect peace if our mind is *stayed* on God. This is living in the flow of the Spirit.

One of the simplest and most powerful ways to monitor your mind is called the experience sampling method. Program a watch or iPhone to beep at random intervals through the day. When it does, write down (or make a mental note if you're a spontaneous non-journaler) where you were and what you were doing.

Then, on a scale of 1-5, monitor your thoughts like this:

	VERY				NOT AT ALL
PEACE	5	4	3	2	1
CONNECTED TO GOD	5	4	3	2	1

Do this for a week, and look for those activities and people that most help you live in the flow of the Spirit. How can you add those? What are the activities and relationships that most block the flow? How can you change or diminish those?

Learn to become aware of the flow of thoughts in your mind without trying too hard to change them. Toddlers who are beginning to walk consistently learn from their falls, but without judgments that paralyze

Here is another exercise for monitoring your mind. Read through the list of words below, which represent the primary patterns that our thinking falls into. As you read through the list, reflect on your own mental habits and think about how other people experience you. Then select which three of the words express patterns that tend to most characterize your thinking. Ask one or two people who know and love you to go through the same list and give you the three words that they think most characterize you.

Grateful	Curious	Stubborn
Defensive	Hopeful	Angry
Self-preoccupied	Passive	Determined
Dissatisfied	Anxious	Engaged
Creative	Courageous	

them. ("Fallen again! What a clumsy oaf I am! I'm crawling the rest of the day. I don't deserve to walk.") Learning to walk in the Spirit takes at least as much grace and strength as learning to walk on two legs, and the Spirit will always help lead us toward God's best version of ourselves. We can picture it this way:

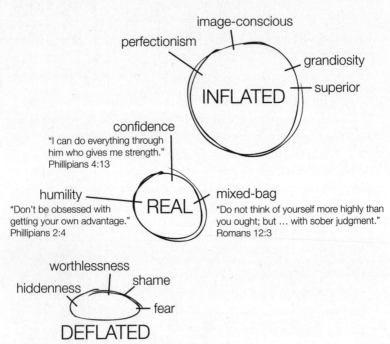

Much like Elijah, we can be tempted to think we are the only one really faithful, the only special or gifted or entitled one. This is related to that old temptation "you will be like God," for when we think of ourselves as god-like, we become obsessed with our own success and happiness and need to prop up an inflated sense of our own competence and worth. Then reality hits, and often when this idealized me crumbles, what is left is a deflated, "shattered" me. Like Adam and Eve, we want to run and hide. We think that we have nothing to offer and that everything is awful.

But the Spirit wants to liberate us, both from thinking as if we are God and from thinking as if we are nothing. There is a God; it is not you. He wants to help you be the real you, the best version of you. He wants to help you become you-ier.

So you move to the next step.

» Learn to Set Your Mind

You can't stop thinking wrong thoughts by trying harder to not think them, but you can do something else. You can "set your mind," for the most basic power you have over your mind is that you can choose what you pay attention to. At any moment—including this one—we can turn our thoughts in one direction or another. It is within our capacity to set our minds; that explains why two people can be in the same set of circumstances and yet have completely different experiences.

A friend sent me passages from a dog's diary and a cat's diary as a means to show me the difference a mindset can make:

Excerpts from a Dog's Diary:

8:00 am—Dog food! My favorite thing!

9:30 am—A car ride! My favorite thing!

9:40 am—A walk in the park! My favorite thing!

10:30 am—Got rubbed and petted! My favorite thing!

12:00 pm—Lunch! My favorite thing!

1:00 pm—Played in the yard! My favorite thing!

3:00 pm—Wagged my tail! My favorite thing!

5:00 pm—Milk bones! My favorite thing!

7:00 pm—Got to play ball! My favorite thing!

8:00 pm—Wow! Watched TV with the people! My favorite thing!

11:00 pm—Sleeping on the bed! My favorite thing!

Excerpts from a Cat's Diary:

Day 983 of my captivity. My captors continue to taunt me with bizarre, little dangling objects. The only thing that keeps me going is my dream of escape.

Two creatures, identical circumstances, but totally different experiences. What is the difference? It is a way of thinking. Gratitude is one mindset; entitlement is another. John Milton wrote in his epic poem *Paradise Lost*, "The mind is its own place, and in itself can make a heaven of hell, a hell of heaven."

Setting your mind is like setting a thermostat. It is creating a target for the climate. Once you set a thermostat, the heating and air-conditioning will have to adjust in relation to the weather. It is a constant process, but the goal is for the system to create a life-giving climate. So too it is with our minds. Many people try to tell themselves to *stop* thinking negative thoughts—which immediately brings to mind the very thoughts they are supposed to stop thinking.

* John Milton wrote, "The mind is its own place, and in itself can make a heaven of hell, a hell of heaven."

Set your mind on things above, not on earthly things. (Colossians 3:2)

Those who live in accordance with the Spirit have their minds set on what the Spirit desires. (Romans 8:5)

There is a better way.

My friend Danny went spelunking in the caves of Iowa. The man guiding took him deep underground, then said he would lead Danny through a passageway into a spectacular chamber. The passageway was small enough that Danny had to stoop at first. Then as it grew still smaller, he had to get on his hands and knees. Eventually the only way to go forward was to lay on his back and push his body forward with his feet. Then the ceiling was so low that when he inhaled he could not move at all! He had to stop, inhale, and exhale, and only then was his chest low enough to allow him to move. By this point it was physically impossible to back out. If the passageway had gotten any smaller they would have lain there and died in that cave.

Danny is a sky-diving, mountain-climbing, hang-gliding thrill-seeker, but there in that cave he felt sheer panic. He was terrified. He tried fighting his fear, but he kept picturing his dead body moldering in the cave. Finally, he told his guide he was about to lose it, and the guide said, "Danny, close your eyes and listen to my voice. I will keep talking, calmly, and guide you through this. We will be okay. I have been here before. I will get you to the other side. But you must listen to my voice. It will not work for you to let your thoughts run wild. Just focus on my voice."

Danny did so. What freed him from panic and fear was *not* trying hard to quit thinking fearful thoughts. It was listening to another voice.

What voice do you listen to when you're in the cave and it's dark, when the ceiling is low and you can't back out? The Spirit longs to flow in our minds all the time. One reason why people have found memorizing Scripture helpful is that it helps us listen to the voice of our guide when we are in the cave. We set our minds on those thoughts that equip us for life. I might miss a second serve, but the Spirit will remind me that I am still God's beloved child. I might be criticized, but the Spirit will remind me that truth and grace are always my friend. The Spirit desires his presence to be a river of life—of love and joy and peace—through each moment of the day.

God's gift of your mind is unbelievably lavish. Before you were born, your body produced about 200 billion neurons, giving you the power to think and react. You had such an embarrassment of riches that by the time you were born, you had killed off around 100 billion of those neurons, and you have never even missed them. Between your second month in the womb and your second birthday, your body was producing 1.8 synapses *per second*. And you weren't even tired!

Your thoughts have enormous power over your life. Researchers have found that tennis players can improve their backhands simply by rehearsing them *mentally*. Neurons that will change you are firing in your mind. Over time, those pathways between neurons were shaped in ways that are absolutely unique to you—and God has no intention of wasting them.

Even twenty years ago, researchers thought the adult brain was genetically determined and structurally unchangeable. But they have since found that even into adulthood the brain is amazingly changeable—it has neuroplasticity. Which synapses remain and which ones wither away depends on your mental habits. Those that carry no traffic go out of business like bus routes with no customers. Those that get heavily trafficked get stronger and thicker. The mind shapes the brain. Neurons that wire together fire together. In other words, when you practice hope, love, or joy, your mind is actually, literally, rewiring your brain!

Researcher Jeffrey Schwartz, echoing pioneer psychologist William James, writes, "The essential achievement of the will is to attend to one object and hold it clear and strong before the mind, letting all others — its rivals for attention and subsequent action — fade away like starlight swamped by the radiance of the Sun."

Because you were made in the image of God, you have the capacity for what might be called "directed mental force." Ever drop a contact lens on a carpet? Your focus causes your brain to suppress attention to anything that could distract you: lint, color, design, or cookie crumbs. All the kinds of sights simply don't register. Neurons don't fire. You have "set your mind" to look for that contact lens, and it responds as if you were giving a bloodhound a shirt with the scent of a fugitive.

It is amazing how often people think they are the victim of whatever thoughts happen to be running through their heads. It is as if they are passive spectators watching thoughts run across the screen, with no control over what's on it.

But there is a fundamental battle in the spiritual life being waged by the Evil One over the nature of the thoughts that run through your mind. The ultimate freedom that you have, the freedom no one can take away even in a concentration camp, is the freedom to decide what your mind will dwell on. I "set my mind" to look for the presence and goodness of God in my life, the river of living water flowing out of my belly.

A wonderful man I know used to stop by a newsstand each morning to get a paper on his way to work. Each day the worker behind the counter was surly, but this man would respond with unfailing good humor and politeness. A friend who sometimes went with him to work asked him why he remained so kind in the face of so much rudeness. He replied, "Why would I let his unhappiness dictate my attitude?"

Somebody is bussing my table at a restaurant. I don't notice him, as he is just a bit character in the movie of my life. Then the Spirit intervenes. The thought occurs in my mind, *Pay attention. Look in his eyes. This is a man with a family, with hopes and dreams. He is bussing tables because he hopes to provide for his children so that they can have more education and possibilities.* For a moment I come alive. I can tell him thank you and mean it. I can bless him — willing good for him before God. And the world moves a tiny little bit toward flourishing.

Sometimes emotions may be leading us down a destructive path, but the Spirit always offers another way. For instance, someone might say, "I'm in love with him. He's married; I know it's wrong, but I can't help it."

Actually, yes you can. You can pray and ask the Spirit to help reset your heart. You could spend an hour a day every day for a month with women who have lost their husbands to infidelity. Listen to their stories. Look into the eyes of their children. Hear the betrayal. See a broken promise through their eyes. You will think new thoughts.

In the flow of the Holy Spirit, your feelings will change. At any moment you can turn your mind to God. The Holy Spirit is flowing, wanting to renew your mind all the time — as if there is a little network called HSN (Holy Spirit Network). I can tune into the Holy Spirit any moment. I can ask the Spirit to guide my thoughts.

I can pause, and listen.

Joshua Bell is perhaps the world's finest violinist. His parents knew he was something special when he was only four years old and he stretched rubber bands to his dresser drawers and played classical tunes on them, adjusting their pitch by pulling the drawers in and out.

As an experiment, he recently played — unannounced — in a metro station in Washington, DC. The people who conducted this experiment were warned by experts that a crowd would certainly gather; they might need extra security. Surely many people would flock to this once-in-a-lifetime opportunity.

Joshua Bell brought his 1713 Stradivarius violin — which cost millions of dollars — and began to play the six most beautiful songs in his repertoire. The world's greatest violinist playing the world's greatest music on the world's greatest instrument.

But no one stopped. A thousand people walked by. You can see it on video. Children would tug on their parents' sleeves, but the adults were too preoccupied. One woman alone recognized him and stopped to listen. She gave him a bigger tip (twenty dollars) than the other thousand people put together. They were in a hurry, hurrying past Joshua Bell because they had other things to do.

Jesus said, "To what can I compare this generation?... We played the flute for you, and you did not dance."

The Master is still playing, but listening is optional. Those who have ears to hear, let them hear.

Chapter 9

Feed Your Mind with Excellence

We once lived across the street from a couple who did not get along. The husband worked in security, but his passion was to be a body-builder. He was strong, sarcastic, and self-centered. His wife was small and timid—and angry.

He had to go to work every morning at 6:00, and she got up at 5:00 to fix his lunch. We wondered why she would do this for someone she was so mad at until she explained that she was secretly packing his lunches with enough calories to put weight on Shamu the Killer Whale. She loaded what he thought were dietary turkey sandwiches with butter and mayonnaise. She put extra sugar in his yogurt and made his protein shakes with half-and-half. He worked out a lot, but he could never understand why his body didn't look like the guys in the magazine.

He never knew she was larding him up when he wasn't looking.

Our bodies are constantly being formed by what goes into them. We may not like this truth, we may not heed it, but we can't evade it. Bodies get shaped by what goes into them.

Sometimes our kids are tempted to feed our dog bad things—things the dog should not be fed. When bad things go into the dog, bad things come out of the dog. We know that about dogs, and we recognize the importance of what we put into what we value. We are careful about what fuel we put into high performance cars, commercial airliners, or thoroughbreds. But we may forget this when it comes to our minds.

In this world we are being bombarded by a steady stream of messages from the media, bosses, co-workers, people we date, books, iPods — and from our own thoughts. Our mind will be shaped by whatever we feed it while the Evil One tries to lard up our mind when we're not looking. He will put depression in our thoughts at breakfast, sprinkle temptation in our mind at noon, and slip us a worry sandwich when it's time for bed.

He will try to keep us from noticing what we are putting into our mind.

» A Flourishing Mind Feeds on Life-giving Thoughts

If I want my mind to be full of life, I will have to pay attention to what it is focused on. One of the greatest gifts God has given the human race is Scripture — yet we often turn it into a burden. Sometimes people will ask me, "How many minutes a day am I supposed to read the Bible? Seven? Fifteen? What is the minimum I can read and not have God be mad at me?"

That is the wrong question. God is not mad at us for not reading the Bible. No matter how much we read the Bible, he won't love you any more than he loves you right now. The question is, *What can you feed your mind with so that it can flourish?*

Other people ask, "How much more information about the Bible am I supposed to know? What if I feel guilty because so many people know so much more about the Bible than I do?" But the reason to read the Bible is not to fulfill a spiritual duty or to gain more knowledge. It is to jump in the river. So let us talk about the feeding of our minds — including how we use the Bible. But let's not try harder. Let's try softer.

> Blessed are those ... who delight in the law of the LORD and medi-
> tate on his law day and night. They are like a tree planted by streams
> of water, which yields its fruit in season and whose leaf does not
> wither — whatever they do prospers.

The phrase "meditate on his law day and night" may sound intimidating, unrealistic, or undesirable. How would I ever get any work done if I spent the whole day contemplating Lamentations? But that's not necessary. That is not the idea.

There is an old saying that if you can worry, you can meditate. Meditating is simply turning a thought over and over in your mind. As you do that, neurons are firing and your brain is rewiring. When you receive information that matters to you, you can't help meditating on it.

When I was in high school, a friend of mine told me about a girl who liked me. I could not believe it, because I knew this girl and she was *way* out of my league.

"This can't be true," I said.

"But it *is* true," my friend said. "I don't understand it either, but it's true."

That night my mind fixated on this thought: *She likes me.* I couldn't stop thinking about it. My mind just went there over and over. *She* likes *me.* So the next day, although I could hardly believe it was true, I called her up and asked her out.

It turned out it wasn't true.

But I had one really good night thinking about it. It was my *delight*, and what I delight in, I can't help thinking about.

What would it look like to delight in the law of the Lord? It certainly is something deeper than being thrilled about a bunch of rules in the Bible. It starts with a vision of being loved by God. God is way out of my league. He is in the *perfection* league; I am in the *fallen* league. This wonderful God, this mysterious, all-powerful, all-holy God—he loves me! Periodically this truth bursts in, and we can't stop thinking about it.

He loves *me!*

When we first learn that, our minds may keep returning to that thought the way they do to a surprise promotion. We can't stop thinking about it. However, the day will come when you *can* stop thinking about it—and not because you're a spiritual failure. Neurons respond to novelty, and what ceases to be novel ceases to cause neurons to fire. If you have been married thirty years, you are able to think about things besides the fact that your spouse loves you. Not because you love that person less, but simply because your neurons have gotten used to that information.

The psalmist is saying that he has actually found ways to carry thoughts of God's love and protection into his mental life—his inner flow—in a way that makes his whole life richer. Being loved by God has become such a deep part of his mental circuitry that now it affects all his other thoughts as well.

There are two ways of looking when it comes to a window. I can look *at* a window. I can notice the glass, see if there are any streaks or dust particles or bubbles in it. Or, I can look *through* a window. I can view the world beyond it by using it as an opening to the world.

Sometimes I look *at* the Scriptures. I study its story. I ask questions. Thoughts of God's goodness, love, and peace lodge in my mind. The idea is that I begin also to look at my world *through* the Scriptures—through the perspective of God's constant care and presence.

» Free to Think about "Whatever ..."

In giving instruction about how to feed our minds, the apostle Paul writes, "Whatever is true, whatever is noble, whatever is right, whatever is pure, whatever is lovely, whatever is admirable—if anything is excellent or praiseworthy—think about such things."

The striking word in that command is *whatever*. Our minds are being shaped all the time, but we have great freedom to pursue minds that flourish. As a bee that can find nectar in all kinds of flowers, we are now free—even commanded—to feed our minds on noble thoughts wherever we find them. The Bible itself commands us to look beyond just the Bible to feed our minds.

Let us meditate for a moment on that phrase "whatever is lovely." Think of something that is "lovely" to you. A sunset. A favorite novel. Tiny robins chirping in the nest. The face of someone you love. Music that makes you dance. Let your mind dwell there for a moment. Give it directed mental focus.

You just obeyed the Bible. That "counts." You just opened up your mind a bit to the flow of the Holy Spirit.

What causes your mind to be drawn to what is true, noble, right, pure, lovely, admirable, excellent, and praiseworthy? Maybe it is taking art classes and learning to see beauty you had never noticed before. One man I know spends much of his time in his car, listening to a list of the twenty best works of English fiction. Maybe you are an athlete, and competition stirs you to admire the pursuit of excellence. What causes your mind to be drawn to those things?

God's desire is for you to have a mind that habitually thinks noble, true, pure, admirable thoughts. You have great freedom—*whatever*—to allow the Spirit to rewire your mind. As that happens, the Holy Spirit's goal is not to get you really good at suppressing angry behavior. It is for you to have a mind characterized by an ever-increasing flow of Spirit-guided, truth-based, life-producing thoughts and feelings.

When we read about what is noble, when we see something praiseworthy, we experience what psychologist Jonathan Haidt called "elevation." We actually feel a slight expansion in our chest; we feel lighter in our bodies. Our emotions are inspired, and we want to become more excellent ourselves. That counts as obedience to Scripture. That is spiritual.

The flow of the Holy Spirit is always available. You do not have to wait for anything.

» How to Get Fed from the Bible

We are free to feed our minds from every good source, but there is no source like the Bible. It is a written revelation of who God is and of what God's purposes are for humanity. No book comes close to it in influence or significance. Eugene Peterson writes, "Christians feed on Scripture. Holy Scripture nurtures the holy community as food nurtures the human body. Christians don't simply learn or study or use Scripture; we assimilate it, take it into our lives in such a way that it gets metabolized into acts of love." Yet consumer researchers say that the average Bible owner possesses nine Bibles and is looking for more. Something is lacking.

Scripture has never been easier to obtain, and Scripture has never been more difficult to absorb. The unspoken secret is that many people find the Bible boring. This is both a serious problem and a quite recent one. Ancient Greek had no word for boredom. The word did not have its current meaning in English until the last few centuries. We look at the ancient world, and they had no television, no Internet, no movies, no iTunes, and virtually no books—and we think of how boring it must have been.

But the ancients were not bored. We are the ones who get bored because our capacity to focus our attention, to delight our minds in sustained thought, has been weakened by our dependence on external stimuli.

Do you know what country has produced the most poets per capita of any country in world? Iceland. Why? Well, they have nothing better to do. If you are sitting around in a hut and the sun is gone for the next six months, that is a long time to just listen to wind. So the Icelanders would make up sagas and tell them by the fire, then repeat them, memorize them, embellish them, and delight in them. This gave them something to think about when they were alone, so their society created poets by the bushelful.

Have you ever read through one of the Old Testament genealogies? One begat after another. "These were the chiefs among Esau's descendants: The sons of Eliphaz the firstborn of Esau: Chiefs Teman, Omar, Zepho, Kenaz, Korah, Gatam and Amalek." Did it seem just a tiny bit boring to you? Want to guess who it did not bore? The people who first wrote them. In the ancient culture, they *loved* reading them! Those genealogies meant that they weren't just nomads wandering around. They had a story. They had an identity. They were somebody.

> Knowing your origins, knowing your relations, creates order out of social chaos. This is still practiced in oral cultures. In ancient biblical times, people actually took delight in memorizing these genealogies, in reciting them and handing them down. The act of memorizing genealogies was a skill that was greatly admired. It gave them a challenge and huge satisfaction when they were able to memorize that list. They were reciting the Bible, but it was also much like a game.

Part of why delighting in the Scriptures is harder for us than for the ancients is that we have many more tempting alternatives. When David was watching sheep, he had nothing better to do, so he wrote psalms, memorized them, and sang them. They shaped his mind. "The LORD is my shepherd; I shall not want...." The pasture became an outpost of God's kingdom.

In a world with so many *easy* options to amuse or distract our minds, we all have to learn to be fed by the Bible.

Read the Bible with Curiosity

We can learn much from the Bible if we just ask questions: *Who is the author of this book? Who was the audience? Is the writing a par-*

able, instruction, a letter, or history? How would the people to whom the words were first written have understood it? Often the biggest barrier to our becoming learners is what we think we already know.

> Philosopher-educator John Dewey wrote, "Genuine ignorance is profitable, because it is likely to be accompanied by humility, curiosity, and open mindedness; whereas ability to repeat catch-phrases, cant terms, familiar propositions, gives the conceit of learning and coats the mind with varnish, waterproof to new ideas."

A friend of mine, a pastor of a church in the Midwest, was delivering the children's sermon one Sunday and quizzed the kids to see how much they knew about the Bible. "See that man with two stone tablets in his hand standing on a mountain?" he asked, pointing to the stained-glass windows. "Can anyone tell me his name?"

"Moses," said one girl.

"Very good. How did you know?"

"Because the name underneath the man says, 'Moses.'"

My friend had looked at the window a hundred times, but had never seen the names.

Our brains are wired to fire in the face of novelty and to shut down under familiarity. This means that when we read Scripture we will be most engaged if we ask questions and look for something we had not noticed before.

One of the most important resources in reading the Scripture is one we always carry around with us—our imagination. When you read a Bible story, take time to recreate the details. In John 21, for example, Jesus has prepared a breakfast of fish over a charcoal fire when the disciples come in from fishing. What does the water sound like, lapping against the boat? What is the smell of the charcoal fire and the fish sizzling in the pan? I imagine the light of an early sunrise streaking the sky. How does it feel to be Peter as Jesus calls his name? How would it feel if it were me, if I had denied Jesus, as Peter had? When I enter into the story, it comes alive and God can speak to me in a new way through a passage I may have read many times before.

Read the Bible with Integrity

A woman I know leads a small group of friends who are reading the Bible together, and one of them recently said, "I have come to realize that I don't believe the Bible is true." Her group cheered for her—not because the unbelief is good news, but because she had finally gotten honest enough to name her doubts.

One of the barriers to feeding my mind through Scripture comes when I am confused or unsure whether I can believe a story, but try to force myself to believe it or avoid reading it so that my faith doesn't get disturbed. Only when I read the Bible with an utter commitment to pursuing what I believe to be true, however, is it able to feed my mind.

So when you read the Bible and you have doubts, don't "try harder" to believe. "Try softer." Let God know about your doubts; he already knows about them anyway.

Read Scripture with Expectancy

Sometimes people bring energy to a gathering; sometimes they just show up. My wife used to head up a ministry to twenty-something folks who were mostly single. I knew, even with my eyes closed, if I was in their presence, just by the smell. They smelled great. In regular church services, with mostly old married people, no one cares how they smell. But when people are hopeful of meeting someone, there is electricity in the air. And a scent in the air. They are alive.

It is the same with God. If I really believe that I may meet with God, I don't just show up. My mind is awake. I am hoping and looking for something beyond myself. If my wife hands me the sports page to read, she doesn't care if I scan it casually. But if she hands me a long letter she has spent hours writing for our twenty-fifth anniversary, it is not time for a casual scan. I approach that reading with a different attitude.

I can't *make* myself be excited about reading the Bible, and it isn't wise to try. How it must disappoint the Spirit if he is waiting to flow through our thoughts, but we are too distracted to hear him.

But if I come to Scripture with an attitude of expectancy, that changes things.

Read Scriptures with an Active Mind

I am thinking of a song that I bet you can sing even if you have never heard a recording of it. We don't know who wrote the lyrics. In fact, it doesn't even have lyrics. It was written by some anonymous genius, and it doesn't contain a single word. But it is the most important song you ever learned.

It is the ABC song.

Until the past few centuries, almost all human knowledge was condensed into forms such as the "alphabet song." To this day, we still use such devices to learn how long the months are ("thirty days hath September ...") or rules of grammar ("I before e, except after c ..."). Television networks spend billions of dollars getting jingles to burrow their way into brains. (I have a hard time remembering my cousins' names, but I can tell you all seven people on Gilligan's Island because I could sing the theme song in my sleep.)

When I study something, I take its order into my mind. I internalize it. It belongs to me; it becomes part of me. Whole new worlds suddenly become available to me.

National Public Radio did a series in which people talked about what they believe in. One person featured was a woman from India who had been sold into marriage at age twelve and abandoned by her husband at fifteen. A few years later she was able to attend a literacy class, where she was mesmerized by the alphabet. When she learned to read the letters in her name, she found it had been mispronounced all her life. The discovery that the alphabet had the power to change her name—and more so, her identity—captivated her. She could not stop saying it, learning it, and reading it.

When this Indian woman's mind became alive to the alphabet, to written words, she became a different person. She received dignity. She was able to work. She could raise her children toward a better future. She had been "dead" to the ABCs. Now she is alive to them.

When I read Scripture, I ask God to put it into my bones the way the ABCs are, so that I am able to read his presence in my world—so that I can learn my new name. We were made for so much more than what the average mind gets filled with.

Read the Scriptures the Way You Watch a Movie

Sometimes when a group of people are together, one of them will mention a movie that everyone has seen, and suddenly a discussion surrounding the movie comes alive. People talk about their interpretations of what happened with great vigor. Nobody "tries harder" to watch a movie, but everybody is engaged. However, when it comes to the Bible, the conversations become stilted. People are so concerned with making sure they get the "right" answer that everyone backs out of the conversation.

Researcher Ellen Langer has studied how our minds work and found we learn best when we view a situation from several perspectives — when we see novel information being presented, when we notice the context in which we are learning, and when we are forming new categories because of what we have learned. Playful curiosity creates much more learning than anxiously filling in the blanks with right answers.

One reason the ancient rabbis read the Scriptures so much is that they created so many wonderful arguments. In the middle of Genesis, for no apparent reason, there is a long list of genealogy of the Edomites. The Edomites were Israel's bitter enemy—yet the rabbis debated over how they made it in Scripture. Could it be that God loves the Edomites too? I grew to love the Bible in college when a group of students and teachers would meet every Friday afternoon, not as a class, but to muse and argue and wonder about why the Bible mentions holy wars or why in the New Testament God is never the subject of the verb for anger. Sometimes we would laugh over our disagreements—as when, after seeking several times to convince me of something, a friend who is much smarter than me shrugged his shoulders and said, "Well, you can't hand a football to a man with no arms."

Because there was space around that table for musing and questions and disagreements, our imaginations and critical thinking were engaged in ways that would never happen if the Bible were simply a series of grocery lists and instruction principles. The characters in the Bible are not sterile moral object lessons; they are real people with flaws and ambiguity through whom God somehow works.

People just like you and me.

Sometimes Try Memorizing Scripture

I know: Memorization scares us. But I also know people who have memorized every episode of the television show "The Simpsons" without trying.

Before written languages were developed, memory was the only way to learn. In our day, memorizing has gotten a bad name as "rote learning." But memorizing never makes our mind a duller place—just the opposite! When we have stored wonderful words in our memory, we will have a much richer inner life than someone who does not. While other people will need external stimulation—such as watching TV or listening to music or going online to keep their minds from drifting into chaos—we will have the joy of being able to savor great words and wonderful ideas without aid.

Eva Hermann spent two years in a Nazi prison camp. She wrote how a young cell mate from a Catholic orphanage one day happened to recite the prayer of Saint Teresa:

> *Let naught trouble thee;*
> *Let naught frighten thee;*
> *All Things pass.*
> *God alone changeth not.*
> *Patience can do all things.*
> *Whoever has God, has everything.*
> *God alone sufficeth.*

When the girl saw how much this helped Eva, she began to repeat the prayer at the end of every day. Eva later wrote of how her time in prison was transformed by the words she had memorized:

We should not imagine that a litany is thoughtless mumbling: real strength can come from it.

"The words were like a stream which carried his soul along with it," says Sigrid Undset somewhere of a person praying. During many a walk in the courtyard I have permitted myself to be carried along by such a stream, by repeating again and again the words of a Psalm: for example, Psalm No. 90, "O God, Thou art our refuge and our strength."

Eva wrote that she met God in a Nazi prison camp in a way she had never met him anywhere else. The words we carry in our minds are available to transform any moment.

When there is a verse that speaks to you, write it on a card. Put it on a mirror in your bathroom, on your Blackberry or calendar, or in your car. If you are an auditory learner, listen to the Scripture being read on CDs or on an iPod. If you are a visual learner, light a candle and read these words: "God is light, and in him there is no darkness at all."

Don't Just Read it ... Do Something

A businessman known for his ruthlessness, arrogance, and religiosity once told Mark Twain he intended to visit the Holy Land before he died, in order to climb Mount Sinai and read the Ten Commandments aloud. "I have a better idea," Twain said. "You could stay here in Boston and keep them."

We would rather cogitate on what we do not know than actually do the things we know we ought to do.

Organizations often suffer from inertia. A company may know they need to improve quality control, so they discuss it, listen to presentations about it, read books, look at state-of-the-art systems—but never actually get around to doing it. Their problem is not one of ignorance. Their problem is one of knowing too much, but doing too little.

People would rather debate protein versus carbs, French cooking versus vegetarian, lifting weights versus cardio. Just spend more carbs than you take in. It's not rocket science.

People love to debate individual stocks versus mutual funds versus real estate. Just save more than you spend. It's not rocket science.

People would rather debate doctrine or beliefs or tradition or interpretation than actually do what Jesus said.

It's not rocket science. Just go do it. Practice loving a difficult person or try forgiving someone. Give away some money. Tell someone thank you. Encourage a friend. Bless an enemy. Say, "I'm sorry." Worship God.

✱ We would rather cogitate on what we do not know than actually do the things we know we ought to do.

You already know more than you need to know.

When I taught tennis, unskilled novices would agonize over which racquet to buy—whether to use nylon or gut strings, whether to string them up at sixty-five or seventy pounds. When they would go practice, they couldn't even hit the ball with their strings. They needed a nylon frame.

Don't debate minutiae. Just go practice.

The most influential talk in the history of the world, Jesus' Sermon on the Mount, ends with a striking story that addresses exactly this knowing/doing gap: "Therefore everyone who hears these words of mine and puts them into practice is like a wise man who built his house on the rock...."

This is our challenge.

> Be doers of the word, and not merely hearers.
> (James 1:22 NRSV)

It is easier to be smart than to be good. You don't need to know more from the Bible; you just need to do what you already know.

We don't become doers on our own, of course. As we read the Scripture, we ask the Spirit to help us understand what to do in response, and the intersection of what the Scriptures teach and how our lives unfold will give us a never-ceasing stream to actually do what Jesus says. And when we forget, another chance will come along.

I was picking up a prescription one Saturday afternoon before a church service, and because I was in a hurry, I had called the night before to make sure it would be there. But when I got there, the man behind the counter told me it wouldn't be ready until the next week. Apparently there was a mix-up between the medical people, the insurance people, and the pharmaceutical people.

"But I've got to have it," I replied. I was scheduled to leave the United States the next day.

"Well, it's not ready," the clerk said.

"But the automated system told me last night it would be ready today."

"There is a flaw in the automated system then," he told me.

All of a sudden I felt unbelievable anger well inside me. *A flaw in the system?* I wanted to say, *There's a flaw in you!* I didn't say that, because people from my church might have been around. (That is an occupational hazard of being a pastor.) But with every gesture and tone that I could, I expressed contempt and irritation with the man behind the counter. I didn't simply *feel* anger, I *wanted* to feel it. I indulged it. I wanted to make him feel small. I was amazed at my own ugliness.

When I returned to the church, I opened a Bible in my office and read a single phrase—"love one another"—and had to call a friend to tell him there was an inner jerk inside me that's scary.

Then, after I got back from my trip, I went to the pharmacy to tell the man behind the counter I was sorry for being so irritated and how much I appreciated his help.

And I was back in the flow.

Chapter 10

Never Worry Alone

When our daughters were three and five years old, we took them to a hotel with a swimming pool. We had a long, stern talk about the importance of water safety and the risk of drowning.

My talk may have been a little too effective.

As Laura was jumping into my arms while I was in the water, three-year-old Mallory slipped from a sitting position on the edge of the pool. She was underwater for less than a second, but when I pulled her up, she was sobbing.

"I drowned!" she cried. "I drowned! I drowned!"

From her perspective, it was terrifying. From my perspective, however, it was actually kind of funny.

"No, honey," I replied sympathetically. "You didn't drown. You were only underwater for a second. You're fine.... So let's not tell Mommy about this."

Mallory was never in danger. I knew that even though she didn't. Her father was always watching her, able to scoop her out of trouble at a moment's notice. I was what you might call "a non-anxious presence."

Jesus knew that no earthly situation has the power to put you outside God's care. You are always in the hand of your Father. So when death itself comes for us, it will be like Mallory dipping in the pool, and we will come up saying, "I drowned! I drowned! I drowned!" and the Father will say, "I had you the whole time."

Try a thought experiment: Imagine not being afraid any more. Imagine facing financial difficulties or an irate boss with inner poise and resolve. Imagine receiving bad news and generating constructive ways to solve the problem rather than spiraling through the worst-case scenarios. Imagine facing rejection and obstacles without giving in to discouragement. Imagine acknowledging the mistakes you have made, moving confidently into the future. Imagine doing all of this with God as your partner and friend. Now imagine people around you coming to you when they are upset or discouraged because they find that your peace of mind is contagious.

The mind controlled by the Spirit is life and peace, and what you are imagining is your mind immersed in the Spirit's flow. There is a phrase that wonderfully describes the role the Spirit wants to play in our minds: *The Spirit is a non-anxious presence.*

» God's Transforming Non-Anxious Presence

A non-anxious presence works like this: A group of people at home or work face a problem, and as one person after another hits the panic button, pretty soon everyone is anxious. They repeat each others' worries and ratchet them up another few degrees. It is contagious.

Then they notice someone among them who isn't afraid, someone fully aware of the problem but calm and able to plan with quiet confidence. That spirit begins to spread. Everyone begins to calm down. That one character brings the gift of a non-anxious presence. It brings the assurance that people's well-being is not at risk.

Jesus was once napping in a boat with his friends when a storm came. They woke him up, terrified, and Jesus looked out at the storm and said, "Peace, be still." And it was.

Jesus was a non-anxious presence. He carried peace with him. He did not say, "If you follow me, you will never have problems," for Jesus himself faced big problems. He was always getting into trouble and eventually got killed.

Peace doesn't come from finding a lake with no storms. It comes from having Jesus in the boat.

God does not want us to live in worry or fear. He wants us to live with bold confidence in his power. "For the Spirit God gave us does not make us timid, but gives us power, love and self-discipline." In the Bible, we see a pattern in which God rarely sends people into situations where their comfort level is high. Rather He promises to be with them in their fear. It is God's presence — not comfortable circumstances — that brings people to the best version of themselves.

> Peace doesn't come from finding a lake with no storms. It comes from having Jesus in the boat.

God told Abraham to leave everything familiar and go to a land he did not know, and he told him that God himself would give birth to a new nation that would change the world. Abraham went, and a nation was born.

God told Moses to confront Pharaoh — the most powerful man on earth — and that God himself would use Moses' faithfulness to deliver his people. Moses confronted, and God delivered.

God told Joshua that if he would be a strong and courageous leader when everyone wanted to return to slavery, God would go with them and give them the land. Joshua was strong and courageous, and God himself gave them the land.

Over and over we see this pattern repeated. David faced the giant Goliath, Elijah faced seven hundred prophets of Baal, and Daniel faced a den of lions — and always there was God in the midst of their fear.

The pinnacle of this pattern is reached in Jesus himself, who said to his followers, "In this world you have tribulation." Nobody had more tribulation than him. But after his death and resurrection, he sent his Spirit to be a non-anxious presence for a whole new community. When Stephen was martyred, Paul rose up to take his place. When Paul was executed, Timothy carried on the torch. Lest we think those stories of courage are all in the past, historian Everett Ferguson calculates that more Christians have been killed for their faith in the past fifty years than in the first three hundred years of the church.

So here is Jesus' word for us when someone doesn't like us, when we get a bad review at work, or when the economy dips south and our 401(k) — which remains the envy of 95 percent of the human race — is down 30 percent: "My peace I give you," Jesus promised. "I do not give to you as the world gives. Do not let your hearts be troubled and do not be afraid."

> "For the Spirit God gave us does not make us timid, but gives us power, love, and self-discipline." ✗

The peace of Jesus is something much deeper than self-help techniques to manage stress. It is deeper than anxiety reduction to make life more pleasant. It is the settled conviction that goes down to the core of your being — to your belly where rivers of living water can flow — that all things are in God's hands. Therefore all things will be well, and you can live free of worry, burden, and fear.

Before we go any further, we need to pause for one very important caveat: *Everybody* worries.

» A Word to the Worry-Prone

Some people don't just worry occasionally. They worry recreationally.

Maybe you are a *champion* worrier. Maybe you can't remember the last time you were not worried. If you ever find yourself not worried, you get worried that there is something you *should* be worried about. And so you worry until you figure out what it is. Sometimes when you hear messages or read books about worry, they can do more harm than good, because what you take away is, *I shouldn't worry so much. I guess I just don't trust God enough.* Then you worry about how much you worry.

Much of our tendency to worry comes from the raw material we were born with. In his book *Emotional Intelligence*, Daniel Goleman writes that from birth, 15–20 percent of children are prone to timidity. They are finicky about new foods, reluctant about new places, and shy around strangers. From birth, their hearts beat faster in new situations. They are genetically predisposed to more guilt and self-reproach. This is so predictable among mammals that exactly the same proportion of cats as humans is prone to timidity. Cats are less curious and are less likely to

a test to worry about

This is a little quiz adapted from Harvard researcher Edward M. Hallowell. Score yourself on each question from 0 (not at all) to 3 (definitely yes).

1. Do you wish you worried less?
2. Do worries sometimes pop into your mind and take over your thinking like annoying, little gnats?
3. Do you find compliments and/or reassurance hard to take?
4. Are you more concerned than you wish you were with what others think of you?
5. How much do you procrastinate?
   (Have you still not finished the last question?)
6. Do you avoid confrontations?
7. Do you ever feel compelled to worry that a certain bad thing might happen out of an almost superstitious feeling that if you don't worry about it, the bad thing will happen, while if you do worry about it, your worrying might actually prevent the negative outcome?
8. Do you "worry about your worry"? Do you sometimes feel God is disappointed at your lack of faith?
9. Are you worried about what your score will be on this quiz?

If you scored a 0, you are either a remarkably confident person or else you are in complete denial.

If your score is 9 or less, worry does not trouble you much.

If you are between 10 and 18, you may often find yourself troubled by anxiety.

If you scored over 18, it may well be that worry is a major source of pain in your life. You may want to talk about this part of your life with some trusted friends, and it may be that telling a doctor or finding a good counselor could be helpful.

go to new territory, and they kill smaller rodents. About 15 percent of cats are just born timid.

Is that a spiritual problem? Are timid cats simply not close enough to God?

No. God is not distant from any of his creatures.

People who wrestle with deep anxiety or panic attacks are some of the most courageous people I know. If you wrestle with chronic worry, don't compare yourself with someone who doesn't. Don't waste time feeling guilty about worry. Guilt may be just what is needed by someone lying, stealing, or lusting. But guilt simply does not help when it comes to worrying. If you only wrestle slightly with worry, don't pass judgment on a chronic worrier. Only God fully understands a person's inner wiring, and the Spirit wants to be a non-anxious presence in *every* life.

We will talk about two ways to grow out of timidity. One of them you will like a lot. The other one you will like only a little, but it will grow on you.

» Let Love Cast Out Fear

Paul said that when we live in the flow of the Spirit, he does not make us timid, but instead gives us power and love. This is not the only place in the Bible where we see a close connection between receiving love and living in power. The apostle John makes the same association in one of the most famous statements in the Bible: "There is no fear in love.... perfect love casts out fear."

> "There is no fear in love.... perfect love casts out fear." ✳

When we live in the flow of the Spirit, we let the perfect love of God wash over us until our fear begins to leave. Modern science has confirmed what John wrote so many centuries ago. Love and fear are literally incompatible in our bodies.

Every child has two needs:

- The need to explore. This is how we learn, grow, develop.
- The need to be safe. If a child doesn't feel safe, she won't explore.

Researchers find that one parent more than the other will push the child to explore, to take a chance, to run a risk, to trust that a little danger's a good thing. Generally, though not in every case, it tends to be the father. Likewise, one parent tends to be the comforter, the soother, the safety net. Again, researchers find that this tends to be the father. (So does this mean that researchers find that moms don't do a whole lot? Just kidding!) Actually, any parent can give both gifts—roots and wings—and every human being needs that secure base from which to explore and grow.

When we experience fear, our body activates the sympathetic nervous system. Our heart races, our breathing grows faster and shallower, our muscles become more tense, and blood leaves the brain and for the heart.

Then we run to our non-anxious presence: our comforter, protector, and parent. As we are held, reassured, and loved, the parasympathetic system takes over. Our heart slows down, our breathing grows deep and even, our muscles relax, and blood flows back to our brain. A little voice inside us says, "I can go out and face the world again...."

Even within our physical body, this is literally true: Perfect love casts out fear.

There is a wonderful picture of this you can see on YouTube if you enter the name "Harry Harlow." Dr. Harlow was a research psychologist in the mid-twentieth century who became famous for his studies of monkeys and their need for love. He found that if little monkeys had perfect conditions for hygiene and food but did not have another monkey present, they languished. Monkeys that had cloth diapers on the floor of their cage did better; they seemed to get what Harlow called "contact comfort"—because they had an innate need for touch that communicated love and strength.

Then Harlow designed two kinds of moms for each cage: a mom made of wire with a bottle of milk so the monkey could be fed, and a terrycloth mom who offered no food—nothing but touch. Much to Harlow's surprise, the monkeys spent less than an hour a day with wire mom and seventeen hours a day with terrycloth mom.

Harlow decided to see what the monkeys would do when they were scared. He devised a mechanical monster with flashing eyes, chomping teeth, waving arms, and a clanking noise—something straight out of a 1950s "Mr. Wizard" television science program—designed to scare the monkey. First the monkey is playing quietly and happily alone. Then one wall of his cage slides up, and he beholds the monster. He is terrified. There is no hesitation. He leaps to his terrycloth mom in a single bound.

Harlow notes that the monkey is not just running *from*. He is running *to*—running to the love that reassures him and drives out fear. Harlow says that contact with his protector "changes his entire personality." He is transformed by love.

At first when the monkey leaps on his terrycloth mom, he is shivering with fear. He wraps his whole body around hers, as if to get her reassurance in as many cells as possible. He is mainlining love and strength. Then he stops shaking. His breathing slows down. The little fellow rotates his head to look at the monster. Then he turns his whole body toward it. His expression changes from fear to menace. He gives a little baby rhesus monkey snarl. Now he is threatening the monster. Perfect love casts out fear.

This is a picture of the mind directed by the Spirit, for God does not give us a spirit of timidity. He gives a mind of life and peace. He calls himself our Comforter, and he will be our refuge, our rock, our fortress, and our safety. He longs to hold us, love us, and watch over us. Perfect love casts out fear.

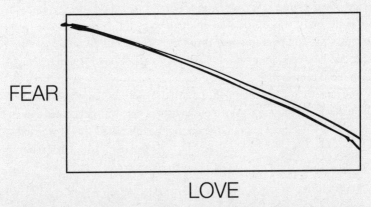

FEAR

LOVE

The kind of anxiety the Spirit wants to free us from is not just the thoughts that are alarming, because such thoughts may alert us to real danger. Toxic anxiety, however, causes our negative, self-defeating, and persistent thoughts to keep cycling over the same ground. Instead of prompting us to take action, they paralyze us. If I worry about finances it will go like this: *Things are not going well financially. The market is probably never going to turn around. I won't have enough for retirement. I am not even saving properly right now. I have never been good with money. I don't understand money really well. I haven't been giving as I should. I can't expect God to bless me. I have to do something to make me feel better. I guess I'll go buy something expensive.*

What are ways in which you most readily experience the love of God, in which his love casts out fear in your body? You have freedom to experiment with all this. God's will is not for intimacy with him to be one more thing you have to worry about!

God wants to love you — and in loving you, to cast out your fear.

Maybe it comes when you are alone with God. Maybe it happens when you pray with a few people. Maybe you find it when reading about the life of Jesus. Or it might come when you are singing a hymn or listening to music.

Often the Spirit will use other people to help love cast out fear. Psychiatrist Edward Hallowell says it like this: *Never worry alone.* When anxiety grabs my mind, it is self-perpetuating. Worrisome thoughts reproduce faster than rabbits, so one of the most powerful ways to stop the spiral of worry is simply to disclose my worry to a friend.

Not long ago I had to speak in front of a large gathering. For some unknown reason, every time I thought about it, I recalled how I fainted twice when giving talks years ago. I could feel the same tightness in my body, and I was afraid it might happen again. For some time I was so embarrassed about this fear that I kept silent. Finally I told a friend, who said he would pray for me; I felt such a relief that I wondered why I hadn't told him sooner.

In fact, when I gave the talk, I started by telling the whole audience about this fear. Now there were thousands of people with concerned expressions, worrying about me fainting during the talk. But I wasn't worried at all. I felt relieved that I didn't have to pretend I was okay. The simple act of reassurance from another human being became a tool of the Spirit

> Never worry alone. One of the most powerful ways to stop the spiral of worry is simply to disclose my worry to a friend.

to cast out fear — because peace and fear are both contagious.

When Israel was to go occupy the Promised Land, God gave them very interesting instructions: "Is anyone afraid or faint-hearted? Let him go home so that the others will not become disheartened too." In an army, in a workplace, on a team, or in a ministry, negativity, fear, and discouragement are contagious. But courage is contagious as well.

God's part in the process is that his peace, "which transcends all understanding, will guard your hearts and your minds in Christ Jesus." By this, Paul means not just peace from God; he is talking about the peace that God *himself* has, the serenity that characterizes God's own eternal being. *That* peace will guard our hearts and minds — and here Paul uses a military term for "guard." It is the word the ancient Greeks used for soldiers who stood guard to protect the city.

"The peace of God, which transcends all understanding, will guard your hearts and minds in Christ Jesus."

Airport security personnel diligently screen every passenger in order to preserve peace and security. Two months after 9/11, I saw that I was just behind a casual acquaintance who happened to be traveling on the same flight. Going through security, I was pulled out of line for some reason and had to go through the security process a second time. The other man went on ahead. He got on the plane and was sitting in the front row as I boarded. In front of passengers and crew as I boarded, this man said, "I wonder why they made you go through security again and not me. Maybe it's your beady, little terrorist eyes." Then he said, "I guess we shouldn't have been talking about bringing those explosives on board, huh?" I made no eye contact. I kept my head down, took my seat, and said nothing. About five minutes later, he got up, took his luggage out of the bin, and was escorted off the plane.

I waited until we took off, then asked one of the flight attendants, "What happened to that guy?"

"Do you know him?" she asked.

"Not very well."

He spent the rest of the day in the San Francisco Airport with four law enforcement officers — and my name ended up on the suspect list.

Airports have resolved that they are not going to board anyone who could threaten the well-being of that plane. They screen anything that can be destructive. In the same way, every thought is a passenger traveling in our mind. Each one has a little spiritual charge that is either positive or negative. Some equip us to deal with life: *God loves me. God is with me. God will guide me. I am never alone.* Some rob us of peace: *I can't handle this. I am alone. I may not be adequate.*

The promise of God is that the Spirit will stand guard over our mind. It's not just our trying harder. When I tell him my concerns, I am "putting off worry." When I ask for his help, I am "putting on peace." And although it takes effort at first, over time it becomes a habit of the mind. This is why prayer is the single most fundamental spiritual discipline when it comes to putting off anxiety and putting on peace.

 "Instead of worrying, pray. . . . It's wonderful what happens when Christ displaces worry at the center of your life."

Prayer—turning any concern over to God when we feel it—is the part we play in allowing the peace of God to stand guard over our mind.

» Take Direct Action to Face Your Fear

Living in peace is not something that involves only our inner thoughts. It also flows from what we actually do. The Spirit will help us grow in peace by leading us in circumstances we would be tempted to avoid in fear. Here our role is to move forward, embracing challenges despite our anxious thoughts.

Hearing messages about how God will take care of us is not by itself sufficient to remove anxiety from our life. In order to open ourself up to the flow of the Spirit, we need to continually expose our mind to certain thoughts and information—but we also need to engage in certain actions. We will need to step out in trust.

I used to take my kids to a summer camp that has a ropes course thirty feet off the ground. It has several sections with colorful names such as "Jacob's Ladder" and "the Leap of Faith." The very last section is called "The Screamer." Want to guess why?

Before going up on the ropes course, we all get a little lecture from the staff, who tell us how strong the harnesses are, how the ropes we are attached to could literally support tons of weight, and how the metal carabiners clipping everything together are virtually indestructible. They explain to us that up on the ropes is a perfectly safe place to be. We have no reason to worry—and in fact face more danger in the car on our drive home.

Everybody hears the same lecture. No one disputes the facts. We all nod our heads. We all believe what they say. But when we get up on the ropes, our stomachs don't believe they are safe. Jesus said that "out of your bellies will flow rivers of living water," but that doesn't feel like what is flowing out of them the first time we are thirty feet up. That is certainly not what is flowing out of our armpits and sweat glands.

The first time you go across ropes, you're afraid. Thoughts flow automatically: *This is too high. This is not safe. I'm gonna fall.* That flow of thoughts has not been changed by the lecture. Your mind has not been renewed. The second time up, you are afraid, but maybe a little less.

But consider the staff. They have been on the ropes hundreds of times — all summer — and because they have put themselves through this experience time and again, their automatic thoughts have changed. Their stomachs and armpits have become convinced that up on the ropes is a perfectly safe place to be. Their minds have been renewed.

> Therefore, I urge you, brothers and sisters, in view of God's mercy, to offer your bodies as a living sacrifice, holy and pleasing to God — this is true worship. Do not conform to the pattern of this world, but be transformed by the renewing of your mind. (Romans 12:1–2)

The pivotal moment during a ropes course comes when you are strapped in, ready to climb, and you say to your instructor, "On belay" — which I would be tempted to think is a French phrase meaning "I've lost my mind." Actually, to belay a rope means to make it absolutely secure, to fasten it to something immovable. It means that now you are connected to something that will keep you from falling, and you will entrust your body to what you say you believe. You will walk by faith. On belay.

The instructor says, "Belay on."

You say, "Climbing."

Your instructor says, "Climb on," and you are on your way.

You could listen to the lecture about the safety of carabiners a thousand times; you could repeat the whole thing by memory — but that alone would not remove the fear from your body the first time you are on the ropes. Yet, once you say "on belay" often enough, it is just a matter of time before your thoughts begin to change.

Information alone will not bring about the transformation of the whole person. We may read book after book, hear talk after talk, listen to sermons — maybe even read the Bible — but still remain just as anxious as we ever were before. There is no way to get the peace of God from our head to the rest of our body besides trusting God enough to directly confront our greatest fear.

Larry needed to confront his boss, but his boss was a powerful steamroller. Larry was intimidated simply by the sound of his voice. When Larry thought about confronting him, Larry's palms got sweaty. His mouth got dry. His wife told him to lick his palms. He read the psalms, he prayed, he thought of how God loves him unconditionally. But he decided not to have the confrontation, and for the moment he felt much less anxious. But he was misusing both the Bible and prayer.

The Bible and prayer were not given to us as forms of anxiety avoidance. In the long run, anytime we avoid doing the right thing out of fear, we die a little inside. When we really place ourselves in the flow of the Spirit's peace is when we say "on belay" to God.

finding the flow in worry

≈ Meditate on a passage such as Psalm 23. Use your imagination to picture being shepherded by the Lord in green pastures beside still waters.

≈ Tell a friend before the worry gets a toehold on your brain.

≈ Use a "breath prayer" such as "God, I'm casting all my cares on you."

≈ Exercise — using our bodies is one of the best ways to fight the buildup of excess adrenaline.

≈ Identify your fear and take one step to help you confront it.

≈ Get adequate rest. "In peace I will lie down and sleep, for you alone, O LORD, make me dwell in safety." (Psalm 4:8)

You are worried about money. Everything in you tells you to hoard it, to hang on to it, to obsess over it. Instead you say "on belay": You manage it wisely. You give it generously. You put it in the trust department.

You are worried about a project at work. Instead of procrastinating, you say "on belay." You give it your best effort with God's help. Each time your worry returns to your mind, you give it to God in prayer.

Your fear of failure tempts you to avoid risk, but instead you say "on belay": *Okay, God, I will take the risk even though I don't know the outcome yet.*

We go through this life one time. Some wonderful things will happen to us; some dreams will come true. Some terrible things will happen to us, bringing with them pain, problems, and disappointment. Of that we can be certain. But we can go through this life worried—or we can go through it at peace.

> *Life is too short,*
> > *joy is too precious,*
> > > *God is too good,*
> > > > *our soul is too valuable,*
> > > > > *we matter too much*
> > *to throw away a single moment of our one and only life on*
> > > *anxious striving.*
> *For the Spirit God gave us does not make us timid.*

On belay.

PART FOUR
redeeming my time

»

Chapter 11

Let Your Talking Flow into Praying

By the time our third child was born, I figured we had been through this drill before and knew what to expect. The doctor was at my wife's bedside for the birth, and everything was going according to plan—until he got a look of deep concern on his face.

"There is a problem," he said.

The umbilical cord had wrapped around the baby's neck, cutting off oxygen to the brain. The doctor had been pretty talkative up to that point, but all of a sudden he wasn't talking at all. Everyone was quiet and focused, and all I could do was say, "Oh God, oh God, oh God, oh God. Make it be okay. Don't let anything happen to that little life."

A few seconds later the doctor was able, inside, to cut the cord. Blood spurted out all over the place, and I started to feel dizzy and queasy.

"I have to sit in a chair somewhere," I announced, "because I'm going to go down." (That did not win me a lot of points with anyone.) So I sat with my head between my knees for the next several minutes while the doctor finished delivering the baby—a beautiful, healthy little boy.

"Is everything okay?" Nancy asked.

"Yes, Mrs. Ortberg," the doctor replied. "Your son and your husband are both pinking up at the same time."

When we are desperate, we call out for God. When we reach the end of our rope, it is only human to reach out to God. When we are thrilled, we thank God. When we are crushed by guilt, we cry out to God.

You pray more than you know. Even in school, we pray. People get concerned about legal issues with that, but experience tells us that as long as there are tests in school, there will be prayer in school, silent though it may be.

> Richard Foster says, "Countless people ... have such a 'stained-glass' image of prayer that they fail to recognize what they are experiencing as prayer and so condemn themselves for not praying."

If someone were to ask you, "How is your prayer life?" what would be your answer? Is the state of your prayer life determined by how long you pray or how often? Is it measured by how many people you are praying for, or how much faith you are praying with, or how many prayers get answered?

If you believe in God, you have already begun to pray — to enter into a dialogue with him — because believing in God means believing he is always present, always listening to what you say. To come to believe is to begin to pray, because of the constancy of God's presence. So let us look at the connection of prayer with "the rest of our lives."

» Is God In on Your Conversation?

We can better understand prayer by thinking about being present with another person, and how being with somebody shapes what we say about them. Sometimes we speak *to* another person. Let's call that Person A. Sometimes, though, we are talking to somebody else about Person A, but we are also speaking in *front of* Person A, so the presence of Person A still influences your words. Then there is a third scenario. Sometimes we talk about Person A in their *absence*, and now what we say may be quite different.

1. Speaking *to* someone.
2. Speaking *in front of* someone.
3. Speaking *in the absence of* someone.

True confession: Have you ever spoken about someone, in their absence, with words you would not have used if they were present? Mark Twain was once riding a train home from Maine after three weeks of highly successful fishing — even though the state's fishing season was closed. He bragged about his huge but illegal catch to the only other passenger in the club car. The passenger grew increasingly glum during Twain's story. When Twain finally asked him who he was, the stranger explained he was the state game warden.

"Who are you?" the warden asked.

"To tell the truth," Twain said, "I'm the biggest liar in the whole United States."

Often when I am speaking *to* someone or *in front of* someone, I hide my real heart. If I am in a job interview, on a first date, or talking to someone in authority, I filter what I say. I may not intend to do this, but I can't help myself. When I am speaking to or in front of somebody — perhaps a boss, a teacher, or a policeman — there is a dynamic at work in my body to manage what I say in light of that person's presence. There is always a sense of effort or strain attached to this, so I long for some place where I can go to be "my real self," where I do not guard my words or body language to manage the impressions of another person.

Now let us bring God into the picture. The reality with God is that we are never speaking or acting in his absence. The psalmist said, "Where can I go from your Spirit? Where can I flee from your presence? If I go up to the heavens, you are there; if I make my bed in the depths, you are there." However, God allows us to sometimes feel as if we are away from him, which I think he does for a reason. Do you ever drive differently when you see a squad car behind you? Why? It is not because your heart is changed. It is not because you see that squad car and think, *Oh, I want to be a good driver.* You don't want to get a ticket! You don't want that little light flashing in the rearview mirror.

You see, God doesn't want forced compliance. God is so immense that if he were "too visible," people would give forced compliance without expressing their heart. So God makes it possible, in enormous love, for us to live as if he were not there.

This reality leads to some dissonance in our spiritual lives. I went to a Christian college, and there was a long-running tradition to determine who was going to pray before meals—the thumbs game, we called it. Everyone would raise their thumbs, and whoever raised their thumbs last was the one to pray. Then we would bow our heads, and that person would say, "Oh God, we love you so much, it's so good to pray to you!"

It didn't occur to me at the time, but years later I thought, *You know, God must be up in heaven saying, "Hey, if it's so good to pray to me, how come the loser of the thumbs game is always the one who has to do it?"* It was as if, when we played the thumbs game, we believed God was not watching. Then when we went to pray, suddenly we were aware that God was tuning in. This is why sometimes people speak in one voice but pray in an entirely different voice. We live with a kind of spiritual split personality.

Anytime I sin, I must remove any thought of the presence of God from my conscious awareness. Then when I pray, I have to put him back in my mind's focus. The goal of prayer is not to get good at praying, as many people think. The goal of prayer is not to try to set new records for how much time we spend praying. *The goal of prayer is to live all of my life and speak all of my words in the joyful awareness of the presence of God.*

Prayer becomes real when we grasp the reality and goodness of God's constant presence with "the real me." Jesus lived his everyday life in conscious awareness of his Father. For example, when he went to raise Lazarus from the dead, he began by "looking up to pray." In our day, most people close their eyes when they pray. But praying with one's eyes open was common for Jewish people in that day. Among other things, it reminded them, *God is right here, right now, in my real world.*

> The goal of prayer is to live all of my life and speak all of my words in the joyful awareness of the presence of God.

> "Father, I thank you that you have heard me. I knew that you always hear me, but I said this for the benefit of the people standing here, that they may believe that you sent me."

Jesus knew the Father was listening not just when he prayed, but all the time, whenever he spoke. God was always responding to Jesus' words, whether they were addressed to the Father or addressed to someone else. For Jesus, the line between praying and just speaking became very thin. Sometimes when Jesus healed a person, he would speak directly to the person he was healing. Sometimes he would speak directly to his Father. It didn't really matter which one he did because he was always speaking in front of the Father and the Father was always responding.

God is the constant gracious listener to our every thought, and prayer begins when we bring what we most naturally think about before God.

» Talk to God about Your Problems

Think about the major categories of your life: your relationships, your financial life, your job, your emotions, your habits, your moral decisions, your health and physical appearance, your mortality. Can you identify at least one problem?

If you can, you have a wonderful prompt for prayer.

One of our illusions is that the reason we worry is because we have problems. If I just didn't have problems, we think, I wouldn't worry anymore. The good news is, *your problems are going to go away.* The bad news is, that won't happen until the day you die. You will be amazed at how your problems stop bothering you then. Until then, however, life will be full of problems.

There is an old equation that helps us understand the dynamics of attention: We tend to be preoccupied by our problems when we have a heightened sense of vulnerability and a diminished sense of power. Today, see each problem as an invitation to prayer. Maybe you are mad at someone. Tell God! An amazing example of this is found in the life of Elisha. One day he was set upon by a gang of young toughs: "Go on up, you baldhead!" they said to him. The Bible says that Elisha turned toward them and called down judgment from heaven, and forty-two of them were chased away by two bears. It doesn't seem like the prayer of a spiritual giant, but Elisha prayed what was in him. Maybe God will send a bear or two down after someone you are mad at. Probably not, but you will never know if you don't pray.

Either way, God will use your problems to grow a better you.

» Talk to God about What You Want

Paul said that we are to pray "in everything," and the implications of that little two-word phrase are enormous. Often we don't pray because our real thoughts seem unspiritual:

- I wonder if I will get a year-end bonus.
- I wonder if I am putting on too much weight.
- I wonder if my boss thinks I am doing well.

When I pray, I end up praying about things I think I *should* be concerned about: missionaries, world peace, and global warming. But my mind keeps wandering toward stuff I am genuinely concerned about. The way to let my talking flow into praying is this: *I must pray what is in me, not what I wish were in me.*

Shel Silverstein once wrote the "Prayer of the Selfish Child": "Now I lay me down to sleep, I pray the Lord my soul to keep, And if I die before I wake, I pray the Lord my toys to break, So none of the other kids can use 'em. Amen." Children come to their parents with all kinds of requests: wonderful, foolish, generous, *and* selfish. What matters to parents, however, is that their child comes to them. They know that

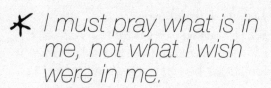
I must pray what is in me, not what I wish were in me.

they can guide the child's growth—as long as their child speaks openly with them. It is the hidden heart, not the selfish heart, that is hardest to change.

This is *"in everything"* kind of prayer. I don't wait to clean up my motives first. I don't try to sound more spiritual than I am. I don't pray what ought to be in me. I pray what's really in me. The "in everything" prayer is the most common kind in the Bible. I just try to attach one sincere rider: "Nevertheless, not my will but yours be done."

As long as we have unsolved problems, unfilled desires, and a mustard seed of faith, we have all we need for a vibrant prayer life.

Chapter 12

Temptation: How Not to Get Hooked

Recently my wife and I went fly-fishing for the first time. Our guides told us that "to catch a fish you have to think like a fish." They said that to a fish life is about the maximum gratification of appetite at the minimum expenditure of energy. To a fish, life is "see a fly, want a fly, eat a fly." A rainbow trout never really reflects on where his life is headed. A girl carp rarely says to a boy carp, *I don't feel you're as committed to our relationship as I am. I wonder, do you love me for me or just for my body?* The fish are just a collection of appetites. A fish is a stomach, a mouth, and a pair of eyes.

While we were on the water, I was struck by how dumb fish are. *Hey, fish, swallow this. It's not the real thing; it's just a lure. You'll think it will feed you, but it won't. It'll trap you. If you were to look closely, fish, you would see the hook. You'd know once you're hooked that it's just a matter of time before your enemy reels you in.*

You'd think fish would wise up and notice the hook or see the line. You'd think fish would look around at all their fish friends who go for a lure and fly off into space and never return. But they don't. It is ironic. We say fish swim together in a school, but they never learn.

Aren't you glad we are smarter?

The governor of a large state has brains, charisma, power, and unlimited potential. He also has an emptiness that he feeds with paid sexual liaisons, and when they are made public, they cost him everything.

A brilliant teacher wins every argument she ever enters. She dominates every conversation. Everyone knows how smart she is—and everyone avoids her. Her misery is the one problem she is not smart enough to figure out.

The leader of a large company is thought of as successful, but everyone in his inner circle feels used. He does not even know how alone he is, for no one will tell him.

Temptation is painful to us because when we give in, it doesn't hurt us from the outside; it hurts from the inside. Temptation tries to get our appetites and will to override our deepest values. Temptation will strike where we are most vulnerable, but life in the flow of the Spirit is about more than avoiding temptation. In fact, temptation will also come to us where we most need to grow. If I need patience, there will be some difficult people in my life to help me develop it. If I am tempted by envy, there will be a shining star in the office next door to help me learn grace. Each temptation I face offers a step in the direction of the me I want to be.

But how can I stay in the flow when I am tempted?

»Ask for Help

Nothing makes temptation more powerful than isolation, but we do not face temptation alone. Paul said that "no temptation has seized you except what is common to human beings. And God is faithful; he will not let you be tempted beyond what you can bear. But when you are tempted, he will also provide a way out so that you can stand up under it." For Joseph, when he was being propositioned by Potiphar's wife, this literally meant running out of the room.

I think the single most common "way out," however, involves talking about our temptations with another person. A friend of mine wrestles with gossip, but early on in our relationship he made one of the most candid confessions I have ever heard: "If you want to keep something confidential, don't tell me—I leak like a sieve!"

There was something so disarming about his honesty that instead of being pushed away, I was drawn to him. This temptation was simply the dark side of his giftedness—he was one of the most delightfully verbal people I have known. We began to talk and pray over why he was drawn to gossip, where it got him in trouble, and how he could get free. He eventually became one of the friends to whom I trusted my deepest secrets.

» Ask, Where Will This Lead?

In the flow of the Spirit, it actually requires more mental gymnastics to walk down the wrong path than to walk down the right one. We disguise most of these gymnastics from ourselves, but they are there all the same. The first thing we must do if we are going to give in to temptation is wrapped up in the single word *quench.*

"Do not quench the Spirit," Paul says. Any time I have a desire, the Spirit will prompt me to set it before God and ask the question, "Lord, what do you want me to do with this?" Or I can simply ask regarding any course of behavior, *"If I walk down this road, where will it lead in the long run—toward or away from the me I want to be?"*

God will never lead us to manage a desire in a sinful way. If I want to walk down the wrong road, I must begin by silencing God's divine voice within me. I must be careful not to pray about this desire with a submitted spirit. I must make sure I don't talk about this desire with wise friends who will hold me accountable. I must make sure I don't look carefully at passages of Scripture on the subject and reflect on them. I must do all these things without recognizing I am doing them. I must keep myself in a state of spiritual and mental vagueness where God is concerned.

This response may become so habitual that we don't even notice. In a restaurant an attractive waitress walks past a husband and wife at a table. The husband starts staring at her. He can't take his eyes off her. He's not thinking of this woman as a person, as someone's sister or daughter. She is just body parts, and he is using her to get a little surge of sexual gratification. He thinks nobody notices—but of course someone notices. His wife feels humiliated.

This is "the look" Jesus warned about when he spoke of "committing adultery in your heart." This does not mean that noticing someone attractive is sinful. The sense of attraction is a good thing. Rather, Jesus warns about looking for the purpose of lusting. An element of will has come into the look, and the husband is allowing his mind to wallow in it. It may have become so habitual that he is hardly even aware he is doing it.

The Spirit will pull us another way, however. Maybe we get "caught" and embarrassed. Maybe we feel a twinge of conscience. Either way, the Spirit wants to remind us of who we were created to be.

»Remind Myself of My Deepest Values

The battle against temptation is a noble fight, but if we simply try to repress a desire, it will wear us out. We need to have a very clear picture of what kind of person we want to become, and why. For instance, one day I wrote down all the reasons why I would like to handle sexuality in an honorable way: what it might do to my wife if I didn't, how my children would be affected, what would happen to my work and ministry, how it would feel to be haunted by guilt and failure, and the inability of sexual gratification to last.

Job put it this way: "I made a covenant with my eyes not to look lustfully at a girl." I deliberately seek to not look at a woman who is not my wife for the purpose of deriving sexual gratification. Suppose I am at a health club and out of the corner of my eye I see a woman and think that if I look over at her, then maybe I'll be able to experience a little sexual pleasure. The next thought that comes because of what Job said is, *I don't have to look. I can* not *look.* The thought that follows is, *Instead of missing out on a little thrill, by not looking I will have a power I didn't know I had. I can be free, and that freedom produced by the Spirit feels good.*

 Real freedom is not the external freedom to gratify every appetite; it is the internal freedom not to be enslaved by our appetites.

Temptation promises that we can be free to gratify our appetites as much as we want. See a fly, want a fly, eat a fly. Temptation promises freedom, but it makes us a slave. There is always a hook. Real freedom is not the external freedom to gratify every appetite; it is the internal freedom not to be enslaved by our appetites, to have a place to stand so that we are not mastered by them. For we are something more than a stomach, a mouth, and a pair of eyes.

» *Monitor Your Soul Satisfaction*

When we are hungry, anything on the menu looks good. When our soul is dissatisfied, sin begins to look tempting. That is why it is important to notice the level of soul satisfaction in our life.

On the dashboard of any car are certain lights that tell us how hot the engine is running or when we are about to run out of oil. They are commonly called "idiot lights"—I suppose because only an idiot would ignore them. Likewise, the main light on the dashboard of our heart is our "soul satisfaction" light. This is why in the Bible there are so many commandments that call us to joy: "The joy of the Lord is your strength" and "Rejoice in the Lord always; again I will say, rejoice!"

Why do intelligent people keep getting hooked? What makes those with high IQs so vulnerable to temptation, when it is obviously such a dumb step? We become vulnerable to temptation when we are dissatisfied with our lives. The deeper our dissatisfaction, the deeper our vulnerability, because we were made for soul satisfaction. We cannot live without it. If we do not find soul satisfaction in God, we will look for it somewhere else, because we will look for it. Then it becomes an idol. What was called idolatry in biblical times we often talk about today as addictions. Our lives get all wrapped up around them. That is why Jesus begins the Sermon on the Mount, not with rules about morality, but with good news to speak right to the yearnings of the soul: *blessed*.

Blessed.

Blessed are not just the winners that society says are blessed. Blessed are not just the super models. Blessed are not just the rich and powerful who can attract trophy partners. Blessed are the wrinkled. Blessed are the misshapen. Blessed are those who never got asked to the prom, who never got asked to dance. Blessed are the single; blessed are the married. Blessed are the prostitutes, the addicted, the shamed, and the regretful.

Blessed, blessed, blessed. Blessed are you, not because you can have every desire fulfilled, but because you are not your desires. Blessed are you because you are more than a stomach, a mouth, and a pair of eyes. Blessed are you because what you really ache for is to be loved by and connected to God, and now Jesus says that love, that life, that connection is yours if you want it through him.

Do you want it?

» Don't Stay Down!

It is instructive that while the devil is called the Tempter, he is also called the Accuser. As soon as he gets someone to give in to temptation, he will switch hats and try to convince us that because we have yielded to temptation, we are beyond redemption.

The Spirit is just the opposite, always seeking to "deliver us from evil." When we do give in, the flow of the Spirit moves us toward forgiveness, redemption, and healing.

I was running on a beach early one morning, discouraged by the lack of progress in my own life and feeling that I was still wrestling with the same selfishness and fear that I had many years ago. Because it was so early, the beach was deserted. Then I saw a man walking toward me — a big old guy, bald as could be, wearing only a long pair of floral swimming trunks, great big paunch leading the way. He looked like Santa Claus on summer vacation.

I intended to just give him the jogger's nod of acknowledgment and keep moving down the beach, but he was having none of that. Looking me right in the eye, he stuck his right arm all the way out to the side and silently held a huge hand in the air. He walked right up to me. He was insisting on a high five. The man had *attitude*. I smacked his hand with mine, and he gave me a nod of satisfaction, as if to say, "We're connected now. It is good that we share this beach together. I am glad you are here."

Immediately I had this thought — whether or not it is from God, only God knows: *I am glad you are here. I am not neutral about your existence. This is a little picture of grace. Do not be discouraged, not even about your own failings.*

To this day, every time I remember the man on the beach, I think about God.

Blessed.

Chapter 13

Recognize Your Primary Flow-Blocker

USA Today once ran an article about the ten most difficult things to do in sports. Number five was returning a professional tennis serve. Number four was hitting a golf ball long and straight (even though it's just sitting there on the tee). Number three was pole-vaulting over fifteen feet. Number two was driving a race car at megaspeed without dying. But the hardest feat in athletics is hitting a professionally thrown baseball.

A few years ago, a friend of mine named Ned Colletti, who was vice president of the San Francisco Giants baseball team, asked if I would speak at a chapel service. He offered to let me take batting practice with John Yandle, the batting practice pitcher for Barry Bonds. I thought it would be a good chance to benchmark my athletic skills.

I never played organized baseball, but as a kid growing up we played on a vacant lot where the best pitcher around was Steve Snail. In fifth grade I could hit his pitches better than anyone else in the neighborhood. (There was only one other kid in the neighborhood, and she was in first grade — but I was still best.)

I did pretty well against Snail, I thought. *Let's see how this goes.*

At the batting cage in AT&T Park, John wound up and let go, and I heard the sound of the ball hitting the net behind me.

He's not just lobbing them in there, I thought. *He wants to see if I can hit his best stuff.*

John wound up again, and the second time I swung, the ball had already been in the net several seconds by the time my bat got over the plate. So I kept starting my swing earlier until eventually I would begin my swing about the same time I saw him start his windup. I hit several foul balls and a few dribblers that might have gone fair. I was feeling pretty good.

Then he said, "Do you want me to put a little zip on one?"

Those *had* been his lobs.

"Sure!" I said. "It's been hard to time these slow balls."

He wound up. I never saw it.

I asked him if that was his best pitch.

"No," he said, "you wouldn't want to see that."

"What level player would hit that well?" I asked.

"A good high school player would crunch it," he said, "and a good college player would strike out a high schooler with his eyes closed. Minor league guys would throw shutouts to college guys. Put a major league arm against minor leaguers and it's no contest."

John sent a scouting report to Ned Coletti: "John Ortberg — bats right, throws right. Took ten minutes of batting practice. As a hitter, John makes a good pastor."

That day I learned there is a vast chasm between sandlot baseball in Rockford, Illinois, and Major League talent in San Francisco. It's not just that I wasn't good — I didn't know enough to know how "not good" I was.

A study done a few years ago showed that the first sign of incompetence is our inability to *perceive* incompetence. We deceive ourselves about our intelligence, for example. I may think I'm pretty smart until I read about a student who did not miss a single question on the SAT, ACT, and PSAT combined. We deceive ourselves about our talent, for people at a karaoke bar sing with far more confidence than reality would allow. We deceive ourselves about our appearance. A grandpa friend of mine boarded an airport tram and noticed an attractive young woman sitting nearby who smiled at him. He thought to himself, *I've still got it.* "Excuse me, sir," she said. "I can stand. Would you like to take my seat?"

Nowhere does this inability to have an objective, accurate, reality-based view of our performance show itself more than in the spiritual realm. When it comes to moral character, the purity of heart, the duplicity in our actions, how many of us have given serious thought to how our lives would grade out — not by the standard of the neighborhood sandlot where we can always find a first-grader to outperform — but in the eyes of a holy, just, righteous, and truth-telling God? That is why the most dangerous force in the world is not sickness or injury or bankruptcy.

It is sin.

Sin is a word not often thought about seriously in our time. Neal Plantinga writes, "Nowadays, the accusation *you have sinned* is often said with a grin, and with a tone that signals an inside joke...." Sin has become a word for hot vacation spots (Las Vegas is Sin City) and dessert menus: "Peanut Butter Binge and Chocolate Challenge are sinful; lying is not. The new measure for sin is caloric."

But sin is the deadliest force because it takes us out of the flow of the Spirit. Imagine the consequences if we did not have a word for cancer or depression. We must identify and understand that which threatens our ability to flourish, and only sin can keep us from becoming the person God wants us to become. All other challenges face us from the outside. Sin works its way inside, strangling our soul.

» Your Own "Original Sin"

We used to have a car with a bumper sticker that read "I poke badgers with spoons." It is a line from a British stand-up comedian named Eddie Izzard.

Eddie grew up in the church and heard early on about the doctrine of original sin, but he was a little fuzzy on the concept. He assumed it meant that priests get tired of hearing the same old boring confessions, so they want somebody who won't just confess sin — they want someone who will confess *original* sin.

He figured that instead of old stand-bys such as greed and lust, he would come up with something that no one has ever confessed before: "I poke badgers with spoons." My wife thought it was so funny, she had it printed on a bumper sticker and put it on her car. We finally peddled the car to another family — on the condition that they had to keep the bumper sticker.

Debates have raged for centuries over the notion of original sin. The theologian Augustine said there is a fundamental moral stain that gets passed on to every human being even before they are born. The classic counterargument was raised by a monk named Pelagius, who claimed that every human being is a blank slate, a morally neutral free agent who has a clean shot at perfect innocence.

Pelagius clearly never had children.

The Bible never actually uses the phrase "original sin," but the writers of Scripture (and any moderately perceptive observers) know that we are remarkably prone to do things that we know are wrong. We have a staggering capacity for self-deception and self-justification.

There is a kind of "original sin" in another sense. Your sin is intimately connected to the passions and wiring God gave you. Sin doesn't look quite the same in anyone else as it does in you. Like your fingerprints, your signature, or your bowling style, your sin pattern is unique to you.

» Needed: A Deeper Understanding of Sin

Author Richard Lovelace noted that for many centuries people who wrote about the soul understood sin's complexity and ambiguity. They knew how much of our character lies beneath conscious control. They understood how superiority and judgmentalism creep into champions of morality and how someone who appears to be dissipated by greed or lust may be capable of nobility and love.

But by the nineteenth century, much of what was written about sin grew superficial and simplistic: Divorced people are bad; married people are good. Sexual sinners are bad; chaste people are good. The "world"—which in Scripture is identified with that broken reality that runs through each of us—became shorthand for talking about people who don't go to church, as in "we're not like 'the world.'" We turned sin into a grocery list of "thou shalt nots."

People latched onto Sigmund Freud and modern psychology partly because they needed language about the human condition that recognizes the complexity and ambiguity in every one of us. We learned how to speak about our psyches, but we still need a way to speak about our souls. No one recognized more clearly than Jesus that some people who look like "huge sinners" actually have hearts that are tender for God.

Others who are thought to be (and think of themselves as!) spiritual giants are actually walking heaps of pride and envy.

Living in the flow of the Spirit requires talking about sin in a way that is balanced, honest, and redemptive.

» Signature Sins

We do not get tempted by that which repulses us. Temptation rarely begins by trying to get us to do something that is 180 degrees in the opposite direction of our values. It starts close to home with the passions and desires that God wired into us and tries to pull them a few degrees off course. That subtle deviation is enough to disrupt the flow of the Spirit in our life, so coming to recognize the pattern of sins most tempting to us is one of the most important steps in our spiritual life.

Author Michael Mangis writes about what he calls "signature sin." It is based on the idea that my life has certain patterns, relationships, temperaments, and gifts that are unique to me—yours does too. My fingerprint is unique and could be recognized by an expert; my sin is similarly patterned. Certain temptations are especially troubling for me, and some sins are more appealing than others. Even if we both struggle with the sin of lashing out in anger, I am likely to have it triggered and express it in different ways than you do. In other words, we don't sin at random. Our sin takes a consistent and predictable course. When a car or a body begins to wear out, it is not equally vulnerable at every point; there are inevitably a few areas that are most distressed that will be the first to go under pressure. So it is with our souls.

My sin pattern is so characteristic that it can be used to identify me. It is my sin profile, and anyone who knows me well will recognize my sin profile in a moment. In fact, other people often know my sin profile better than I do myself.

Because we live in a physical environment, we sometimes speak of leaving a carbon footprint. But we also live in a spiritual environment and leave a sin footprint, which damages our spiritual environment. This is part of the power of temptation, because *the pattern of your sin is related to the pattern of your gifts.*

> The pattern of your sin is related to the pattern of your gifts.

Just as home-run hitters also strike out a lot, the areas of our gifts and passions will also indicate our areas of vulnerability. Extroverts who can inspire and encourage can also be prone to gossip. People who love to learn will be tempted to feel superior and talk down to others. Those who are spontaneous and have a great appetite for life will struggle with impulse control. Good listeners may become passive enablers. Optimists wander toward denial. Tell me your gifts, and I'll tell you your sins.

Greek mythology spoke of the nemesis, your mortal enemy. Your nemesis is like you in almost every way, except that he is the ruined version of you. Sherlock Holmes's nemesis was Professor Moriarity, also a brilliant man—but like Holmes would have been if Holmes had gone wrong. You are your own nemesis, your own biggest problem, because there is a relationship between the best version of you and the worst version of you. What they have in common is that both of them are *you*.

Mangis identifies nine of these patterns, using an ancient system called the enneagram. It is somewhat controversial, because it is used by many different spiritual traditions, but it is thought to have originated out of considerations of the seven deadly sins and the fruit of the Spirit, and it can be applied in a Christian framework. (For a few other references, see Richard Rohr's book *The Enneagram*.)

These nine patterns are as follows:

Reformers have a deep love of perfection. They naturally have a high standard of excellence, and their greatest fear is to be flawed. (They also make good surgeons and excellent golfers.) At their best, they are crusaders, watchdogs, and prophets. But they wrestle with perfectionism and self-righteousness. They will be tempted to judge others whose standards are not so high.

A friend of mine in Chicago, a surgical pathologist, fits the reformer profile. He was charming and eligible, but he cycled in and out of relationships because no one could ever quite measure up. I once asked him if he thought there was any connection between his inability to find a woman good enough to marry and his profession—cutting up dead tissue and putting it under a microscope to see what is wrong with it. Reformers are prophets and idealists who call us to be our best selves—but they can also be hard to live up to.

Servers love to be needed. They are natural caregivers who will fluff up your pillow even if it doesn't need fluffing. They remember birthdays and are the first ones up to do the dishes. Often servers work in positions where they support someone else, and they will feel most comfortable in a social gathering when they have something to do.

While they are drawn to help, their helping can sometimes come out of their *own* neediness. As a result, they can drain others if their giving becomes a form of taking. Underneath their servanthood sometimes lurks low self-esteem that demands to be fed but can never get filled up. Sometimes servers marry an addict because that forms a kind of symbiotic relationship.

Achievers love to conquer challenges and perform before others. At their best, they are motivated to grow, stretch, and learn. They can inspire and move people to action, and they often like to be in front of crowds. Giving a talk, which is the most common fear in America, often energizes them. If they don't have a chance to develop and shine, they will lose motivation. Achievers want to make an impact on the world around them.

Their temptation is that they can live for their image, idolizing their own performance. Unredeemed, they will be prone to measure their success in terms of applause and recognition. When John the Baptist said about Jesus, "He must increase, but I must decrease," he was stating the surrender that comes most difficult to an achiever. In the book of Acts we read about a character named Simon Magnus who offered to give Peter money in exchange for a dose of the Spirit that would let Simon have a spectacular ministry. An unredeemed achiever can turn what looks like serving God into serving himself.

Artists love beauty and carry inside a strong desire to be unique. They love to express their individuality in bold ways and enjoy living on the margins. In different eras they were beatniks, hippies, or punk rockers. They often have a very strong sense of what kind of look they want to effect or what life they want to create that they cannot express in words but that emerges in art or action.

While they bring color and flair to a world that might otherwise be drab, their sensitivity can enslave them to emotional swings, and their desire to be special can become preoccupying. Their temptation is connected to the need to be different. In their need to be special and stand out, they may look down on "ordinary people." They want to be bohemian—unless they live in Bohemia.

Thinkers like to know—*everything*. At their best, they are the investigators, scientists, and inventors among us. They love to discover truths that no one else has ever seen and to master a body of knowledge, a skill, or a hobby on their own. They often have amazing memories for the information that they are interested in, and they are often quite introverted. If you are a thinker, you probably like your own space.

While thinkers love knowledge, knowledge can "puff up." Sometimes thinkers love being right more than they love the people around them. They often don't express emotion or affection directly; more often they will express it through gestures or indirection. So it can feel as if they are takers and not givers.

Thinkers do not like to lose an argument, and in their minds that has never happened. They don't like to be interrupted, and they can go into solitude for hours, if not days. That doesn't mean that they are more spiritual; they just have a low need to be around people. Thinkers are not fun to argue with—unless you are one.

Loyalists were born to be part of a team. They crave a cause to which they can give themselves and a community that they can believe in. At their best they help everyone else become better. They are usually quite bright and often articulate, although they may not volunteer their thoughts. But they can grow cynical when they feel let down—which is inevitable at times. They are tempted to want to shift responsibility to somebody else.

Of all animals, dogs are most famous for their loyalty, and oddly enough the ancient Greek word for dog is *kunos*, from which we get the word *cynic*. Loyalists' suspicion of God is that he is fickle, hard, or unfair, and their signature sin is fear. When Jesus told the parable about the three servants and the talent, the third servant—the one who buried his gift because he was afraid the master was hard and cruel—was behaving like a bruised loyalist.

Enthusiasts are wired to be the life of the party. They can add zest and color to the lives of everyone around them, and in their perfect world they would be the bride at every wedding and the corpse at every funeral. The enthusiast will often have a gift for storytelling—and they may talk about themselves a lot. If you talk with them about their problems, they may listen to you at first, but they are like Teflon—it just doesn't seem to stick with them.

I was in a restaurant with a friend, and every time we ordered something, the server said "superb" or "excellent choice" or "brilliant." We finally asked her, "Do you ever say, 'That was really stupid,' or, 'That's going to taste terrible'?" The mask came off, and she said, "No. In the kitchen we actually have a list of affirmations, and every time somebody orders something, we have to give them one of those affirmations."

Enthusiasts do not need a list of affirmations because they are *always* saying "cool," "awesome," "wow," "fabulous," or "great." They can live for years without seeing the pain or darkness in other people or themselves. They are also tempted to make life revolve around the pursuit of positive feelings — the desire for gratification — and they become miserable if they feel they are not getting enough attention.

Commanders are created to understand power and leadership, to know how it works and to feel a natural pull toward it. If this is you, being strong is very important to you. You have a need to lead. Opposition actually energizes you, but power can become an end in itself, and you can get frustrated when you are not getting your own way. Other people may be frightened by you if they don't agree with you.

Winston Churchill was a commander who was easily bored by agreement and whose greatest moments were inspired by opposition. He once said that British Prime Minister Clement Attlee was a modest little man with much to be modest about. He had a running battle with Lady Astor, who once said to him, "Mr. Churchill, if I were your wife I would put poison in your coffee!" To which Churchill famously replied, "Lady Astor, if I were your husband I would drink it." When Adolf Hitler came to power in Germany, Churchill found the enemy that he had been waiting for his whole life.

When we took our dog for obedience training, the instructor said, "When you're giving your dog an order, you must always be above your dog. Never get down and look your dog in the eye when you're giving him an order, because you must establish your dominance. If the dog wants to go outside and scratches at the door, you never respond to the dog and let him go out. You make the dog do a trick first, and then you let him go out the door."

I immediately thought of someone I know who treats people this way, someone with an instinctive understanding of how power works and who always seeks the dominant position. If you are a commander, you do not like to be coached, taught, corrected, or led.

Peacemakers have a natural love for serenity and tranquility; they thrive when life is calm. Peacemakers love the verse, "How good and pleasant it is when God's people live together in unity!" Peacemakers can make excellent therapists and mediators, and in their redeemed state they bring reconciliation to families, neighborhoods, and workplaces.

But peacemakers can be tempted to seek peace at any price, using their relational skills to blend in and avoid taking initiative or assuming risks because of their undue attachment to comfort. They often suffer from "terminal niceness" when courage is required instead. A peacemaker friend of mine used to leave the table to empty the wastebasket anytime a conflict broke out at dinner time.

REFORMER

Strengths: Lives with an internal standard of what is good, noble, and beautiful. Calls others to live better lives

Weaknesses: Can be arrogant when unredeemed. Has high standards that can lead to a secret, inner sense of inadequacy

Example: The prophet Amos, who carried a plumbline to show Israel the standard God expected of society

SERVER

Strengths: Lives out love in action. Has a natural other-centeredness that makes people feel cared for

Weaknesses: Can use "giving" to manipulate others. Sometimes mistakes servanthood with fear or low esteem

Example: Martha, who was busy serving while her sister Mary sat at Jesus' feet

ACHIEVER

Strengths: Has a strong desire to grow. Has the ability to accomplish things and add value in the lives and world around them

Weaknesses: Has the temptation to be preoccupied with one's own success. Sometimes uses other people to receive applause or approval

Example: Solomon, who sought achievement in education, finance, culture, statecraft, and the arts

ARTIST

Strengths: Loves beauty and goodness. Brings imagination to life, love, and faith

Weaknesses: Finds that the need to be different can become an end in itself. Can be tempted to give in to impulses and live an undisciplined life

Example: King David, who had strong gifts as a poet, dancer, and composer of many psalms

THINKER

Strengths: Is a discoverer, inventor, and lover of logic. Holds a passion for truth — even when it is costly

Weaknesses: Having conviction of being right can lead to arrogance. Can be tempted to withdraw from relationships and love

Example: The apostle Paul, who loved to study, reason, explore, and teach

LOYALIST

Strengths: Is faithful and dependable when the chips are down. Loves to be part of a great team

Weaknesses: Is prone to skepticism or cynicism. When threatened, can be pushed into isolation by fear

Example: Elisha, who became Elijah's steadfast companion and protégé

ENTHUSIAST

Strengths: Has high capacity for joy and emotional expression. Has enthusiasm that is contagious for others

Weaknesses: Can have a need to be the center of attention. Has a need to avoid pain that can lead to escape or addiction

Example: The apostle Peter, who was the first one to leap out of the boat — even if it meant sinking

COMMANDER

Strengths: Has a passion for justice and desire to champion a great cause. Has charisma to lead that inspires others

Weaknesses: Has a need for power that can cause others to feel used. Sometimes relies on fear and intimidation to get one's own way

Example: Nehemiah, who was moved to action — rallying followers and defying opponents — when he heard Jerusalem was in ruins

PEACEMAKER

Strengths: Has a natural ability to listen well and give wise counsel. Has an easygoing, low-maintenance relational style

Weaknesses: Has a tendency to smooth things over and avoid conflict. Is passive

Example: Abraham, who was a peacemaker with his wife, his nephew Lot, and foreign leaders — even attempting to mediate between God and Sodom and Gomorrah

- Which category best describes you?
- Tell a friend or two, and see if it matches their observations of you.
- What does this tell you about your sin pattern and temptation?

It is critical to learn the patterns at the core of the me you want to be and the corresponding sin patterns, for no one is more vulnerable than the person who lacks self-awareness. Jesus warned about people who go around taking specks out of others' eyes while failing to notice the two-by-four in their own. My signature sin is my own two-by-four—so appealing to me that it is my biggest danger, so close to me I am apt not to see it.

As I become more aware of my signature sin, I sometimes wish I could be like someone else. I fall into the "achiever" category, so I sometimes think I would be less sinful if I were a "server." But every category wrestles with sin, only in different ways. Knowing every category has its own hidden temptations helps me be less likely to envy someone else when I am doing badly and less likely to judge someone else when I think I am doing well.

Knowing our signature pattern also tells us what we need to be most fully spiritually alive. If you are a reformer, you will need to be aware of the risk of self-righteousness, but you will also know that you have been wired by God with a passion for justice and that this passion is a good thing. You will feel God's presence most fully when you can express it with freedom and love.

Finally, knowing other people's patterns helps us live in community better. As we learn about others' patterns, we become more patient with those whose signature sins are different than ours. We can make sure helpers don't always get stuck in "serving" mode; we can encourage peacemakers to speak honestly when they are angry. We grow into a way of talking about our sin so that we challenge each other in ways that include laughter and lightness about our common brokenness.

I had lunch last week with a friend and co-worker who tends to be a peacemaker. At the end of our lunch, he had one more thing to tell me, which was to remind me of a group conversation we had both been part of a week earlier where I had communicated frustration and anger in inappropriate ways. He was gently telling me that I had sinned, and it was not fun for me to hear that. One difficulty of being in relationship with this guy is that he only sins about once a decade. But I am watching him very carefully, so that when it happens I can be there for him too.

For when we know ourselves and each other, when we walk in love, we are free to be called to the best version of ourselves—God's handsigned version of ourselves.

That is the signature we really want.

Chapter 14

When You Find Yourself Out of the Flow, Jump Back In

The one pair of eyes into which you can never gaze is your own. There are parts of yourself you will never see without a mirror, camera, or outside help.

So it is with your soul.

In one sense, you know yourself better than anyone in the world. You alone have access to your inner thoughts, feelings, and judgments. In another way, you know yourself worse than anyone else can know you, for we all rationalize, justify, minimize, forget, and embellish—and we do not even know when we are doing it.

There is a me I cannot see.

Carol Tavris and Elliot Aronson have written a wonderfully disturbing book called *Mistakes Were Made (But Not by Me)*, which charts the mental tricks we play to deceive ourselves. We all fall for the self-serving bias. We claim too much credit and too little blame. Most faculty members rate themselves as above average teachers, and virtually all high school students rate themselves as above average in social skills. Most people in hospitals due to car crashes *they* caused rate themselves as above-average drivers. Even when people have the notion of self-serving bias explained to them, most people rate themselves as above average in their ability to handle the self-serving bias.

We suffer from the fundamental attribution error. When I see bad behavior in you, I attribute it to your flawed character. When it happens in me, I attribute it to extraordinarily trying circumstances. When you yell at your kid, you have an anger problem. When I yell, it's my kids' fault for misbehaving.

We are also guilty of confirmation bias. We pay attention to experts who agree with opinions we are already committed to, ignoring or discounting contrary evidence.

Our memories are not simply faulty; they are faulty in favor of our ego. People remember voting in elections they didn't vote in, voting for winners they did not vote for, and giving money to charities that they never gave to. They remember their children walking and talking at ages earlier than they did. (I know these are findings of credible research, but I can't remember who the researcher was—I think it might have been me.) The book *Egonomics* tells of a survey in which 83 percent were confident in their ability to make good decisions, but only 27 percent were confident in the ability of the people they worked closely with to make good decisions.

We are all viewing ourselves in the fun house mirror. People who know me well can always see these trends in me more easily than I see them in myself. This is why we are often stunned when someone else sees past our defenses into our souls. It is not that they are geniuses. It is just that I am sitting right in my blind spot.

»Acknowledge Your Own Blind Spot

Apart from the flow of the Holy Spirit, we can't even see our sin. Here is a vivid picture of how this works: When we lived in Chicago, there was a season when we would often get heavy snow. (It started in August and ended in June.) To melt snow and ice, the street crews would cover the roads with rock salt, which ended up coating car windshields. At night, driving by headlights in the dark, you don't know the film is there. Then the sun comes up, and sunlight is 500,000 times more intense than moonlight. The intensity of the sunlight illumines all the salt on the windshield, and suddenly you can't see out of it. You can't go anywhere. You have only two choices: Get the windshield cleaned up, or drive only at night. Avoid the light.

> This is the verdict: Light has come into the world, but people loved darkness instead of light. . . . (John 3:19)

We connive with each other not to see sin.

In South Africa I talked about apartheid with many church leaders who are about my age. Several of them said that they didn't favor it and knew it was a bad idea—but they look back now and ask, *Why didn't we say more? Why didn't we protest it?*

There was a system that sustained the sin of apartheid. If you were white, you talked mostly with other whites. The evil and injustice of it all did not enter your mind with sufficient force to move you to act. Millions of victims lived in injustice and cruelty, and the evil still ripples out.

> The same dynamic that sustained apartheid is always at work in us when it comes to greed, gossip, judgment, hypocrisy, flattery, bitterness, and hatred. Our insensitivity to sin is as dangerous as the inability to feel pain. However, the awareness of sin cannot be recovered simply by trying to crank up the volume. Merely *saying loudly and often* that sin is bad will not create the tectonic shift needed in our souls. You don't have to work hard to get people to hate cancer. They just have to love life. If they love life, people will always be opposed to whatever can destroy it.
>
> "The thief comes only to steal and kill and destroy; I have come that they may have life, and have it to the full." (John 10:10)

» Invite the Spirit to Examine Your Soul

Trying to see the truth about myself is like trying to see the inside of my own eyeballs. "Who can discern their own errors? Forgive my hidden faults," the psalmist asked. Fortunately, we are not left on our own. The Spirit is already at work in us. Our job is simply to listen and respond.

Once, in the middle of the night, Nancy and I were lying in bed and there was a tremendously loud beeping sound. Nancy gave me an elbow to the ribs and said, "What is that sound?"

I knew that if I acknowledged hearing the sound, it would be my job to go check it out. So I said, "What sound?" But I had to say it very loudly so that she could hear me over the tremendously loud beeping sound.

And she said, "That tremendously loud beeping sound."

"Oh, *that* sound! Let me go find out."

I went into the hallway, found the problem, and took care of it. When I got back to bed, Nancy asked, "What was it?" I told her it was the smoke detector.

"What made it stop?"

I told her I took the battery out.

"You can't do that," she said. "There could be a fire in the house somewhere."

"Nancy," I explained patiently, "we're upstairs. There's no smoke, we can't smell anything, there's no heat coming from anyplace. I checked. Do you smell any smoke? I don't smell any smoke. It was clearly a battery problem. Trust me. I took care of it."

We went back to sleep.

The next morning I had an early breakfast meeting, so while everyone else in the family was still sleeping, I went downstairs to leave the house. There were some odd malfunctions. The hall lights downstairs didn't work. The garage door wouldn't open automatically. That was strange, but I didn't think much more about it. Forty minutes into breakfast the server asked me if I was John Ortberg.

"Your wife called," she said. "She asked you to come home. She said the house is on fire."

I went home. Fire trucks were parked all over the cul-de-sac. I watched the outside of our white house turning brown, great clouds of smoke escaping into the neighborhood.

It turns out that a few delinquent birds built their nest inside the chimney casing. It eventually started smoldering and set off that loud beeping sound. Because we didn't do anything (and when I say "we," it is my way of saying that mistakes were made, but not by me), a fire started behind the wall and did unbelievable damage. All from a little bird's nest. A stupid little bird's nest. What kind of an idiot would take the batteries out of a smoke detector so he could sleep better during a fire?

That would be me.

The smoke detector wasn't my enemy; the fire was my enemy. The smoke detector was simply trying to help me.

I have a life. That's my house. I have a soul. You do too. Do you hear any beeping sounds there?

Beeping can sound like this: A parent neglects his children. They complain, misbehave, or increase the level of conflict around the house, and the parent has a nagging sense of failure. But instead of looking closely at his parenting — instead of talking directly about it with his children — he buries himself more fully in work, hobbies, or television.

A woman feels a twinge of pain when she sees a documentary about famine in Africa. She vaguely wonders about how little money she gives. But she doesn't like the discomfort, so she distracts herself by going shopping.

An angry man blows up at those closest to him. His "beeping sound" is his loneliness. He takes the batteries out of the smoke detector by drinking a little more, convincing himself his relatives are all difficult people.

Guilt is not my enemy. Sin, which blocks off life, is my enemy. The Spirit will often bring a sense of conviction, and when he does, the best response is not to suppress the guilt, but to get out of bed, take a look around the house, and put out the fire before it does more damage.

» Don't Get Used to the Beeping

One of the most poignant statements in the Bible is about Samson, who had been created by God to be a man of great strength and power. After a lifetime of disobedience, Samson had pushed God out of his life. At a great moment of crisis, he rose to exert his strength, but we are told that Samson "did not know that the LORD had left him." He had lost all sensitivity to God's divine presence in his life.

I too am insensitive. I don't know the truth about myself. But God will help reveal to me what truth I am able to handle. Our bodies have an amazing capacity to warn us about what ails them, if we learn to read the signs. Some warning signs are obvious: Chest pains may indicate heart trouble. But some are remarkably subtle: Shortened eyebrows could signal hyperthyroid problems; yellow bumps on our eyelids can mean high cholesterol; a diagonal crease in our ear lobe is linked to risk of heart attack. It makes you want to go look in a mirror, doesn't it?

In the same way, God will enable us to find the truth about our souls if we are patient and open and willing. The psalmist asks God to do the fearless searching inventory, for only God can give enough grace, strength, and truth to overcome our distorted vision. Left to myself, I will rationalize or excuse or defend myself. I will "call evil good and good evil," as Isaiah says. Or I will be neurotic about it. Madame Guyon, a wise writer on spiritual life, warned against "depending on the diligence of our own scrutiny rather than on God for the knowledge and discovery of our sin." So let's try. Allow your thoughts and responses to be guided by the Spirit.

One of the most important metaphors the Bible uses for sin is that of clothing. It speaks of "putting off" anger, slander, rage, greed, sexual impurity, and so on. And then it speaks of "putting on" those characteristics that flow from life in the Spirit. One of the ways you can think about sin is to use the acronym R.A.G.S. Those characteristics we are to "put off" by and large fit into one of these four categories:

R.A.G.S.

Resentment: mismanaged anger and bitterness

Anxiety: an inability or refusal to trust God; sins of passivity and timidity

Greed: mismanaged desire of all kinds

Superiority: self-righteousness and contempt for others

To make it concrete, you can respond with an A, B, or C response

   "A" means things are going well

"B" means there is not much change either way

"C" means this is a matter of concern

Let the Spirit prompt you as you walk through this.

Resentment

≈ What is your irritability these days?
≈ Are you becoming less and less easily irritated?
≈ How about bitterness and unforgiveness?
≈ Do you attack or withdraw from others?
≈ Is your handling of resentment getting better, getting worse, or in neutral?

Pause for a moment. Does the Spirit bring to mind anyone with whom you need to reconcile? Seek to set things right.

Anxiety

≈ What is the discouragement factor in your life these days?
≈ Do you find that you are more frequently allowing concerns to motivate you to prayer?
≈ Do you have more or fewer fears these days about money, your job, or what other people think of you?
≈ Do you allow your fears to keep you from doing what God wants?

Greed (and Mismanaged Desire)

≈ Are you becoming more or less a victim of your appetites now than you used to be?
≈ Is self-control going up, down, or in neutral?
≈ Are you living with more openness and less hiddenness than you used to, living more of your life in the light?
≈ Do you find that what you desire and enjoy is increasingly in line with what God wants for you?

Superiority

≈ Respond to this statement: "I have become so humble, I amaze myself." (It's hard to give yourself an "A" on this one.)

≈ Are you becoming less self-preoccupied these days?

≈ Do you find yourself thinking more about other people and God as well as the work God has for you to do?

≈ How often in conversations do you remark on the positive characteristics of others?

≈ How often do you tell negative stories or communicate cynicism?

≈ Are you spending more or less time serving?

≈ How much clarity did you have? Often we have to grow before God can show us deeper and more subtle layers of sin.

≈ Where did you find yourself "B" or "C"? Are there any particular behaviors you need to go back to apologize for or clean up?

≈ Find a close friend and talk with him or her about what you are learning.

» Recognize the "Ministry of Conviction"

Jesus said that when the Holy Spirit came, he would convict people of sin. But conviction is not simply the same thing as "getting caught." After we moved from California to Illinois, I was driving home from preaching—a short mile-and-a-half drive—and got pulled over.

"Do you know why I pulled you over?" the officer asked.

I hate that question.

"You came to a stop sign, but you didn't come to a complete stop. You just came to a roll. I noticed your license plates. In California they may be fine with it if you slow down to a roll at a stop sign, but you're in Illinois now, and in Illinois stop means *stop.*"

I told him that I was sorry, that I was distracted because I was coming home from church—did I mention I work at a church? Did I mention I work for God?

He told me he would let me go if I would say a Mass for him.

Sometimes people get caught doing something wrong and feel pain. But pain is not necessarily conviction over sin. It may just be embarrassment over being caught. Sometimes pain is pain over how other people are thinking about them. If no one knew, they would not be in pain.

Conviction is not the same thing as fear of punishment. Conviction is when I get a glimpse of what I am capable of, as in, *How did I become the kind of man who can do* that? *How did I become the kind of person who cheats on tests? How did I become the kind of person who tells lies to get what I want? How did I become the kind of person who is so cowardly about what I say?*

When God is at work in me, however, the pain is not about other people knowing or about consequences. That is all external. The pain of conviction is internal—over who *I am.* I respond by asking, *God, please send as much light as I can stand. Clean off the windshield of what I cannot clean.*

Cleanse me.

» The Indispensible Hope

Repenting of our sin is never despairing of our sin; it is always done in hope. Guilt may be an important stop on the journey, but it is never meant as the end of the line. We get our car checked by a mechanic, not so we can blame the car, but so it can get fixed.

Repenting is a gift God gives us for our own sake, not his. Repenting does not increase God's desire to be with us. It increases our capacity to be with him.

Ever see an animal repent?

We have a dog and a cat. Our dog sleeps in a little house every night, and he always gets a treat before he retires. He expects it. He feels entitled to it. When I stand up after 9:00, he goes crazy with anticipation. He stands at the door of the closet where the treats are and won't go into his house without a treat.

But sometimes the dog does a bad thing. When that happens, and when we find the bad thing, he does not expect a treat. He will run from us. He will actually kennel himself without a treat. He knows he's been bad.

Sometimes our cat does something wrong. Do you think the cat repents? No. Do you know why? Cats are evil. Somebody once said the difference between a cat and a dog is that a dog has a master, while a cat has staff.

We often think we need to repent because God is mad at us and needs some time to cool off. We think of repenting as a way of punishing ourselves so that perhaps God will be less severe with us.

> Low self-esteem causes me to believe I have so little worth that my response does not matter. With repentance, however, I understand that being worth so much to God is why my response is so important.

Repentance is not low self-esteem. Low self-esteem causes me to believe that I have so little worth that my response does not matter. With repentance, however, I understand that being worth so much to God is why my response is so important. Repentance is remedial work to mend our minds and hearts, which get bent by sin. When David murdered Uriah and slept with Bathsheba, he went a year without repenting. He had to train his mind to separate his deed from his worship of God. Then his friend Nathan told him a story about a wealthy man who stole the one sheep a poor man possessed. Notice what happens: David looks at Nathan's story through the eyes of the wronged person, and he feels compassion for the victim and indignation for the oppressor. Then Nathan says to David, "You are the man!" For the first time, David sees his deed from the perspective of those he has hurt. He now *thinks* and *feels* differently.

Repentance is always done in the gracious promise of forgiveness.

» Can We Really Expect to Change?

Imagine an alcoholic going into an AA meeting and hearing, "We re so glad you're here! We want you to know that you are loved and forgiven through nothing you have done. Of course, don't expect to change. Don't expect to stop drinking. We don't like it when people suggest sobriety is possible. We believe it breeds arrogance and self-sufficiency when people think in terms of actually not drinking. We have a little bumper sticker: 'Twelve-steppers are not sober, just forgiven.'"

The whole point of Alcoholics Anonymous (which grew out of an attempt to recapture classic Christian spiritual practices) was to bring freedom from a spiritual power (what the *Big Book* calls the "cunning, baffling, powerful, patient" enemy of addiction) that was destroying lives.

Sometimes people are afraid that if they don't change fast enough, God will get impatient with them. They don't generally use these words, but they wonder, *How much sin can there be in my life before I need to start worrying? Is there a level of sin that is acceptable for a Christian, then if you go higher you're in danger—like with the level of mercury in Lake Michigan? Is there a limit to impurity such as the Food and Drug Administration has? Is the standard high like that for homogenized milk, or is it like the standard of purity required for hot dogs, with lots of room for junk? Is it possible to be a Christian and just never grow?*

The issue is not whether God will get tired of forgiving sins. Forgiving is always the right response to sincere repentance. God is not worried that he might be taken advantage of. He is not afraid that some bad boy will use his charm to put one over on heaven.

The danger is not that God won't respond to our sincere repentance; the danger is that we might become so ensnared in the distorted thoughts that sin inevitably produces that we become simply unable to repent.

It is because of this that sin is to be taken so seriously. Paul told the church at Galatia, "Brothers and sisters, if someone is caught in a sin, you who live by the Spirit should restore that person gently. But watch yourselves, or you also may be tempted."

When the Spirit is helping us, we don't turn to that person in a judgmental way, because we are in no position to judge the amount of spiritual growth that has taken place in someone else. Missionary Frank Laubach preached the gospel to a tribe that had a long history of violence. The chief was so moved by Laubach's presentation that he accepted Christ on the spot. He then turned to Laubach in gratitude and said, "This is wonderful! Who do you want me to kill for you?" That was his starting point.

Only God knows what everyone's starting point is.

» Cling to a Bigger Hope

The bigger hope I cling to in the face of sin is not my goodness, but God's.

This year we had a daughter graduate from Azusa Pacific University. My wife spoke at the commencement, so we gathered with a group of fifty or so faculty, alumni, and administration before the ceremony. A few dozen people had graduated fifty years earlier, and they were there also to celebrate with their freshly minted co-alums.

At one point, Jon Wallace, the university president, pulled three seniors into the center of the room and told us all they were going to be serving under-resourced people in impoverished areas for several years after graduation. The graduating seniors said a few words about where they were going and why, and we applauded. They thought that was why they were there. Then Jon turned his back to the rest of us, faced the three students, and told them the real reason they were in the room.

"Somebody you do not know has heard what you're doing," Jon said. "He wants you to be able to serve the people where you are going without any impediment. So he has given a gift. He has asked to remain anonymous, but here is what he has done for you."

Jon turned to the first student and looked her in the eye. "You have been forgiven your school debt of $105,000."

It took a few moments for the words to sink in. The student shook her head at first. The thought registered. She began to cry at the sheer unexpected generosity of a mountain of debt wiped out in a moment by someone she had never met.

Jon turned to the next student. "You have been forgiven your debt of $70,000."

Jon turned to the third student. By this time she knew what was coming. But it was as if she could not believe it was happening until she heard the words. "You have been forgiven your debt of $130,000."

All three students were trembling. Their lives had been changed in a twinkling by the extravagance of someone they had never met. All of us who watched were so moved, it was as if we had experienced the forgiveness ourselves. There was not a dry eye in the room. (I wanted so badly to say, "I have a daughter who's graduating this weekend....")

An unpayable debt. An unseen giver. An unforgettable gift. And the freedom of the debtors becomes a blessing to the world.

Grace.

The joy of forgiveness.

There is a bigger debt we labor under. We give it labels such as regret, guilt, shame, or brokenness — sin. But God was in Christ reconciling the world to himself. We know what is coming, yet we need to hear the words just the same: Forgiven. Forgiven.

Forgiven.

PART FIVE
deepening my relationships
»

Chapter 15

Try Going Off the Deep End
with God

Researchers once surveyed people about their favorite room in the house. The top answer was the kitchen. People love that one. Most husbands' top answer was the bedroom. Want to guess what the top answer was for mothers of young children?

The bathroom.

Why? You lock the door. You keep those little rug rats out of there for at least a couple of minutes. You keep your husband out of there for at least a couple of minutes. The idea is that you find some place where you know you are alone. You are free of stress. You find sanctuary—a holy place.

God wants to give us sanctuary. There is another kind of presence when we are gathered together, but there is a unique way in which we experience the presence of God when we are alone.

I have one friend who finds this special solitude with God at a little Italian restaurant. Another friend experiences it most often while driving country roads. One finds it on airplanes. Another likes to go to a retreat center in the hills of Malibu Canyon. Still another finds it in the early hours of the morning in his office. You will recognize the place where you can be yourself before God.

Sometimes we are to pray privately. It is good to pray with people, but when I am praying and other people are listening, the fact that I am aware they are listening changes how I pray. Being alone with God, however, I can fully be myself.

In Jesus' day, almost no homes had private bedrooms. The "room" he refers to when he said, "When you pray, go into your room, close the door and pray to your Father," might be a supply room where they kept feed and tools or a few small animals. That would be the only place where there might be a door. It would be the most humble room in a humble home.

Being alone with God, you can fully be yourself.

> "When you pray, go into your room, close the door and pray to your Father, who is unseen. Then your Father, who sees what is done in secret, will reward you." (Matthew 6:6)

What is your room?

» Speak to God about Your Deepest Concern

Dutch theologian Abraham Kuyper wrote that there is a similarity between the structure of each individual life and the structure of the tabernacle in the Old Testament, which was divided into three compartments.

There was the outer court, where everyone had access. Likewise, there is a public you. You too have an outer court, which is you when you go to work, shop, or play. This is your appearance or your image, and everyone sees this part of you.

In the tabernacle there was also an inner chamber called the Holy Place. Not everyone had access to this area, and most were not allowed in. You too have a holy place, the place where you only allow certain people to enter, such as your friends or family. You decide who comes in and who doesn't, and no one can force their way in. Someone may hold power over you vocationally or financially, but that does not allow them entrance. Maybe someone wormed their way in, and you have to see a therapist to get them out. But ultimately everyone gets to decide who they allow in that inner chamber.

Then there was one more chamber—a very small, carefully guarded place, deep inside. It was the most sacred, and they had a beautiful name for this: the Holy of Holies. It was entered only by the chief priest, and there was room there for only one person and God.

This is the mystery and depth and amazing truth about *you*, because whether you are young or old, high or low on the totem pole, you have one of these places inside you too. Only God is allowed in there. No other human being can come into your Holy of Holies.

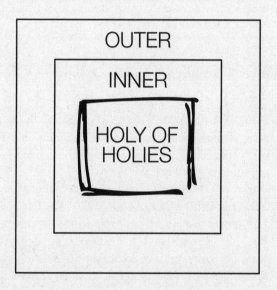

Early in our marriage I used to say to Nancy, "I know you so well, I know you better than you know yourself." Do you think she took that as a compliment? No. That is one of those "how could you be so dumb as to say that?" comments of mine, because there are depths in each one of us no one else will *ever* know—even if we wanted them to know. That is not because we are closed mouthed or secretive. There are parts of us we simply cannot put into words. There are depths in us that we don't even know ourselves.

In the Bible we often see characters addressing their own soul. The psalmist says, "Bless the LORD, O my soul," and, "Why are you downcast, O my soul?" Recognition of the unconscious, of thoughts and desires living far beneath my awareness, was around long before Sigmund Freud. The soul is so deep that I do not even know it fully myself.

You carry your soul around with you all the time. It may be filled with joy and peace; it may be empty and neglected. People who just look at the outer you—sometimes even people who are in the inner court—do not see your soul.

No one knows about this but you and God.

»Private Prayer Is Your Soul Alone with God

Jesus prayed. We are told that when he was baptized, "as he was praying, the heavens opened," and the Spirit came upon him. The flow of the Spirit is closely connected to prayer, and Jesus immediately went into forty days of fasting and prayer.

Jesus prayed *when his life was crowded and draining.* After he began his public ministry, privacy became difficult. "The news about him spread all the more, so that crowds of people came to hear him and to be healed.... But Jesus often withdrew to lonely places and prayed."

Jesus prayed *when he faced important choices.* When it was time to select his closest friends, he sought guidance. "One of those days Jesus went out into the mountainside to pray, and spent the night praying to God. When morning came, he called his disciples to him and chose twelve ... [as] apostles...."

Jesus prayed *when he was sad or frightened.* During Jesus' ministry his cousin, John the Baptist, was arrested and eventually executed. "When Jesus heard what had happened, he withdrew ... privately to a solitary place" to be alone with his Father.

Jesus prayed *when he needed strength for his work.* One morning, "while it was still dark, Jesus got up, left the house and went off to a solitary place where he prayed." When Simon Peter came looking for him,

Jesus said, "Let us go somewhere else—to the nearby villages—so I can preach there also. That is why I have come."

Jesus prayed *when he was worried about people he loved.* When he was about to die, Jesus knew that his disciples would fail. He told Simon Peter, "Satan has asked to sift all of you as wheat. But I have prayed for you, Simon, that your faith may not fail. And when you have turned back, strengthen your brothers."

Jesus prayed *when he faced an insurmountable problem.* "Jesus went out as usual to the Mount of Olives, and his disciples followed him." He said, "Pray that you will not fall into temptation." Then "he withdrew about a stone's throw beyond them, knelt down, and prayed, 'Father, if you are willing, take this cup from me; yet not my will, but yours be done.'"

When Jesus prayed, things happened. One time he took Peter, James, and John with him up on a mountain to pray, and "as he was praying, the appearance of his face changed, and his clothes became as bright as a flash of lightning."

I often find myself feeling guilty when I read those descriptions of Jesus at prayer, but I am not sure guilt helps us pray much more over the long haul. So consider this question: Do you think Jesus prayed a lot because he *wanted* to pray, or because he thought he *should* pray?

> If you ever feel guilty about your praying, know that someone who is better at it than you is already at work. Scripture says, "God's Spirit is right alongside us helping us along. If we don't know how or what to pray, it doesn't matter. He does our praying in and for us, making prayer out of our wordless sighs, our aching groans. He knows us far better than we know ourselves ... and keeps us present before God."

I think Jesus *wanted* to pray. I think that for us to pray much, or deeply, we need to move from what we think we *should* do to what we *want* to do. But that won't happen if we simply tell ourselves that we have to pray more. So let us put "shoulds" aside for a moment. How can we begin to pray in a way that will help us *want* to pray?

Almost twenty years ago, I felt frustrated at my own lack of prayer. So

I found a kind of prayer coach, who advised me to spend a few moments after praying just jotting down what had gone on while I was praying. The single most frequent observation for me was that while I was praying I was aware of being very tired.

"Did you tell the Lord about this?" my coach asked.

"No."

"Do you think it would be a good idea to talk to him about this?"

"Yes."

I began to learn that although I was trying to set aside time to pray, I had a hard time being *fully present*. We all know what it is to be with another person when their mind is a million miles away. I began to think that is how God felt when I was praying. After a period of frustration, my prayer coach had the suggestion I mentioned earlier; to go outside alone and simply invite Jesus to come with me.

The next day I went to the ocean, took my shoes off, started to run, and invited Jesus to come along. I found the strangest thing. When I thought I was *supposed* to be talking to him, I found it effortful and difficult. Now that all I had to do was invite him, I couldn't stop thinking about him. My mind kept reflecting on his being with me. I found myself wanting to point out the pelicans and the waves to him. People and concerns would pop into my mind, and I would find myself telling Jesus about them.

Everything changed.

» The Spirit Will Invite You to Pray

We can look for cues that embed prayer into our daily lives. In the Bible we are commanded to practice hospitality. In ancient times this usually involved hosting overnight visitors; now it might start with welcoming a telephone call that feels like an interruption. Out of habit I may find myself answering with a grudging spirit. *What do you want? Make it fast. You're bothering me.*

But there is another way. Wil Derske, a Benedictine monk, writes about the monastic value of hospitality and says that to accept a phone call is an opportunity to receive a guest. We can pause a moment before answering, in order to change our inner attitude from irritation to welcome. Derske says he will say a prayer of blessing just before taking the call: *Benedicamus Domino*—it might be the Lord!

Another way to accept the Spirit's invitation to pray is what might be called "paper prayers." Hezekiah was king of Israel when he received a letter from the much more powerful king of Assyria. The Assyrian king demanded the capitulation of Israel and warned Hezekiah not to trust in God. He warned that resistance meant that they would have to "eat their own filth and drink their own urine" before they died.

Hezekiah took the letter, went up to the temple, "and spread it out before the Lord." Then he prayed, beginning by remembering God's greatness: "O LORD Almighty, God of Israel, enthroned between the cherubim, you alone are God over all the kingdoms of the earth. You have made heaven and earth. Give ear, O LORD, and hear; open your eyes, O LORD, and see."

What piece of paper would you spread out before the Lord? Maybe it is a financial statement that is overwhelming. Maybe it is a divorce certificate or a medical diagnosis or a pink slip or a flaming e-mail. Any piece of paper that causes distress can be an invitation to prayer, a candidate to be spread out before the Lord.

» Use Your Body in Prayer

Body language is an important part of communication, and we can use our bodies in many ways to help us pray. We saw earlier that in Bible times people generally prayed with their eyes open. A friend of mine who knows church history said people closing their eyes and bowing their heads to pray did not become common practice until the 1800s — and then it was mostly to get children to settle down in Sunday school. There are records in Scripture of people praying as they stand, kneel, lie prostrate on the ground, sit, stretch out their hands, lift faces toward the sky, or bow them toward earth.

I find that my mind often works better in prayer when my body is moving. My wife and I take walks in our neighborhood, and there is one very steep hill that I usually run up. It takes two minutes and twenty seconds on a good day, and my heart is beating like a hummingbird's wings by the time I reach the top. Not long ago, I was running and was seized by the thought that this time I could not make it. So I began to repeat, "I can do all things through Him who strengthens me." Repeating that, one step at a time, I made it to the top. I was facing a difficult conflict at the time — my own king of Assyria. At the top of the hill the thought came, *Just as I received the power to go up the hill, I will receive the power to face the conflict.* And the flow of the Spirit came in a running prayer.

You are free to use your body and posture to help you turn your mind and heart to God:

≈ In confession, I often have my head bowed and will kneel; it helps me remember and experience the humility of the moment.
≈ In worship, you may want to turn your face toward the sky.
≈ Asking for guidance, I will sometimes place my palms upward as a way of expressing with my body "whatever you want...."
≈ When praying with someone, say at a restaurant, I may look that person right in the eye while talking to God: *Father, I am so grateful for this person. You know what they need. Give them what is required by their hearts.*
≈ To praise God, I will often use music to sing prayers.

» When Your Mind Wanders — The Spirit Is There Too

Does your mind ever wander when you pray? Sometimes it is good for us to take a few moments at the beginning of a prayer to slow down our mental metabolism and help us focus. It can be helpful for us to look at a candle or meditate on a verse or a word. But I have discovered that sometimes my wandering thoughts themselves can guide me into prayer.

I begin praying, and then I imagine myself being wildly successful at something. Or I replay a conversation with a person I am upset with. Or I try to figure out how to solve a problem I am worried about.

I used to think of those kinds of thoughts as obstacles to prayer, but I have come to think of them as prayers waiting to be offered. Maybe the reason they pop into my mind is not simply my short attention span, but rather what my mind is really concerned about. Instead of trying to suppress these thoughts, it is better to begin to talk to God about them. And just like that, I am back in the flow of prayer. Indeed, we are free to pray in the ways that will best help us live in the joyful awareness of God's presence.

» Let God's Face Shine on You

God gives us a remarkable picture of what can happen in prayer when we watch a parent and a little child. Imagine a one-year-old who looks at you and holds his gaze. You are charmed. He looks shyly at first, tilting his head away and looking out of the corner of his eye. You do the same. It's fun. He turns his face to look directly at you. You mirror the turn. There is a sudden noise behind him, and he looks startled—and you mirror his surprised look. He is so startled that he is getting ready to cry, so you shift into a smile. He does the same, and he is soon gurgling with joy.

We are hard-wired for this interaction. In fact, it is more than a game. When a child makes eye contact like this, when someone lets him know through their own body that they understand what he is feeling, his brain and nervous system make crucial connections inside his body. He is experiencing what is called "neural integration." When his amygdala gets terrified, it gains rapid access to his cerebral cortex, which can tell him to calm down while it works on solving the problem. By playing the face game, you are literally giving the child peace. Therefore, he wants to play. No one has to tell a child they should play. Children are hard-wired for it. It heals them. They find delight there.

In the Old Testament, God instructed Moses to give the Israelites the following blessing: "The LORD bless you and keep you; the LORD make his face to shine upon you; ... the LORD lift up his countenance upon you, and give you peace."

Is this what happened when Jesus prayed?

Prayer was not an energy-drainer for Jesus; it was an energy-giver. So it can be for us, if we come to see God's face shining on us. When I meet with a critic who wants to argue with me, I lose energy. When I meet with my best friend, I gain energy. God wants to meet with us as our friend.

The ability of love to speak to the deepest places of our hearts never goes away. Have you ever noticed how people in love sometimes speak to each other in baby talk? It is immensely intimate and private—and it's off-putting to a third party. If you do it, I wouldn't want to hear it. But we do it because it is the tenderest language we know.

Jesus' prayer life demonstrated this intimacy, because he called God "Abba," an Aramaic word much like "Dada" or "Momma." (Jesus spoke in Aramaic, and some portions of the New Testament are written in Aramaic rather than Greek.) "Abba" was a Jewish child's first word, because it was so easy to say. Somehow when Jesus was with God, the tender love that an adult offers to a child to give strength is what he received from his Father. It rewired his nervous system.

It does not stop there, for Jesus told his followers that they could have this same experience. This is why Paul wrote that by the Spirit we too can say, "Abba, Father." This is what happens when we are praying in the flow.

> God's Spirit touches our spirits and confirms who we really are. We know who he is, and we know who we are: Father and children. (Romans 8:16 *The Message*)

Prayer, more than any other single activity, is what places us in the flow of the Spirit. When we pray, hearts get convicted, sin gets confessed, believers get united, intentions get encouraged, people receive guidance, the church is strengthened, stubbornness gets melted, wills get surrendered, evil gets defeated, grace gets released, illness gets healed, sorrows are comforted, faith is born, hope is grown, and love triumphs.

In prayer—in the presence of God—we come closest to being fully ourselves.

Chapter 16

Make Life-Giving Relationships a Top Priority

When I turned fifty, my sister Barbara brought two stacks of boxes that were four feet high. When I opened them, I found they were filled with the foods of our youth. She had brought for me all kinds of food that I had loved, that were part of life growing up in Rockford, Illinois, and that I hadn't eaten in thirty-plus years.

There was a bag of "Mrs. Fisher's Potato Chips," which you can only get in Rockford. These chips are just grease and fat and salt and vinegar. Fabulous! Barbara brought almond tarts with white frosting that we used to get at a Swedish bakery that, sadly, went out of business years ago. Barbara had to track down a baker and get him to teach her how to make those tarts. She also brought a box of homemade popcorn, because our grandmother used to pop popcorn in bacon grease. She would fry up bacon, pop popcorn in the bacon grease, and then throw the bacon into the popcorn. Nobody in my grandmother's family lived to be very old — but we ate well.

When I grew up, we had "Sara Lee Banana Cake," so another box from Barbara had banana cake in it. I was a frosting guy, and Barbara was a cake girl. I would give her my cake, and she would give me her frosting. They don't make it anymore, but there is a group of "Sara Lee junkies" online who track down these recipes and swap them. My sister went online, found the recipe, and practiced it for months.

Only my sister could have gotten me those gifts. Love in a box. Our life together in food.

I was struck by how much a part of my life Barbara is. For fifty years I have been loved, believed in, and called to my best self by this remarkable, slightly older woman. My sister Barbara was my first and best friend. We played "spies" together, shared secrets, and went through school, church, piano lessons, plays, college, adult life, and therapy. When she gave me that birthday food, it struck me that as the body is nourished by food, so the soul is nourished by people.

More than anything else, we are shaped by people. Some naturally help me live in the flow and make me want to be the best version of myself. They see that best of me when I cannot see it. They cheer me on when I grow toward it. They get in my face when I move away from it. They encourage me when I am tempted to give up.

Plus I like them.

» The Power of Connectedness

God uses people to form people. That is why what happens between you and another person is never *merely* human-to-human interaction — the Spirit longs to be powerfully at work in every encounter. Referring to this dynamic, some writers of Scripture speak of "the fellowship of the Spirit." *Fellowship* has become a churchy word that suggests basements and red punch and awkward conversation. But it is really a word for the flow of rivers of living water between one person and another, and we cannot live without it.

An academic journal called *The Journal of Happiness Studies* publishes studies using the tools of research to identify what makes human life flourish. When researchers look at what distinguishes quite happy people from less happy people, one factor consistently separates those two groups. It is not how much money you have; it is not your health, security, attractiveness, IQ, or career success. What distinguishes consistently happier people from less happy people is the presence of rich, deep, joy-producing, life-changing, meaningful relationships.

Spending meaningful time with people who care about us is indispensable to human flourishing. Social researcher Robert Putnam writes, "The single most common finding from a half-century's research on life satisfaction, not only from the U.S. but around the world, is that happiness is best predicted by the breadth and depth of one's social connections."

> Connectedness is not the same thing as knowing many people. People may have many contacts in many networks, but they may not have any friends.

Part of what it means to be made in God's image is our capacity for connectedness, because God created human beings and then said, "It isn't good for man to be alone." Paul paints a picture of that connectedness in writing to the church in Ephesus that they are "being rooted and established in love."

When a tree puts roots into the ground, those roots are able to take in nutrients and water, and the tree grows and has life and strength — but *only* if it is rooted. In the same way, we are rooted and our souls are nourished in the love of God and other people. We experience this both physically and emotionally when we connect with somebody.

You are walking down the street, and someone you know smiles at you. They care about you through words, through touch, through listening, through prayer together. Whenever there is an exchange of genuine caring, it is as if the roots of your soul are getting fed. Every life has to have that connectedness.

How necessary is it? British scientist Donald Winnicott found that children who play in close proximity with their mother are more creative than children playing at a distance from her. Winnicott found that children are naturally inventive, curious, and more likely to take risks in what might be called the "circle of connectedness." When they are within this circle, they take more risks. They show more energy. If they fall down, they are more likely to get back up. They laugh more than children who are outside the circle.

Why? It is not that Mom is doing for the child what the child could do for himself. She is not solving problems for this little kid or generating ideas about how he ought to play. Instead, when love is present, when that child feels safe and cared for in her presence, something gets released in his life. He gets a little stronger. He gets bolder and more creative. Love releases life in that child that would otherwise remain dormant and unsummoned.

When you are loved, it is not just that you receive more from someone else, but also that you become more yourself. *You-ier.* Love brings the power to become the me I want to be. Loving people are literally life-givers. That is connectedness.

As children grow older and capable of more abstract thought, the circle gets bigger. When they are a one-year-old, maybe they want to be within a few inches of their mom. When they are two, they can be several feet away, but still in the circle. When they are three, the circle may be as big as a house.

How about when they are fifteen—how far away do they want to be then? The circle is now the size of the solar system. They want to be tracing the orbit of Haley's Comet.

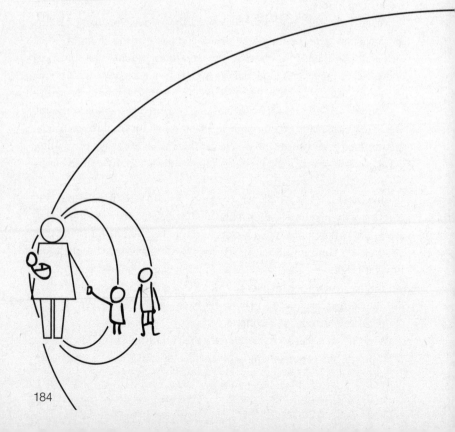

When love is working correctly, this sense of connectedness becomes internal. Initially, it is a very physical connection. When life begins, there is actually physical attachment. As we get older, we carry it around inside of us, and eventually we can take it with us wherever we go.

Likewise, we flourish when we are connected with God and people, and we languish when we are disconnected. Emotionally, isolated people are more prone to depression, anxiety, loneliness, low self-esteem, substance abuse, sexual addiction, and difficulties with eating and sleeping.

Physically, the destructive aspects of isolation are powerful. Even animals that are isolated experience more extensive arterial sclerosis than animals that are not isolated. A friend of mine used to have a dog and a cat, and the dog and the cat fought for ten years. Then one year the cat died, and the dog didn't want to eat. Day after day the dog wouldn't eat, until six weeks later the dog died. That is the power of connection.

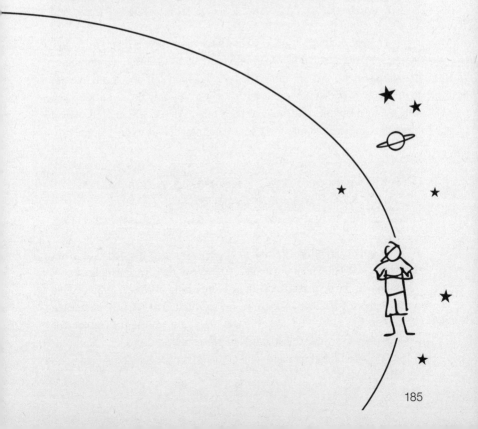

People who are socially disconnected are between two and five times more likely to die from any cause than those who have close ties to family, friends, and other relationships. People who have bad health habits like cigarette smoking, overeating, elevated blood pressure, and physical inactivity — but who still remain connected — live longer than people who have great health habits but are disconnected.

We see the physical, life-giving power of connection in Winston Churchill. He had a wonderful marriage with his wife, was deeply connected to his family, his friends, his nation, and his work. His health habits were terrible. His diet was awful. He smoked cigars all the time. He drank too much, had weird sleep habits, was completely sedentary — yet he lived to be nearly ninety. Somebody asked him, "Mr. Churchill, do you ever exercise?" He replied, "The only exercise I get is serving as a pallbearer for my friends who died while they were exercising."

Spiritually, as John says, "Anyone who does not love remains in death." When we live in isolation, we are more likely to give into temptation or discouragement. We are more likely to become self-absorbed. We are more likely to spend money in selfish ways. Not only do *we* suffer when we live in disconnectedness, but then other people whom God placed around us get cheated out of the love God intended us to give them.

"Loners who care only for themselves spit on the common good." (Proverbs 18:1 The Message)

We were designed to flourish in connectedness. This does not mean that we have to become more extrovert. Some of the shyest people I know have some of the deepest friendships. Flourishing in connectedness does mean that we will have to learn to identify who the life-giving people around us are, as well as discover how to give the power of connectedness to others, so that we can cultivate those relationships.

So let's open the boxes and look at the gifts connectedness brings.

» The Gift of Delighting

Love is mostly something you do, not something you feel. The circle of connection is marked by servanthood. "You, my brothers and sisters," Paul says, "were called to be free. But do not use your freedom to indulge the sinful nature; rather, serve one another humbly in love," because what marks God's kingdom is when people serve one another.

A therapist I know asked a client how he knew when his marriage of several decades had gone bad. "It was when she stopped putting tooth-paste on my toothbrush in the morning," the man said. When they were first married, whoever got up first would put a roll of toothpaste on the other spouse's toothbrush. Then somewhere along the line, they stopped squeezing for each other and squeezed only for themselves.

A son drives for five hours to be with his mother on her birthday. A friend mentions a book he is interested in; his friend remembers and finds a copy to give him for no visible reason. A middle-aged couple in a restaurant see a young husband and wife with little money and secretly pay their check. A father knows how much his daughter likes having a clean car, so he sneaks over to wash it for her by surprise. People in a small group email each other throughout the week as a way of expressing their care.

A wise man once said that just as the three laws of real estate are "location, location, location," the three laws of relationship are "observation, observation, observation." People who give life to us are people who notice us. They know what we love and fear. When we work to truly notice someone else, love for them grows. When we work to truly observe another person, in that self-forgetfulness our own soul flourishes.

If you can't do great things, Mother Teresa used to say, do little things with great love. If you can't do them with great love, do them with a little love. If you can't do them with a little love, do them anyway.

Love grows when people serve.

» The Gift of Commitment

One of the marks of the early church was their commitment to connectedness because they knew connectedness doesn't just happen. They met together every day. They ate together with glad and sincere hearts. Over time, however, that value began to fade. So the writer of Hebrews said, "Let us consider how we may spur one another on toward love and good deeds, not giving up meeting together as some are in the habit of doing." In other words, keep committed to community.

I have never known anyone who failed at love yet succeeded at life. I have never known anyone who succeeded at love yet failed at life. We need love to live.

Robert Putnam made a staggering comment: "As a rough rule of thumb, if you belong to no groups but you decide to join one, you cut your risk of dying over the next year in half." It is difficult to imagine anyone not interested in cutting their risk of dying in half. That is why the new motto for small groups at the church where I serve is, *"Join a group or die."*

In sports, the more an athlete needs encouragement from the fans, the less likely he or she is to get it. Rarely do fans of a losing team think when a slumping player comes up to bat: "Let us consider how we can spur him on to good deeds." Too often, people who need the cheers the most get them the least.

Every day, everyone you know faces life with eternity on the line, and life has a way of beating people down. Every life needs a cheering section. Every life needs a shoulder to lean on once in a while. Every life needs a prayer to lift them up to God. Every life needs a hugger to wrap some arms around them sometimes.

Every life needs to hear a voice saying, "Don't give up."

» The Gift of Love

The deepest words of the soul are the simplest: "I love you."

My father grew up in a Swedish home where he knew he was loved, but love didn't get expressed much verbally. So when he and my mom formed a family, they wanted to make sure they said those words. And so I grew up hearing those words: *I love you, Johnny.*

Let no debt remain outstanding, except the continuing debt to love one another, for whoever loves others has fulfilled the law. (Romans 13:8)

My dad is actually John Ortberg Sr., and I am John Ortberg Jr., so I was always "Johnny." Those were the last words I would hear at night: "Love you, Johnny." I would hear them when I got discouraged or sad. I would hear them when I felt lonely. I would hear them when I messed up.

My mom always said two things when she was really worried. One of them was, "I thought you were dead in a ditch somewhere." And it wasn't just "dead." You would think "dead" would be bad enough, but it's not just dead. It's "dead in a ditch." You might have been dead in a lovely meadow or something. That wouldn't be so bad, but dead in a ditch—that was awful.

The other was, "I was afraid someone had hit you over the head." Not just "hit you"—that would be bad enough. But "hit you over the head" because the head is such a vulnerable place. If she was *really* worried about us, she would combine them: "I was afraid someone had hit you over the head, and you were lying dead in a ditch."

Which is another way of her saying, "I love you."

Maybe there is someone in your life who just needs to have you look them in the eye and say it: *I love you*. The Spirit of God is at work in us all the time, prompting these expressions of love.

I was driving someone else's car yesterday morning, and I noticed that the gas tank was about empty, so I stopped and filled it up with gas. I can give a small gift of love like this in other ways, such as noticing what kind of coffee delights someone in a coffee bar and surprising them with it. I can let someone who is obviously in a hurry cut in front of me in line at a grocery store when I am not rushed. I can notice something admirable about one of my kids' friends and write a note to their parents to congratulate them.

Every moment is an opportunity to practice a gesture of love.

» The Gift of Joy

In the circle of connectedness we learn what a good thing joy is. One time my sister, brother, and I came home from school, and my mom had put on some kind of a rejuvenating facial mud mask that hardens and makes your face look like you are 187 years old. With all the wrinkles and cracks, she looked like something from a science fiction movie.

"Mom," we said, "take that off your face. That looks terrible!"

She looked at us sadly. "Children, I can't take it off. I haven't put anything on my face. This is a skin condition. It just happened today. I went to the doctor, and he said there's nothing that can be done. This is it."

"Mom, stop teasing us. It's awful! Take it off now."

"Children, stop saying this. You will make me feel bad. My face will look like this for the rest of your lives, so get over it."

We lost it. My little brother started to weep. My sister ran to call my dad. I kept pleading. Finally my mom couldn't take it anymore, so she told us the truth and she laughed and laughed.

We all ended up in therapy.

> A cheerful heart is good medicine, but a crushed spirit dries up the bones. (Proverbs 17:22)

We hunger for joy. "Satisfy us in the morning," writes the psalmist—but not with more money or power or applause. "Satisfy us in the morning with your unfailing love so that we may sing for joy and be glad all our days."

Joyful people make us come alive.

When the book of the law was read to the people in Nehemiah's day, they were overwhelmed by inadequacy and guilt. Nehemiah gave to them and us a remarkable statement: "The joy of the LORD is your strength." We know we love joy, but we often forget the power of joy. Joy gives us the strength to resist temptation. It brings the ability to persevere. Joy is the Velcro that makes relationships stick. Joy gives us energy to love. A person who brings joy to us is an oasis in a desert land. We don't just need air and food and water. We need joy.

> A twenty-year study of more than 4,700 people found that joy is contagious. People who become happy make it more likely that their friends will become happy, for happiness travels through relational networks like ripples on a pond. It is so robust that it continues through three degrees of separation, so you are more likely to increase in happiness if even a friend of a friend of a friend becomes happy. Having a happy friend is more likely to increase your happiness than getting a $5,000 raise. So if you get a $5,000 raise, try giving it to your friend. He will be happy, and you will both win.

» The Gift of Belonging

When I am loved, I belong to someone and they belong to me. This is why the most common designation for people in Jesus' community is "brother" or "sister."

When our family moved from Illinois back to California, our oldest daughter was entering college and wrestled not with just leaving the family, but with having all of us leave the home where she had grown up. She told us an unforgettable metaphor that a very wise friend used to explain her situation. It is as if she were getting her boat, sailing away from the dock, and then turning to find her dock was going away too. It is hard to be a little boat heading out to sea when you have no more dock to return to.

As our daughter spoke, I looked over at Nancy. She was immediately thinking of her own life growing up. In her family there was lots of independence early on, but not so much all-togetherness. "It's like I got a boat right away," she said, "but I never had a dock!"

I was struck by just the opposite. We prized closeness, but independence was the bigger struggle. "I had a great dock," I said. "I just never got my boat!"

When you were born, God gave you a boat—your life—designed to be an adventure for all your days on the earth. God also created a dock—your family—that could be the place of safety and security to give you the courage to sail.

Belonging. This is God's gift to us.

One day God says to the angels, "I have an idea. I am going to create the family."

An angel asks, "What is it?"

"I am very excited about this idea," God says. "Of course, I am excited about all my ideas. One of the great things about being God is you just never have a bad idea—but this one is special. *Family* is going to be the way I connect people in love. It will work like this. Adult people will sign up to take care of a tiny little stranger."

"Are they going to get paid?" the angel asks.

"No, that little stranger is actually going to cost them a lot of money. Not only that, but the little stranger won't even be able to talk at first. It will just cry and scream, and you will have to guess why. It will make you lose sleep. It will make messes all the time that you have to clean up. It will be utterly vulnerable. You have to watch that kid twenty-four hours a day, seven days a week. Then when it's two, that little stranger will be able to say words like "no" and "mine," and it will throw tantrums. And then I am thinking about inventing puberty. I am not too sure about that one yet, but if I do, they will get these strange things called hormones that will go crazy. Odd things will happen to their bodies. They will get pimples, their voices will crack, and their limbic systems will melt down. Then they will grow up, and just when they are mature and beautiful and interesting and able to contribute, they will move away. That's the idea. What do you all think?"

The angels shuffle around and look at their feet. *Who's going to tell him?* they think. *Lord, who would sign up for that? Why would they do it?*

Here is where God really gets excited. "They won't even know why. They will just look at that little body, those little hands and feet, and they will think that this tiny little stranger is beautiful, even though he looks like every other baby and all babies look like Winston Churchill. Then one day that little stranger will smile at them, and they will think they have won the lottery. That little stranger will say 'Dada' and 'Mama,' but it will say 'Dada' first because daddies are just so self-sacrificial and noble and ... how I love them. But moms are good too. So it will say 'Dada' and 'Mama,' and then those little arms and hands will open up and reach out and wrap around that neck, and it is going to feel to that grown up that for the first time now they understand why arms and hands were created.

"What it's really all about is just grace.

"Children, the new generation, will learn that they are prized and belong before they have ever done a single thing to earn it. The old generation will learn that when they give, they will receive. When they give the most, they receive the most.

"And then one day I will tell them, *Human race, I am your Father. You are my daughter; you are my son.*

"They will get it and they will be undone."

Teilhard de Chardin wrote, "Someday, after we have mastered the winds and the waves, the tides and gravity, we will harness for God the energies of love, and then for the second time in the history of the world man will have discovered fire."

connectedness inventory

When something goes wrong, do I have at least one friend I can easily talk with about it?

Yes   No

Do I have a friend I can drop in on at any time without calling ahead?

Yes   No

Is there someone who could accurately name my greatest fears and temptations?

Yes   No

Do I have one or more friends whom I meet with regularly?

Yes   No

Do I have a friend I know well enough to trust their confidentiality?

Yes   No

If I received good news like a promotion, do I have a friend I would call immediately just to let them know?

Yes   No

If I can't say 'yes' to most of these questions, I may want to look for a small group to join, or invite someone out for coffee as a first step toward connecting.

Chapter 17

Be Human

In the church, we have a sin problem.

The problem is not just that we sin—everyone has *that* problem. Our problem is that we can't talk about it. Our problem is that we pretend we don't have a problem. We are comfortable with stories about people who *used* to sin, and people often get invited to give testimonies as long as they have happy endings, the way television sitcoms used to in the 1950s: *I used to have a problem, but then I met God, and now I'm doing much better.*

Imagine going to see a counselor and saying, "I only want to talk about problems I *used* to have. Please do not ask me to acknowledge having any current problems. It would be embarrassing. I'm afraid you might reject me."

Why would anyone go to a counselor to try to convince the counselor that they don't need a counselor?

Why would anyone go to church to try to convince the people there that they don't need a church?

Years ago in southern California, I was part of a small group in which we were all relatively new husbands. We talked about our adjustments to married life, our sexuality, our jobs, our faith, and our money. We went to movies, baseball games, and weekends in Palm Springs. But one day one of the guys didn't show up, and we found out that week that he had struggled with compulsive gambling for years. This put him in huge financial problems, which then led to financial dishonesty at work. Eventually he got fired and got divorced. He had lived in fear, compulsion, and self-loathing for years — but none of us knew. Maybe he didn't have the courage to tell us. Maybe we sent subtle signals that talking about such deep problems would be unwelcome. I found myself wondering afterward, *How deep did the roots of these issues go in his life? When did they start? If we could have talked about them, would his life have gone differently? How much did my own need to look better than I am contribute to a culture of superficiality?* All I know for sure is that what should have been the place of greatest safety and healing was not.

People are okay telling a doctor that their body has a problem or telling a mechanic that their car has a problem. Couldn't sinners be okay telling other sinners they have a sin problem? If I want God (or anyone else, for that matter) to love the *real* me, I will have to work at getting real.

David was Israel's greatest king — but he was also a polygamist. He was a terrible father. He coveted another man's wife, committed adultery with her, attempted to deceive the husband, eventually had the husband murdered, and covered up his crime for a year. He was a liar, an adulterer, a coveter, and a murderer. As a friend of mine noted, no one at the time was wearing a "What Would David Do?" bracelet.

Yet he was called "a man after his [God's] own heart."

Is it possible for someone to be struggling so deeply with sin and yet still long for God at the same time?

I heard a Christian leader speak about the two great sins that plagued his spiritual life. One was that there were times when he was on an airplane and was not as bold in witnessing to the passenger next to him as Jesus would have been. His other confession was that there were times when his mind wandered while he was praying. He expressed great angst over these sins.

What hope does that leave for those of us who, as the author Anne Lamott says, do things that make Jesus want to drink gin out of the cat dish? Even in writing this, I confront a strange problem. If a pastor confesses to serious sin, people think he should leave the pastorate. If he only confesses to safe, non-scandalous sins, people think he is inauthentic and hypocritical. So at this moment I find myself wanting to make some confession that will look vulnerable and honest, yet not be so scandalous as to cost me my job. I cannot confess sin without sinning in the act.

You don't have to be victorious to join Alcoholics Anonymous — just needy. There are no "recovered addicts," only people in the process of recovering, because as soon as sobriety leads to self-righteousness, for disaster to come is just a matter of time.

However, relationships grow deep when people become real, which is to say, honest about the sin common to us all.

» The Spirit Flows in Transparency, So Come As You Are

I have a recurring problem that periodically requires treatment. It is a little embarrassing to mention, but recently it became very troublesome, and I had to go to the urgent care center. Andrew, the medical student on call, asked me what the problem was, and I didn't want to tell him. Want to know?

I'll tell you anyhow.

I had wax in my ears that had been building up over time, and then, when I went swimming, water got behind the wax until I could barely hear. People would come up to me after church, and I couldn't tell if they were saying "hi" or confessing deep sin.

So I finally went to the urgent care center, but I didn't want to name my problem. When I at last told Andrew, my vulnerability melted when he smiled.

"That's *tremendous*!" he said. "We're going to get that wax right out. I love getting wax out. It's one of the things I do best. All kinds of people have that problem. I'm a wax specialist."

Andrew took out a high pressure hose and an ice pick and removed a piece of wax the size of a small grapefruit. He said, "Man, your body really produces a lot of wax." I felt much better, and he was so happy to get it out.

My wife used to be a nurse, so when I arrived home, she asked, "Did you bring the piece of wax home? Can I see it?"

"I just left it there," I said. "But I could go back and see if they saved it or something."

Why was I embarrassed about my wax? Andrew is my friend. My wife was so proud of me, she wanted to see it. Their acceptance helps me accept that I am a wax machine. Now I don't care who knows.

When you can step into openness and stop pretending, you find yourself coming alive. Hiddenness and pretense are always the enemy of flourishing.

There is an old but uncertain story about the derivation of the word *sincere*. The ancient Romans used to prize Greek sculptures for their aesthetic excellence. The statues were already a few centuries old, however, and some of them had cracks or gaps where marble was missing. Vendors discovered that if they put wax in the sculptures, these figures looked great — for a season. The wax looked like real marble, but over time, the wax would yellow and harden until it became apparent that the statue was not totally authentic. So if vendors wanted to sell a statue and it was all marble — the real deal through and through — they would mark it *sine*, the Latin word for "without," and then *cera*, the Latin word for "wax."

Sine cera. Without wax.

When the Christian church started, people met together in their homes "with glad and sincere hearts" — without wax — because now there was a circle of connectedness where everyone could come on in just as they were.

Where hearts are sincere, they will be glad.

In writing to this early community of believers, the apostle Paul said, "Accept one another, then, just as Christ accepted you, in order to bring praise to God." Acceptance is more than just being liked by someone. Jesus didn't say to me, "John, if you just clean up a bit, if you just dress better, and read the Bible more, *then* I'll let you into my family." Of course he is going to help me become my best self, but I don't have to pretend to be any better than I am to be in Jesus' circle. *How* did Jesus accept you? Just the way you are. When someone knows the embarrassing, humiliating truth about me and still accepts me, I come alive.

A few friends and I from college days get together once a year for an extended weekend to experience the fellowship that comes from knowing each other deeply over a long period of time. Most of the time I was with them, I tried to listen to myself speak as I might hear someone else, and I was struck by how much of what I say is designed to show how smart, how clever, or how funny I am, often at someone else's expense. I found myself making my achievements sound more impressive than they are. I wasn't sure that — if I were not me — I would actually *like* me.

I read recently that one sign of narcissism is that the desire to be admired is stronger than the desire to be liked. It was painful to read that, because I thought of how much it describes my own wound. While I was telling these things to my friends, I was suddenly seized by the thought of how *lucky* I was to have friends who love me, for I am broken. When I am in superficial relationships, I can forget my brokenness. But when I am with people who know me deeply and accept me fully, their acceptance touches my brokenness as a doctor touches the injured place on a patient's body. Their very touch begins to heal, and through the mystery of the fellowship of acceptance, God's Spirit flows.

> Henri Nouwen wrote, "When we honestly ask ourselves which person in our lives mean the most to us, we often find that it is those who, instead of giving advice, solutions, or cures, have chosen rather to share our pain and touch our wounds with a warm and tender hand. The friend who can be silent with us in a moment of despair or confusion, who can stay with us in an hour of grief and bereavement, who can tolerate not knowing, not curing, not healing and face with us the reality of our powerlessness, that is a friend who cares."

» Give the Gift of Confession

One of the most important moments of my spiritual life was when I sat down with a longtime friend and said, "I don't want to have any secrets anymore." I told him everything I was most ashamed of. No wax. I told him about my jealousies, my cowardice, how I hurt my wife with my anger. I told him about my history with money and my history with sex. I told him about deceit and regrets that keep me up at night. I felt vulnerable because I was afraid that I was going to be outside the circle, to lose connection with him. Much to my surprise, he did not even look away.

I will never forget his next words.

"John," he said. "I have never loved you more than I love you right now." The very truth about me that I thought would drive him away became a bond that drew us closer together. He then went on to speak with me about secrets he had been carrying.

I can only be loved to the extent that I am known.

If I keep part of my life secret from you, you may tell me you love me. But inside I think that you would not love me if you knew the whole truth about me. I can only receive love from you to the extent that I am known by you.

I cannot be fully loved unless I am fully known.

To be fully known and fully loved is the most healing gift one human being can give another. James writes, "Confess your sins to one another, and pray for one another, so that you may be healed." We are all forgiven, recovering sinners, and no one can be secure in a relationship if they are loved only because they are smart, pretty, strong, or successful. Sin isolates us, and sin and isolation will make us sick in our soul and even our body. Confession and then prayer, connectedness to each other and to God, ushers in the Spirit and helps bring healing.

> **You can only be loved to the extent that you are known.** ✱

» No Pedestals

It is a remarkable thing how the writers of Scripture never do what churches are so tempted to do, which is put people on a pedestal. To illustrate how grittily honest the biblical writers are about human nature, answer this question: *Who in the Bible would you say had the best marriage?*

Adam and Eve had their honeymoon in paradise, and it all went downhill from there. Abraham lied that Sarah was his sister—twice—and impregnated her servant, Hagar. Isaac and Rebekah spent their marriage battling because he favored Esau and she favored Jacob. Jacob had children by two wives and the wives' servants. About all we know of Moses' wife, Zipporah, is that they had an argument over circumcising their son and she called Moses a "bridegroom of blood." David was a disaster as a husband; Solomon was worse. When Job's life got hard, Mrs. Job told him to "curse God and die!" I am not making this up: Someone online said they thought the best marriage in the Bible was between Noah and Joan of Ark.

In fairy tales, life is a difficult adventure until you get married—and then you live happily ever after. But nowhere in the Bible do a couple get married and then live "happily ever after." Marriage doesn't save anyone. Only Jesus does that.

The Bible is remarkably transparent about the flaws and brokenness of the marriages of every character—yet how often in churches do couples sit in silent agony? They have an image of spiritual success to project, but under the surface the reality is that they have not slept together for months. Or there is verbal or physical abuse going on. Or they have a young daughter who is pregnant and they don't know what to do. Or one of them is a secret alcoholic. Or they are facing bankruptcy.

Often the people who need help the most receive it the least, because that would mean leaving the pedestal. But what if real people could be as honest as the Bible about marriage? In a community gathered around a cross, there is no room for pedestals. In the Bible, marriage is not the fulfillment of our dreams; it is a place where we learn.

» Recognize the J-Curve

Experts in the learning field sometimes talk about the J-curve, a graph measuring performance, in which someone initially does worse before they start improving. Their progress looks like a letter "J" when graphed, with an initial dip before things head upward.

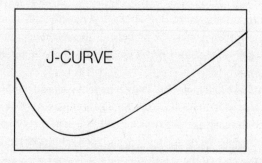

If you have been hitting tennis backhands the wrong way, when someone teaches you the correct grip, proper form, and right footwork, when you begin to try to hit them the right way—you will actually hit them worse than when you were trying the wrong way! If you stick with it, however, eventually your backhand will be far better than before. But you have to accept that at first it will be worse.

When the disciple Peter first exercised enough faith to get out of the boat, he sank and looked worse than any of the other disciples. When he tried to defend Jesus, he cut off a man's ear. When he promised to be loyal, he fell flat on his faith. When he tried to advise Jesus, he was a devil's advocate.

Eventually, though, Peter's faith and boldness and loyalty and wisdom enabled him to become a leader of the church. But he got worse before he got better. Notice that this did not surprise or discourage Jesus. In fact, Jesus was so patient with his disciples that we might think of the J-curve as the Jesus-curve. He will never stop helping a follower of his who is sincerely seeking to grow.

Jesus will always lead us toward growth, and growth always requires risk, and risk always means failure. So Jesus is always leading us into failure. But he never gives up on a student just because he or she fails.

If you haven't been confronting when you should and you begin, you will do it badly at first. If you have rarely encouraged people, your initial attempts may be clumsy. If you have never shared your faith with someone, the first time you do it you may stumble all over yourself.

Go ahead and stumble. Failure isn't falling down; failure is refusing to try. We ought to celebrate failure.

We are living on the J-curve.

» The Gift of Honest Language

Being human means being honest about what we want, but all too often we can wallpaper over human difficulties with a veneer of pious language. There is the story about a boy who comes home and doesn't see his mom is visiting with their pastor. He holds a rat in his hand. "Mom, you'll never guess what. There was a rat running around behind the garage. I saw it and threw a stone and hit it. It just laid there, so I went over and stomped on it. Then I picked it up and threw it against the wall as hard as I could. And I picked it up and threw it again." Then he sees that the pastor is there and that if looks could kill, he would be a dead kid. He holds the rat high in the air and adds in a pious voice, "And then the dear Lord called him home."

When we try to look more spiritual, we actually make ourselves less human. Pretending always cuts us off from the flow of the Spirit. Author Scott Peck once wrote of a couple who constantly used "God talk" to cover up their cruelty and attempts to control. In the Ten Commandments we are told not to take the Lord's name in vain. Usually we think about this in terms of using profanity, but maybe it happens more often when we hide behind spiritual language.

We were in a small group many years ago with a very diverse group of people. One of them was a teacher with a traveling ministry doing "Holy Ghost Explosion Revival" meetings. One of them was uninitiated enough that she did not know whether "Jesus" and "Jesus Christ" were the same person. The uninitiated one was once talking about her most dysfunctional relationship with a former boyfriend who had belittled her and betrayed her and abused her in humiliating ways. "Now he has cancer," she said, "and I hope he dies."

"You can't say that!" said the teacher. "You have to pray for him. You have to pray that he will be healed. The Holy Ghost can heal him right this moment. I'm going to pray right now. You've just got to love him!"

"But I don't love him. I hate him. I hope he dies."

Why is it that the psalms are so full of human anger, that they express so much raw, unfiltered hostility and lust for vengeance and fury and demands for divine justice to come pretty quickly — and that the prayers prayed in churches feel so ... well, decaffeinated? Is it possible that God could actually handle our anger?

There is an old hymn that includes the lines, "Just as I am, without one plea." This song speaks of coming to God without hiding, knowing that I am loved simply as a gift. A few people in my life allow me to relate to them "just as I am," and I cling to them the way a drowning man clings to a raft.

If ever there were a true "just as I am" church, if ever there were a community where everybody could bring all their baggage and brokenness with them without neat and tidy happy endings quite yet, if ever there was a group where everyone was loved and no one pretended — we could not make enough room inside the building.

---

in the flow ≈

- ≈ Who is the friend I am most transparent with?
- ≈ What are my secret regrets and temptations? Is there someone I could talk with about them?
- ≈ Spend some time reflecting on your regrets and temptations. Schedule some unhurried time to meet with the person you trust most deeply. Share with them — at a level appropriate to how well you know and trust them — the condition of your heart and soul.
- ≈ Laugh at yourself at least once today.

Chapter 18

Find a Few Difficult People to Help You Grow

Some people tempt me out of the flow of the Spirit. They judge me, and I feel discouraged. They dislike me, and I feel rejected. They are a black hole of need and drain me. They throw roadblocks in my path and discourage me. They anger me. They scare me. They depress me. Plus I don't like them.

The playwright George Bernard Shaw sat next to a pompous bore at a dinner party one evening. After listening to an interminable monologue of useless information, Shaw observed, "Between the two of us we know all there is to know."

"How's that?" asked his fascinated companion.

"Well," replied Shaw, "you seem to know everything except that you're a bore. And I know that!"

Shaw and Winston Churchill famously found each other to be difficult. Shaw once sent two tickets to Churchill to the opening night of one of his plays, with instructions to "bring a friend—if you have one." Churchill sent them back because he was busy opening night. He said he would come on "the second night—if there is one."

We all have difficult people in our life, but hear this: God can use them to help you become the best version of you—maybe even more than the people you like. Jesus said,

> You're familiar with the old written law, "Love your friend," and its unwritten companion, "Hate your enemy." I'm challenging that. I'm telling you to love your enemies. Let them bring out the best in you.... If all you do is love the lovable, do you expect a bonus? Anybody can do that. If you simply say hello to those who greet you, do you expect a medal? Any run-of-the-mill sinner does that. In a word, what I'm saying is, *Grow up*. You're kingdom subjects. Now live like it. Live out your God-created identity.

Other people don't create your spirit; they reveal your spirit.

In fact, if God wants to grow some quality in you, he may send you a person who tempts you to behave in just the opposite way. If you need to develop love, then some unlovable people will be your greatest challenge. If you need to develop hope, maintaining it in the face of discouragers will make it strong. If you want to grow in your ability to confront, a hard-to-confront intimidator will give you serious practice. As lifting weights strengthens a muscle and cardio exercises strengthen a heart, difficult people can strengthen our ability to love.

Why does God allow difficult people in my life?

What other kind are there?

If God were to get rid of all the difficult people in the world—if he were to remove everybody with quirks, flaws, ugliness, and sin—you would get awfully lonely.

We always wish that God would give us a life without difficult people in it. But how many great characters in the Bible had difficult people in their lives? Moses had Pharaoh, Elijah had Jezebel, Esther had Haman, Jacob had Laban, David had Saul, John the Baptist had Herod. Even Jesus had Judas. If God loves you and wants to shape you, he will send some difficult people your way. But take heart. You are the difficult person he is sending to shape somebody else!

If we can learn to have rivers of living water still flowing through us in these relationships, we will be unstoppable.

» Recognize the Impact

We are far more affected by the impact of people on our lives than most of us realize. We are always—*always!*—being energized or drained by every interaction.

Dr. Jill Taylor was a thirty-seven-year-old, Harvard-trained brain scientist who suffered a massive stroke. The left side of her brain, which regulates speech and linear thinking, was devastated. For many months she lay in a hospital bed, unable to carry on a conversation. She writes of how even though she could not understand the words people were saying to her, she became intensely aware of whether the people approaching her were enhancing her sense of life or depleting it.

> I experienced people as concentrated packages of energy ... although I could not understand the words they spoke, I could read volumes from their facial expression and body language. I paid very close attention to how their energy dynamics affected me. Some people brought me energy while others took it away.

At a level deeper than words, deeper than exchanging information, every interaction with another person is a spiritual exchange. Some people are life-bringers to us. They increase our energy, deepen our hope, add to our joy, and call out the best in us. Other people are life-drainers. They add to our anxiety and invite us to cynicism. We find ourselves becoming defensive, depressed, or exasperated.

How do we grow through difficult relationships?

» Keeping God between You and Me

Before some friends of mine went on a trip, they dropped their hunting dog off at a summer camp. I didn't even know there were such places. It was a refresher course on obedience school to retrain their dog, to make sure that every time he gets a command, his response is prompt, eager, wholehearted, unquestioning obedience. When he came home, it was as if he were a new creature. It was summer camp and reform school all wrapped up into one.

Wouldn't it be nice if there were such places for people? If there were, they would be full. Of course, that's what kills us, because we can't fix *people*. There is a good reason for this, however: Everyone has a soul. Everyone has a "Holy of Holies," where only that person and God can meet. Only God can touch the deepest place of another's soul. We may think, *I can intimidate, lecture, flatter, manipulate, reason, cajole, reward, or withdraw to get the behavior I want out of that person.* And maybe I can, out on the outer edges of their personality; but I can't touch the deepest part of another person. Only God can.

Prayer is the closest we come to being able to influence people at their deepest level, to be able to go with God into another person's soul, because always between me and the most inner part of another person stands Jesus. The most direct way to another person is not talking to them. The most direct way is talking to Jesus.

I can remember as if it were yesterday the hardest conversation I have ever had. It was with a person I had known more than a decade, over long-standing and complicated problems in our relationship. I had avoided speaking truthfully about our problems for years, so picking up the phone to schedule the talk felt like the hardest thing ever. I was afraid the conversation would be grueling and painful, that we would not see eye-to-eye. It ended up being worse than that!

But here was the thought that enabled me to have the talk: *I do not have to control the outcome. I do not have to make the other person agree. I don't even have to do the talk well. I just have to show up. The rest is up to God.*

At the end of the conversation, even though it had not produced the results I wanted, I felt alive because I was trusting Jesus with a challenging relationship. When I keep God between you and me, I begin to be less afraid of you.

Another time I was desperately concerned about someone I love, whom I wanted to fix, but they would not let me fix them. A wise friend said the best thing I could do was to pray, offering "gentle, non-frantic prayer." When God is present, prayer does not have to be frantic. When I keep God between me and you, I begin to be less controlling.

In driver education we learn to reduce accidents by keeping the right distance between ourselves and other cars—one car-space of distance for every ten miles per hour of speed. In spiritual education we learn to keep a kind of spiritual space between ourselves and the souls around us. That space is where God flows between you and me. Jesus advised, "When someone gives you a hard time, respond with the energies of prayer, for then you are working out of your true selves, your God-created selves. This is what God does."

» What Makes Someone Difficult for You?

The space between me and my enemy is the space where love can grow. Many studies have been done on what causes us to like someone. Out of all the causes—physical attractiveness, IQ, ability, personality type—the number one factor that determines whether or not you will like another person is whether or not they like us. If they like you, you will like them. If they don't like you, you will not like them.

This is humbling.

If there is someone I have never liked and then I find out that they have said something good about me, I think, *Man! This person is more on the ball than I thought. This is a person with some hidden depth in them.*

That person could be wonderful in every other respect, but their dislike of us shapes our perceptions more than anything else. *Gandhi doesn't like me? I always thought he was a little shallow.*

God's not that way. God loves people who love him. He loves people who don't love him. He doesn't do it because he has to. He doesn't say to himself, *Well, I am God, so I guess I'm stuck with having to love people. Boy, I sure wish I didn't have to!*

God does it because love is the only way to life.

» Staying in the Flow with the Spirit Takes a Quarter-Second

Anger is prone to take me out of the flow. This is why Paul wrote,

> Do not grieve the Holy Spirit [in other words, don't cut yourself off from the flow of the Spirit] with whom you were sealed for the day of redemption. Get rid of all bitterness, rage and anger, brawling and slander, along with every form of malice.

Difficult relationships can give the Evil One a foothold, but God has wired us so that in times of intense difficulty we have a kind of built-in moment to turn to the Spirit for help. As we noted in chapter 15, the primary place in the brain that processes strong negative emotions such as rage and fear is called the amygdala. When this is removed from certain animals, they become incapable of rage and fear. Normally, when input comes into the brain, it goes to the neocortex for processing. In about 5 percent of cases, however, when something extremely emotional happens, it goes to the amygdala, and the thinking part of the brain gets short-circuited.

Mom is in a grocery store, in a hurry, so she is tense. She has her three-year-old next to her and her eighteen-month-old in a shopping cart. Suddenly the three-year-old grabs a box of cocoa puffs.

"Put it down," says Mom.

But the three-year-old is determined to have them.

"Put it down!" Mom repeats.

At this point the eighteen-month-old, who has been holding a glass of jelly, throws it to the ground from the cart, and it shatters. What happens to Mom next is what researchers call "an amygdala hijack." The amygdala takes over the thinking process, and Mom goes ballistic. She picks up the three-year-old, drapes him over one arm, carries him doubled over like a pretzel, and she is shaking the shopping cart. The kid is yelling, "Put me down! Put me down!" Mom is out of control, suffering from what researchers call "cognitive incapacitation." Rational thought is no longer an option.

But there is an aspect of our circuitry that gives us hope.

Impulses formed in the brain can be measured during neurosurgery. I decide that I am going to move my hand, and then that impulse travels to the hand. But in between the brain activity and the movement of the hand, there is what one researcher calls the "life-giving quarter-second."

There is a quarter-second between when that impulse takes place in your brain and when that action takes place in your body. And that quarter-second—although it doesn't sound like very long in the life of the mind—is huge. The apostle Paul wrote, "In your anger do not sin . . . and do not give the devil a foothold." That quarter-second is the time when the Holy Spirit can take control. That is when you can give the foothold to the Holy Spirit or you can give it to sin. That one quarter-second in your mind can be an opportunity to say, "Spirit, I've got this impulse right now; should I act on it?"

It was a long hot day, the car had broken down once, the air conditioning wasn't working, the kids weren't behaving, and Nancy wasn't being too good either. I tried enticing the kids into "the quiet game," but they weren't going for it. I got lost. I was frustrated. The kids spilled food. Finally, the noise level went beyond what I could bear. There was a life-giving quarter second, but I blew right past it. I wasn't interested. And I used language on my kids that I had never used before, that I never thought I would.

It is amazing how the desire to hurt someone you love can be so strong in your body one moment and then lead to such pain when you indulge it. But another piece of good news is that when you blow it—and you will blow it—God sends another quarter-second right behind.

And you can get right back into the flow.

» Learning from the Master

No one mastered the art of dealing with difficult people better than Jesus did. He had lots of practice. The Romans wanted to silence him; Herod wanted to kill him; Pilate washed his hands of him; religious leaders envied him; his family thought he had lost his mind; his towns-people wanted to stone him; Judas betrayed him; soldiers beat him; the crowds shouted for his crucifixion; and his own disciples ran out on him. Yet Jesus never prayed for God to remove difficult people from his life.

If he had, there would have been no people left at all.

Sometimes even prayer can be misused as a way of avoidance. Some-times people will ask God to remove a difficult person from their cir-cumstances because they are too anxious to confront the person honestly. If God answered that prayer the way they wanted, they would actually lose the opportunity for growth that is his great desire for them.

Jesus' teachings about dealing with difficult people flowed out of deep, intimate, painful experiences and wisdom. They have influenced world civil rights leaders and movements like no other words ever spo-ken, from Mahatma Gandhi to Martin Luther King to Desmond Tutu. We will look at two of Jesus' teachings here: How you deal with those who insult you, and how you deal with those who would use you.

Insulters

Jesus begins, "You have heard that it was said, 'Eye for eye, and tooth for tooth.' But I tell you, ... If anyone slaps you on the right cheek, turn to them the other cheek also." The "eye for an eye" statement comes from the Hebrew Scriptures, and although it sounds harsh to us, it was actually an enormous step forward in the ancient legal world. When there were no policemen, no Constitution, and no Bill of Rights, powerful people might kill someone for a slight injury. So this law limited retribution by teaching proportional justice.

But it still leaves us with a problem. My instinct is that if someone hurts me, I will hurt them back — and the pain I experience always seems worse to me than the pain I cause the other person. A group of subjects was paired up, and people received pressure against their finger. Then they were told to exert the same amount of pressure on the other person's finger. When it was their turn, they always inflicted more pain than they received. Always. The result is an "eye-plus-a-little-something-extra" for an eye.

But Jesus gives another option. A key for understanding him comes from his mention of the "right cheek." Society in Jesus' day was built around shame and honor. The left hand was considered unclean; it was not to be used for eating—or for hitting. So a blow to the right cheek would be done with the backhand. It was a way to publicly insult someone. The main intent was not physical harm, but public disgrace. A backhanded slap was something done only to a social inferior, such as a slave or a child.

When someone insults us, what should we do? Everyone expects one of two responses: retaliation or cowering. Jesus is saying, "Your safety and your honor are in the hands of your heavenly Father."

So now we can get creative.

One possibility is that we could turn the other cheek. Our enemy can't backhand our left cheek. Either he has to fight you as an equal, which he doesn't want to do, or he has to find a nonviolent, nondestructive way to resolve conflict.

Who do you get insulted by? "Slaps" in our day often take the form of barbs, digs, and "backhanded" comments. Someone demeans your idea at work. Someone accuses you falsely at home. A relative says something judgmental about you. What is your first instinct: retaliation, fear—or both?

Now, with the Spirit there is a new possibility. Don't run and hide. Don't strike back. Confront the other person with honesty and strength. Be creative, patient, and active. Work toward reconciliation.

Users

Jesus gives another case study: "If anyone forces you to go with them one mile, go with them two miles." His listeners would have understood this situation, for Roman soldiers were allowed to force Jews to carry a burden a mile for them.

This is the kind of person who would use us, thinking of us not as a person, but as a tool. What do you do in that situation? Jesus invites people to see their enemy as a human being. This Roman soldier is a young boy, a stranger here, probably poor himself. All he receives is local hostility. So here is an idea. You finish the mile, look him in the eye, and say, "You look tired. Can I give you a little more help? Can I go with you another mile?"

That would blow the soldier's mind. Nobody does that! Who sends in a tip to the Internal Revenue Service?

Often when someone is difficult to me, I want to think of them as deliberately unlikable rather than as a real person with their own story. A friend offered to introduce English essayist Charles Lamb to a man whom Lamb had disliked for a long time by hearsay. "Don't make me meet him," Lamb said. "I want to go on hating him, and I can't do that to a man I know."

We can give the gift of empathy. We remember that the person we don't like is also a human being. We put ourselves in their place. We take the time to imagine how they feel, how they're treated. We ask what would help them become the best version of themselves, and in turn the interaction becomes an opportunity for me to practice becoming the best version of myself. We actually *need* difficult people to reach our full potential. (If you don't have enough, take the Monvee online assessment mentioned earlier and hone in on the "difficult people" section.)

» Being the "Difficult Person"

I once gave a talk about difficult people that I thought was terrific. That is, until I found out that someone I knew quite well and worked with closely told another friend about who his difficult person was.

It was me.

I wanted to run and hide when I heard that. He was not a casual acquaintance either, and I realized that I had been speaking and behaving in ways that were painful and life-draining to someone quite close to me. Our conversations often left him feeling that he was just an audience. He got clear signals that I regarded my opinions as more accurate and important than his. All this left him wanting to hide. On top of that, I had been clueless.

It is hard enough to try to reconcile something wrong that we have done. But to heal what we have *been*—to overcome being the difficult person for somebody else—requires grace from a higher source. My own defensiveness and embarrassment made me want to hide. We were able to overcome this somewhat, though I am afraid it remained in a high-maintenance category. But I have never forgotten the emotion of discovering that I was someone else's difficult person. I hope it has made me more aware in other relationships. I know it has made me more grateful for grace.

Maybe you have difficult people who haven't just troubled your world but have rocked it. Shattered it.

What happens then?

» The Reconciling Power of Tenacious Love

Often we find our difficult people right in our own family. One of the great stories about shattered relationships is the biblical story of Joseph and his brothers. You may remember that Joseph was hated by his brothers because he was his father's favorite. Joseph is then betrayed and sold into slavery by his brothers — but the end of Joseph's story looks odd to us.

His brothers head to Egypt to get food and don't recognize Joseph, who is now serving as the prime minister. Because they don't recognize him, he puts them through some odd circumstances. He gives them a feast, but gives the youngest brother Benjamin "five times more" than anyone else. Why does he supersize Benjamin's meal? He then sends them on their way, but frames Benjamin for stealing a silver cup. He tells the brothers they can have their food and go home, but that Benjamin must be left behind to die. Isn't he being a little passive-aggressive?

> Children between the ages of two and four average 6.2 fights per hour. That's about ninety fights per day, or about three thousand fights per year. If you are parenting little kids, no wonder you're tired!

The reality is that there is something beautiful in this story that serves as the climax to the book of Genesis. Up to this point in Genesis there has not been the healing of a broken relationship through confession and repentance at the expression of forgiveness. In the accounts of the brokenness of Adam and Eve, Cain and Abel, Isaac and Ishmael, and Jacob and Esau there is no record of true reconciliation.

But now it will happen.

Here are Joseph's brothers, one more time with their youngest brother, Benjamin, whom their father loves, and they can be rid of him. This time, however, they don't even have to do anything. They don't have to sell him into slavery. As far as they know, it is Benjamin's own fault. All they have to do is not lift a finger, and the favorite is gone once more.

But Judah stands up:

But Benjamin is so young. It would kill my father. Let me take the place of the boy. I know the law must be upheld. I know the debt must be paid. I understand. Let me pay it. Let me pay it. Let his punishment fall on me. I love him too much. I love my dad too much. I'll pay it. I'll pay. Take me.

For the first time in the Bible, in this story of God's, we see the possibility of a substitutionary act of suffering on behalf of someone to save someone else. We see that maybe a community could be healed by the voluntary atonement of one person who is willing to suffer the punishment that belongs to somebody else.

In the ancient world the rabbis had a saying, "Full repentance is shown when a person is subjected to the same situation in which he had sinned ... in which he had fallen once before ... only this time, he does not sin." The rabbis said that Judah was the ultimate example of true repentance. The second time around, Judah gets it right.

Now Joseph knows that the hearts of his brothers have changed, and this strange charade ends. He weeps so hard that the Egyptians could hear him sobbing through the thick walls. That is the power of reconciliation.

Where in your life is there a relationship that needs reconciliation? Maybe you have been so badly hurt by somebody who lied or cheated or betrayed you, and that hurt goes so deep, that you are thinking right now, *He doesn't deserve it!*

Probably not. Neither did Joseph's brothers. Neither do I. Neither do you.

Do it anyway.

God was in Christ, reconciling the world [the whole world] to himself." (2 Corinthians 5:19 KJV)

Do it because another young dreamer came into the world, and he too was stripped of his robe. He too was betrayed and deserted by his brothers.

He too loved sacrificially so that love could prevail in the end.

PART SIX
transforming my experience

»

Chapter 19

Let God Flow in Your Work

Once there was a man who loved to work.

He loved creating value. He loved the way his work made him grow. He didn't always like the problems he ran into, but he felt joy when he came up with a solution that ... well, *worked*.

He loved being a part of a team. He managed people and felt it was what he was born to do. He liked getting to know his co-workers; he asked about their lives and families and interests. He loved when a team got inspired about an idea. He loved watching people gain new skills and confidence. He valued the chance to spot each person's abilities and help them move toward becoming the best version of themselves. He even enjoyed getting ready for work. Sometimes in the shower he would yell, "Focus!" to himself just to get psyched up. He liked looking ahead at what each day would hold. He enjoyed the feeling at the end of the day when he could look back on how he had been productive.

He didn't tell people at his church this, but secretly he felt the presence of God more at work than he did at church services. He often found himself praying for ideas and wisdom. He would get excited when a solution to some problem seemed to pop into his head. When it was time for evaluations, he looked forward to the chance to learn and grow. His joy at work made him a better husband, father, friend, and volunteer. The skills he learned at work made him better at other relationships. His children grew up believing that the chance to work was a gift.

When he was sixty-five, someone asked him if he was going to retire. He looked up the word *retire* in the Bible, but he couldn't find it. So he just kept working. After a while he cut back to part-time, and eventually his work was all volunteer.

When he was very old and ill, all the people he had loved and worked with over the years gathered around his sickbed. They thanked him for how he had enhanced their lives. He thought of all the joy and purpose that his work had given him over the years, and these were his final words:

I wish I could have spent more time at the office.

I'm not sure where the cliché first arose that at the end of life no one wishes they had spent more time at work, but it wasn't in the Bible. In the Bible, everyone works. Dennis Bakke, in a wonderful book called *Joy at Work*, notes that most of the heroes in the Bible had what we would think of as secular vocations. Isaac developed real estate, Jacob was a rancher, and Joseph was a government official (in charge of agriculture, the economy, and immigration policy) who served a pharaoh in a foreign land that did not honor Israel's God. Joseph did not decide he could serve God best by leaving his well-paying government job and starting a non-profit, faith-based organization to do charity work. Moses spent forty years as a sheepherder, Esther won a beauty pageant and went into government service, and David worked in animal husbandry, the military, and statecraft. Daniel was an immigrant who attended Babylon's version of Oxford and became prime minister. Lydia was a successful business-woman in textiles. Paul was a tent-maker.

Perhaps the ultimate expression of how much God values work is Jesus the carpenter. Jesus spent more than three-quarters of his working life in the building profession, fashioning benches and tables and probably involved in construction. The word we translate *carpenter* comes from the Greek *tekton*—from which we get our word *technology*—and would include the ability to do stone or masonry work.

The Bible is a book written by workers about workers for workers, but too often in discussion about spiritual life our work gets ignored. Or all we get are warnings: "not too much," "not too hard," or "not too long." One writer on spiritual life lamented how some pastors call their work space an office rather than a study, "thereby further secularizing perceptions of pastoral work." By this line of thinking, "study" is somehow by its nature "spiritual," but "office work" is "secular."

Yet far more human beings will spend their lives in offices than in studies. Most adults spend about half their waking lives at work. Your work is a huge part of God's plan for your life, and God intends the Spirit to fill and energize workplaces. Work that gets done in offices and elsewhere—building up people, creating teams, managing the resources of creation—desperately requires the guidance and energy of the Spirit.

The fourth commandment covers all seven days of the week, not just the Sabbath: "Six days you shall labor and do all your work ... for in six days the LORD made the heavens and the earth." I have often heard sermons designed to make people feel guilty about not keeping the Sabbath, but I have never heard a sermon designed to make people feel guilty about not honoring the six-day work week. The point is not how many days or hours we are punching the clock. The point is that just as God made and loves the Sabbath, so he also made and loves work.

So how do we find God in our work? How do we allow our work to move us toward the person God wants us to become?

» First, Discover Your Strengths

Do you know the first person in the Bible who was said to be "filled with the Spirit of God"? Here's a hint: It was not Adam, Noah, Abraham, Joseph, Moses, Elijah, Daniel, Mary, Jesus, Paul, Jonah, or the whale.

It was Bezalel.

That name doesn't ring a bell?

Bezalel was not a prophet, priest, king, or apostle. He was a craftsman, skilled in design. He had an eye for color and a flair for management, so when it was time to build a tabernacle for the people of Israel, he oversaw the job.

> See, I have chosen Bezalel son of Uri,... and I have filled him with the Spirit of God, with wisdom, with understanding, with knowledge, and with all kinds of skills—to make artistic designs for work in gold, silver and bronze, to cut and set stones, to work in wood, and to engage in all kinds of crafts.

Imagine being Bezalel. From your youth you love to work with your hands. You don't know that God is involved in this—but he is! He has actually placed these desires in you, which will one day bless people around you. When you are working, the joy and power you feel is actually the presence of the Spirit.

"Discover your strengths" is a phrase made famous by Marcus Buckingham and what has been called the "strengths movement." It calls us to stop focusing on improving weaknesses rather than naming and developing strengths — which also reflects God's design. God did not say, "Moses, your craftsman skills are weak. Let's have you stop leading this people for a while, and work on improving your craftsmanship skills." God's plan was that the community would be enriched when people were doing what he had created them to do.

> Each of us has certain strengths. We were born with them, they will always be our strengths, and we delight in them. Work happens best when we discover these strengths, put them to use, and focus on developing them. Trying to improve our weaknesses is like trying to teach a rabbit to swim or a snail to race. God's design for work is best when it goes "from strength to strength." (If you haven't discovered your strengths yet, the book *Now Discover Your Strengths* by Buckingham and Donald O. Clifton is a great place to start.)

According to Marcus, the simplest definition of a strength is an activity which, when you do it, makes you feel strong. There are certain activities that thrill and challenge you, and others that bore and drain you. When you discover this, you are not simply engaged in "career planning" — you are studying the handiwork of God. It matters that you do this, because the single little patch of creation that you are most responsible for stewarding is your own body.

> Dorothy Sayers said, "Work is not, primarily, a thing one does to live, but the thing one lives to do. It is, or it should be, the full expression of the worker's faculties, the thing in which he finds spiritual, mental, and bodily satisfaction, and the medium in which he offers himself to God."

God himself works with strength, freedom, and joy. When you discover your strengths, you are learning an indispensible part of what it means to be made in the image of God. When you help other people discover their strengths, you are helping the image of God to be restored in another human being. You are part of the work of redemption—the liberating of work from the curse. You are doing the work of the Spirit.

George comes alive when he picks up a guitar. Emily comes alive when she leads a team. Rick comes alive when he counsels someone who is hurting. Verna comes alive when she finds someone she can help.

Speaking is my craft. When I get to read, study, and think, then figure out how to communicate it all in front of a group of people—trying to sense the room and gauge where people's hearts and minds are, thinking about what to say next, listening to the Holy Spirit—I feel as if every single cell of my body has been switched on.

That's work—just what you and I were made for.

» Understand What You Receive When You Work

Amazingly enough, research shows that the best moments of our lives don't come from leisure or pleasure. They don't involve sex or chocolate. They come when we are totally immersed in a significant task that is challenging, yet matches up well to our highest abilities. In these moments, a person is so caught up in an activity that time somehow seems to be altered; their attention is fully focused, but without having to work at it. They are deeply aware without being self-conscious; they are being stretched and challenged, but without a sense of stress or worry. They have a sense of engagement or oneness with what they are doing.

This condition is called "flow," because people experiencing it often use the metaphor of feeling swept up by something outside themselves. Studies have been done over the past thirty years with hundreds of thousands of subjects to explore this phenomenon of flow. Ironically, people experience it far more in their work than they do in their leisure. In fact, the time of week when "flow" is at its lowest ebb in America is Sunday morning, because so many people do not know what they want to do. Sitting around does not produce flow.

I believe this picture of "flow" is actually a description of what the exercise of dominion was intended to look like. God says in Genesis that human beings are to "rule" over the earth, or to exercise "dominion." We often think of these words in terms of "dominating" or "bossing around." But the true idea behind them is that we are to invest our abilities to create value on the earth, to plant and build and write and organize and heal and invent in ways that bless people and make the earth flourish.

> Draw a graph in which the vertical axis represents the strengths God has given you and the horizontal axis represents the challenge of the task before you. If your skill level is very high, but the challenge of the task is too low, you experience boredom. If your skill level is too low, and the challenge of the task is too high, you experience frustration and anxiety. But when the level of the challenge you face matches the level of the skills you possess — then you are set up for flow.

All skill is God-given, and we are invited to live in conscious interaction with the Spirit as we work, so that he can develop the skills he gives us. Work is a form of love. We cannot be fully human without creating value.

We do not work mainly for money, recognition, promotion, applause, or fame. We work for flow. We live for flow. We hunger for the experience of flow, and when it is present, something happens in our spirit as we connect with a reality beyond ourselves and partner with God. This is why the psalmist says, "Unless the LORD builds the house, those who build it labor in vain." Flow is part of what we experience in that partnership, and in that, God in turn uses flow to shape us.

Bezalel experienced flow when he crafted wood, David when he played the lyre, Samson when he used his strength, Paul when he wrote a brilliant letter, Daniel when he ran a government, Adam when he gardened, and Jesus when he carpentered. If other people report to you, whether in paid or volunteer activities, one of the great spiritual acts of service you can perform is to ask whether they are experiencing flow in their work and seek to help them experience more flow.

When we are working in the flow of the service of God and his kingdom, when we are experiencing flow in activities that enhance and bless the lives of others around us — then we are working in the Spirit.

Then we are growing rich.

When we work, we grow. Marcus Aurelius wrote, "When you arise reluctantly in the morning, think like this: 'I arise to accomplish a human task. Should I then complain, when I am about to do that for which I was born, and for which I was placed on earth? Or was I created to pamper myself under the blankets, even if that is more pleasant. Were you born, then, to enjoy and, generally to feel, but not to act? Don't you see the plants, the birds, the ants, the spiders, the bees who all perform their own tasks and in their own way helping to let the cosmos function? Don't you then want to do your work as a human? Don't you hasten to do what is befitting your nature?"

Chapter 20

Let Your Work Honor God

Journalist William Zinsser's first job was writing for the *Buffalo News*. Traditionally cub reporters often start by writing obituaries, but Zinsser was frustrated with his assignment. *I could be doing Pulitzer Prize-winning investigative reporting*, he thought to himself, *and I'm stuck writing obituaries*. Writers don't win Pulitzers for obituaries. Finally he worked up enough courage and asked his editor, "When am I going to get some decent story assignments?"

"Listen, kid!" his crusty old editor growled at him. "Nothing you write will ever get read as carefully as what you are writing right now. You misspell a word, you mess up a date, and a family will be hurt. But you do justice to somebody's grandmother, to somebody's mom, you make a life sing, and they will be grateful forever. They will put your words in laminate."

Things changed.

"I pledged I would make the extra calls," Zinsser said. "I would ask the extra questions. I would go the extra mile."

That is essentially from the Sermon on the Mount—write obituaries for others as you would want others to write an obituary for you—obituaries that deserved to be laminated—because someday, somebody will. Zinsser eventually moved on to other kinds of writing, including a book on writing itself that has sold more than a million copies. But none of it would have happened if he had not devoted himself to obituaries.

God himself can only bless me in my circumstances today. If I cannot experience the Spirit in the work I am doing today, then I can't experience the Spirit today at all.

My friend Andy Chan headed up the placement office for the Stanford School of Business, helping graduates find work. He says that someday he wants to write a book called *The Myth of Passion*. This is the myth that somewhere out there is the perfect job, the idealized calling that fits my soul the way a key fits into a lock, and if I could just find that job, torrents of passion would cascade out of my heart like water going over Niagara Falls. We have this romanticized idea that we will find "job-love at first sight."

Passion for our work is not usually a subterranean volcano waiting to erupt. It is a plant that needs to be cultivated. It is a muscle that gets strengthened a little each day as we show up—as we do what is expected of us, and then some.

Paul wrote, "Don't just do the minimum that will get you by. Do your best. Work from the heart for your real Master, for God, confident that you'll get paid in full when you come into your inheritance. Keep in mind always that the ultimate Master you're serving is Christ. The sullen servant who does shoddy work will be held responsible. Being Christian doesn't cover up bad work."

Maybe it would help to put a little sign on your desk: "For God's sake—do your best!"

» My Best Self Works Wholeheartedly

We almost never get to know ahead of time the full significance of what we do or don't do in our work. We are simply told, "Whatever your hand finds to do, do it with all your might."

Judaism, Christianity, and Islam all trace their roots to Abraham—not a priest, but what we would think of today as a rancher. When he was "now old and well advanced in years," he realized the time had come to find a wife for his son Isaac. Since there was no eHarmony, he assigned the task to the "chief servant in his household, the one in charge of all that he had."

The servant set out with a caravan of ten camels to the region Abraham had directed him. Finding a wife for your boss's son was a high-stakes assignment that required considerable thought. So the servant began his work with a prayer: "O LORD, God of my master Abraham, give me success today...."

Do you ever pray to ask God to make your work successful? People sometimes wonder if it's okay to pray for work to be successful. Of course! If success is becoming my god, I will have to find a way to dethrone it. But generally speaking, if you can't pray for the success of what you're doing, start doing something else!

When the servant arrived in the town of Nahor, a young woman named Rebekah greeted him and offered to get the servant a drink. When he had finished drinking, Rebekah said, "I'll draw water for your camels too, until they have finished drinking." We are told she "quickly" emptied her jar into the trough and "ran" back to the well to draw more water. It all sounds fairly unremarkable, until you read between the lines:

One gallon of water weighs eight pounds;
    a thirsty camel can drink up to thirty gallons of water;
        and there were ten camels.
            Do the math.

Rebekah is running to the well. This girl is drawing three hundred gallons of water for a stranger. She does all that could be reasonably expected of her and then some.

This was the pivotal moment of her life. Because of her act of service, Rebekah became the wife of Isaac and went on the adventure of a lifetime, becoming part of sacred history. To this day, her name is remembered and revered by people of faith.

But Rebekah did not know all this was at stake. She did not offer to draw three hundred gallons of water because she knew what the reward could be. It was simply an expression of her heart.

We often hear people say that we should put family above work. Oddly enough, we will not find this thought expressed in the Bible. I will say that again: Nowhere in the Bible does it say that family is more important than work. What the Bible does say is that love matters above all. Families are to be one vehicle through which we express love. Our work is to be another. We will be accountable for our families; we will also be accountable for our work. Often, from a biblical perspective, families were (and are) a place where work gets done.

When we discover the gifts God has given us and the passions that engage us, and we put them to work in the service of values we deeply believe in — in conscious dependence on God — then we are working in the Spirit. Then our work is helping each of us to create the me I want to be.

We are the ones who make our work significant — not the other way around.

» Make Work Part of Your Calling

In our first year of marriage Nancy and I went to Ireland to visit the town of Kilrush at the mouth of the Shannon River in the County Clare, where Nancy's grandmother had been born. While Nancy was visiting some of her relatives, I met a man named Father Ryan.

Father Ryan had actually assisted the priest who helped christen Nancy's grandmother in that remote village in an obscure corner of Ireland, where they seldom saw Protestants. So when Father Ryan found out that I was a pastor at a Baptist church, he wanted to talk shop.

"So you're a Baptist, are you?" he said to me. "Tell me, do you believe in God?"

"Yes," I replied.

"Do you believe in Mary?" he asked slyly.

"Yes," I said again — though we didn't go into detail.

Then we talked about our job descriptions, and he told me what a priest does. "We christen them when they're born. We marry them when they get wed. We hear confession and pronounce forgiveness over their souls. We preach over them when they die. We do it all. We hatch 'em, match 'em, patch 'em and dispatch 'em."

When Nancy came into the room, I introduced her to Father Ryan.

"Ah," he said, "your calling comes with benefits."

A priest is sometimes described as one who represents God to the earth and the earth to God. But the reality is that that was the original job description of the human race. We were made in God's image to continue his work of making the earth to flourish and then, by our flourishing, to give voice for the whole earth to praise God. All work was designed by God to be priestly work. It is not just professional clergy or missionaries who are called by God.

The scholar N. T. Wright has a wonderful image of this. Picture human beings as mirrors set at a forty-five degree angle between heaven and earth. We were created to reflect God's care and dominion to the earth, and we were made to express the worship and gratitude of creation up to God. This is what we do when we work.

You have a calling. You have been gifted. You are a priest.

This is not just something that relates to volunteering at a church. Your work is a primary place—maybe *the* primary place—where your calling gets lived out. Maybe we should issue robes to electrical engineers, clerical collars to accountants, and vestments to auto mechanics every once in a while just to remind us of this.

In his book *Habits of the Heart*, sociologist Robert Bellah describes three orientations people take toward their work. The first is to treat your work as a job. When you do this, you focus on it as a way to get money and pay bills. When asked, most people list money as the primary reason why they work. In the words of that old bumper sticker, "I owe, I owe, so off to work I go." But if your focus is mainly on what you receive from your work, you will most likely come to resent it.

A second orientation is to approach your work as a career. Here your motivation will be higher, but your focus is on advancement and prestige. In a career orientation, your feelings about your work are based on how much success it is creating for you. If your career is not going well, it may feel to you as if your worth is on the line.

The third orientation is to look at your work as a calling. The language of vocation or calling is widespread, but it is rooted in the life of faith. If there is a "calling," then there is someone making the call. That someone is God. That is why you cannot do just anything you want. You are not the call-er; you are the call-ee.

Any work that has meaning, that can be a blessing to people and to the earth, can be a calling. A doctor or pastor might get sucked into viewing work as a means to get a good income, and therefore they only have a job. A garbage collector, however, may see what he does as part of making the world a cleaner and safer place and therefore have a calling.

On our street lives an older woman with many health problems, and a younger woman helps care for her. Often in the afternoon the two of them walk very slowly down the street. The younger woman holds her tightly, makes sure her walk is safe, tries to make her laugh, and listens to her heart. She has a calling.

Lottery winners often make the same comment: "Winning the lottery is not going to change my life." But six months later they have quit their job and bought a new house. A survey of one state's lottery winners had two main findings. One, a majority were more unhappy now than before winning. Two, none of them would give up the money they had won. People whose primary motivation for work is money will always feel resentful and dissatisfied. It is perhaps not so ironic that the song "Take this job and shove it" was famously recorded by a man named Johnny Paycheck.

Isaiah wrote, "When a farmer plows for planting, does he plow continually?... Does he not plant wheat in its place?... His God instructs him and teaches him the right way.... All this also comes from the LORD Almighty, wonderful in counsel and magnificent in wisdom." God wants to meet you in your work.

> Miroslav Volf says, "All human work, however complicated or simple, is made possible by the operation of the Spirit of God in the working person; and all work whose nature and results reflect the values of the new creation is accomplished under the instruction and inspiration of the Spirit of God."

»View Work as Service to God

I have a friend who used to work at Disneyland, and he said that when he was trained, there was one value emphasized above all others: What puts the magic in the Magic Kingdom is servanthood. They are told that when you are in the kingdom, when you walk through those gates, you serve. Whatever your job is, you are a servant.

You treat every encounter with people as if they were your personal guest. If they need directions, escort them. If they ask a question and you have heard it a hundred times, answer it as if you have never heard it before.

There is a ride called the Jungle Cruise, and the most common question asked of the Disneyland staff about it is, "How long is this ride?" So the staff is given a prepared, standard answer: "The Jungle Cruise is an exciting adventure ride that lasts ten minutes." They are supposed to repeat that every time.

Well, one employee had been asked it once too often, so when a couple asked, "How long is the Jungle Cruise?" he looked at them and

---

in the flow at work ≈

- ≈ Ask God to make your work go well *today*.
- ≈ Continually seek to identify and develop your God-given strengths rather than focusing on improving your weaknesses.
- ≈ Take five-minute breaks throughout the day to relax, get refreshed, and ask God for strength to work well.
- ≈ Identify the larger meaning of your work that makes it a calling.
- ≈ Periodically review your attitude — get water for the camels.
- ≈ Solicit feedback on how you can grow.
- ≈ Make friends with the people you work with.
- ≈ Seek to enjoy your work.

---

said, "Three days." That couple got out of that line, left the park, went back to the Disney Hotel where they were on their honeymoon, packed up their suitcases, checked out of their hotel, and came back to the line at the Jungle Cruise. The next day that Disneyland employee was gone, and someone else was standing at the line and saying, "The Jungle Cruise is an exciting adventure ride that lasts ten minutes."

Jesus said that what puts the magic into his kingdom is serving, because "the Son of Man did not come to be served, but to serve." His is not a kingdom about status and climbing ladders and getting attention. The best you is built by serving, and God's kingdom is one of those kingdoms where if you don't want to serve, you won't really want to be there. Sometimes God will interrupt us in our work, not to give us a chance to show off our giftedness, but simply to give us a chance to serve.

Jesus tells a story about three men who are given bags of money and then are accountable to their master. The first man received five talents' worth — a talent being a unit of weight — and he "went and traded with them, and gained five more talents." He had skill, initiative, drive, and broad scope to make decisions. He made a 100 percent profit and was commended by his master.

The second man had a smaller talent share, but was equal in his work. His commendation was just as big. In the life of the Spirit, visible outcomes do not determine the gift given or the gift received.

But the third man buried the single talent he was given. He punched the clock. He called in sick. He did not dream, try, dare, or do. His job review did not go well.

In the end, he too said, "I wish I had spent more time at the office."

Think about your work today. If Jesus were your direct supervisor, would you have done your work any differently than you did? How would you have done repairs, answered phones, typed documents, or taught classes if Jesus were checking your work?

In this world, the hardest work sometimes is the most overlooked. A husband came home from the office one day, and the house was a mess. Dirty clothes were all over the floor, dirty dishes filled the sink, the kids were crying, the beds were unmade, the bathrooms smelled bad, and the TV set was blaring. He asked his wife what was going on.

"You know how you ask me every night what did I do all day?" she said. "Well, today I didn't do it."

> Martin Luther once said, "What you do in your house is worth as much as if you did it up in heaven for our Lord God."

The day is coming when God will look at his faithful servants and say, "Well done." He will say it to faithful employees who give themselves diligently to work that never earns much human recognition. He will say it to workers who know they could have climbed higher if they had cut corners or manipulated others. He will say it to single parents who cared for kids—bathing them, feeding them, cleaning up after them—when they were tired and thought nobody was looking.

Somebody is looking. Someone is keeping track.

It *is* worth it.

Chapter 21

You Have to Go through Exile before You Come Back Home

Imagine you have a child and you are handed a script of her entire life laid out before you. Better yet, you are given an eraser and five minutes to edit out whatever you want. You read that she will have a learning disability in grade school. Reading, which comes easily for some kids, will be laborious for yours. In high school your child will make a great circle of friends, then one of them will die of cancer. After high school she will get into the college she wanted to attend, but while there she will lose a leg in a car crash. Following that, she will go through a difficult depression. A few years later she will get a great job, then lose that job in an economic downturn. She will get married, but then go through the grief of separation.

With this script of your child's life before you and five minutes to edit it, *what would you erase?* That is the question psychologist Jonathan Haidt asked in this hypothetical exercise. *Wouldn't you want to take out all the stuff that would cause them pain?*

We live in a generation of "helicopter parents" who constantly swoop in to their children's lives to make sure no one is mistreating them and that they experience one unobstructed success after another in school, sports, and relationships. Whoa! If you could wave a wand and erase every failure, disappointment, and suffering, are you sure it would be a good idea? Would that enable your children to grow into the best version of themselves? Is it possible that in some way people actually need adversity and setbacks—maybe even something like trauma—to reach the fullest level of development and growth?

Paul believed that as we live in the flow of the Spirit, suffering can lead to growth. Suffering can actually produce more flourishing people.

> We rejoice in the hope of the glory of God. Not only so, but we also rejoice in our sufferings, because we know that suffering produces perseverance; perseverance, character; and character, hope. And hope does not disappoint us, because God has poured out his love into our hearts by the Holy Spirit, whom he has given us. (Romans 5:2–5 NIV)

» Three Attitudes toward Adversity

There are many ways to look at the ups and downs of our futures, and philosopher Robert Roberts describes three attitudes we can hold: hope, despair, and resignation.

Hope is the belief that my future holds good prospects. I genuinely *desire* what I think this future holds, and I *believe* this future prospect to be on the way. Hope is not hype. Of course, hope involves waiting, and hope can include uncertainty, so it can be scary. But when I hope, I delight in the thought of the future. I welcome tomorrow. You can always tell if you are around a hope-er.

Despair, on the other hand, creeps in if I desperately want something but believe it will not happen. In despair, my longing is still strong, but I believe that it will go unfulfilled. The thought of the future becomes painful: *This depression will never go away. I will never be loved.* Despair paralyzes. The soul cannot survive for long with deep despair. Despair is so toxic, people will manage it by *resignation*.

Resignation is a kind of halfway house between *hope* and *despair*.

In resignation, I ratchet down my desire, trying to convince myself that what I wanted so badly isn't a big deal. *The job is not that great. She's not that pretty, and there are plenty of other fish in the sea. When it comes to aging or taxes or being a Chicago Cubs baseball fan, learning to accept the inevitable with serenity is the course of wisdom.* But can resignation alone sustain a life?

The best version of you is a hoper, because the Spirit of life is a Spirit of hope. The Spirit never leads us to despair, and there is always hope—which is not based on circumstances, but rather is an inner disposition. In fact, researchers have identified a personality variable they call *dispositional optimism*, a capacity to anticipate the future.

Give yourself a five-second hope test by answering yes or no to these two statements:

- In uncertain times, I usually expect the best.
- If something can go wrong for me, it usually will.

If you answered yes to the first question and no to the second, you will naturally love this chapter. If you answered any other way, you will *need* this chapter, because the good news about hope is that it can be learned!

» Normal Life and Crisis

In what we call "normal life," we drift along under a set of assumptions that may work for a long time: I may feel secure because I have a certain amount of money. I have an identity because I have a certain job, title, degree, or list of achievements. I have a purpose because I am going to achieve more than I already have. Life seems to "work."

Then a crisis comes. Maybe it's a financial crash. Maybe you lose your job. Maybe you lose someone you love. You go to the doctor's office and find you have a malignancy. There is a scandal, and you lose your reputation. Your son or daughter rejects you, running down a road that violates everything you believe in.

Any crisis carries in its wake the question, *What can I build my life on that circumstances cannot rob me of? What really matters?*

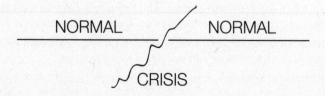

Sometime ago someone came into my office and told me to check my rear passenger tire. It appeared to be getting low, so I took it to the service station to get it patched. After a few months, somebody else told me the same thing. For several months, I would have to reinflate it, then it would slowly leak out. Eventually, the car doctor said, "This tire is tired and worn out. It's time to face reality. You have to get a new tire."

Then last weekend my car wouldn't start. It was a battery problem. I thought I could get the battery recharged, but the car doctor said, "This battery is tired and worn out. It's time to face reality. You have to get a new battery."

At breakfast, after too much coffee and too little sleep the night before, I noticed my wife looking at me with a tender look, and I asked her, "What are you thinking?"

"You're looking tired and worn out," she said.

I did not like where this was headed.

What do you do with a broken person? I can resign myself to a tire that can't be reinflated or a battery that can't be recharged. But what if the problem is closer to home? Ernest Hemingway wrote, "Sooner or later, the world breaks everyone, and those who are broken are strongest in the broken places."

Sometimes that is true. But sometimes people write beautiful things and believe them to be true — or hope that they are true — and yet they don't help. Hemingway himself had a brokenness that couldn't get stronger, and he ended his life because the pain was too great.

Something happens to us amid adversity.

For a long time, researchers have looked at what enables some people to endure suffering. But over the last decade or so, the focus has shifted from looking only at how some people make it through to how people are able to go through adversity and actually come out the other side stronger than before. Just as there is a condition called "post-traumatic stress disorder," researchers are now talking about "post-traumatic growth."

One line of thinking is that adversity *can* lead to growth. Another line of thinking is that the highest levels of growth cannot be achieved *without* adversity. It may be that somehow adversity leads to growth in a way that nothing else does.

But adversity does not automatically bring growth. It can cripple people, and much of the outcome depends on how people respond to adversity. Jonathan Haidt writes about three ways in which post-traumatic growth can happen. I modify them here a bit, add a fourth, and look at how God can grow us in adversity.

1. *Rising to a challenge reveals abilities hidden within you (and beyond you!) that would otherwise have remained dormant.*

It is in adversity that we find out what we are really made of, just as we find out what is inside a tube of toothpaste when it gets squeezed. People often say, "I could never go through what that person went through. I would die." Then they go through it. Their heart keeps beating. Their world goes on.

We don't know what we are capable of until we have to cope.

I cannot ensure my circumstances will work out the way I want them to, but I can always ask, "How would the person I most want to be face this situation?" We don't even have to believe in the Bible to see this. Wise people have always understood the connection between suffering and growth. Meng Tzu, a Chinese sage from the third century BC, said,

> When heaven is about to confer a great responsibility on any man, it will exercise his mind with suffering ... place obstacles in the path of his deeds, so as to stimulate his mind, harden his nature, and improve wherever he is incompetent.

But nowhere do we see this idea displayed more prominently than in the Bible. God could have let Abraham stay in the comfort of Ur, Moses stay in the splendor of Pharaoh's courts, and Aaron stay in the safety of the crowd. He could have kept David away from Goliath; Shadrach, Meshach, and Abednego out of the fiery furnace; Daniel out of the lion's den; Elijah away from Jezebel; Nehemiah out of captivity; Jonah out of the whale; John the Baptist away from Herod; Esther from being threatened; Jeremiah from being rejected; and Paul from being shipwrecked. But he didn't. In fact, God used each of these trials to bring people closer to himself—to produce perseverance, character, and hope.

One of the classic stories of adversity in the Bible is about Joseph. At the beginning of his life, Joseph is the favorite son of his father, envied by his brothers, with dreams of being the one everybody bows down to. Then he is kidnapped by his brothers and ends up serving as a slave in the home of Potiphar. He loses his home, his culture, his security, and his status as favorite son. What does Joseph have left? He is in a strange bed, in a strange house, in a strange land, with no friends, no prospects, and no explanation. But he has one gift—and that one thing makes all the difference.

Scripture says, "The LORD was with Joseph...." Joseph is not alone.

What happens to someone who loses everything but God, then finds out that God is enough? As a powerless stranger, he experiences the presence of God in his life in a way he never did in the comfort of his own home. Rivers of living water begin to flow from his belly that he had never known before, because hope comes from the promise that "we know that in all things God works for the good of those who love him." God wasn't at work producing the circumstances Joseph wanted. God was at work in bad circumstances producing the *Joseph* that God wanted.

> God isn't at work producing the circumstances you want. God is at work in bad circumstances producing the *you* he wants.

One of the most misquoted "verses" you will never find in the Bible is this one: "God will never give me more than I can handle." Huh? Are you kidding me? Where is that one? Poverty, holocausts, genocide, war—people are given more than they can handle all the time!

The Bible does say that no temptation is given to people without a way out, but that is about temptation, not adversity. The Bible does not promise that you will only be given what you can handle. In fact, the one certainty of your life is that you will die—and you definitely can't handle that! You will never be placed in a situation God can't handle. Nothing—including death—will place you beyond his flow of living waters.

Maybe you are in a situation—a relationship or a financial condition—that is not what you wanted. You want to lie down and die. But when you don't—when you show up, when you offer the best you have—something good is happening *inside* you that far outweighs whatever is happening *outside* you.

Jesus was facing adversity when he told his followers that if they had faith, they could command a mountain and it would be cast into the sea. When my focus is on the mountain, I am driven by my fear. When my focus is on God, however, I am made alive by my faith. But if I did not have the mountain, I would not know that faith could be in me.

Your circumstances—even the best of them—are temporary. But you—the person you become—go on forever.

2. *Adversity can deepen relationships.*

Somehow suffering can soften a heart and deepen friendships in a unique way.

> The Trappist monk Thomas Merton wrote, "As long as we are on earth, the love that unites us will bring us suffering by our very contact with one another, because this love is the resetting of a Body of broken bones."

Nancy went to nursing school with a classmate we will call Shelly, who was intelligent, engaging, and beautiful—everyone loved her.

Shelly fell in love and married Steve, an architect and basketball player who looked like a male model. They had more good genes than any couple has a right to expect. But when Shelly walked into her bridal shower, she was grieving that everything was not as it should be: she had broken a nail putting gas in her car.

"But it's okay," she said in her deep southern drawl. "Steve said that once we're married, I will never have to put gas in my car again."

To resurrect a phrase from those days, *gag me with a spoon.*

On that day, a trial was a broken nail. But storms have a way of coming to every life.

Shelly and Steve were married and wanted to have children, but were disappointed for years, through two miscarriages and the pain of watching other people walk baby strollers and complain about their lack of sleep. They wished that little cries would keep them up at night, but finally Shelly was diagnosed with a condition that was treatable, and she eventually gave birth to a little girl.

By this point they had reached an age when they thought it better not to have any more children, so Steve went through a surgical procedure. The next month, Steve was hurt playing basketball and knocked unconscious. In the emergency room, the doctor took one look at his x-rays and turned pale:

"Don't move; don't breathe deep; don't have a deep thought," the specialist said.

The staff put him in traction and flew in a surgeon, who told Steve that if he had so much as sneezed or turned the wrong way, he could have ended up quadriplegic or dead. Steve could die during the operation.

But he didn't, and the surgery was a success.

Because of all this, the doctors never did check to make sure Steve's minor surgical procedure to avoid having more children had been effective. Next month, Shelly called to tell us she was pregnant. They hadn't planned on this. A few weeks later she called back, and for the first thirty seconds all she could do was groan.

The baby still inside her had been diagnosed with severe heart defects and massive cognitive deficits. Friends did not know what to say. Some said, "Your baby will be healed. God has told us. You just have to have faith. We'll pray — you watch."

Steve and Shelly watched. They prayed. The baby was not healed. All that the doctors said came true.

Others said, "People will be watching you. Don't grieve. Don't look sad. Show how much faith you have." Another person said, "God must love you very much to give you a retarded child." I won't even tell you what that response did to them.

If they were writing this, Steve and Shelly would tell you that their little baby is precious to them beyond words. They would tell you they have grown through this pain. They would also tell you they would give all that growth back in a heartbeat if it meant health and wholeness for their child.

Loss is not simply something to be recovered from. Hope does not mean returning to happiness as soon as possible. God comes to us in our grief and shares it. In that shared grief, we find love. "Mourn with those who mourn," Paul says. Love meets in shared suffering and broken souls like no other kind of love.

One of the most common results of people who go through deep grief is that they come to have a deeper appreciation for other people. People diagnosed with a serious illness often describe this paradox. They hate having their body invaded by the illness, but they wake up to how much people matter. They quit wasting time and emotion on what doesn't count.

Recently I visited a twelve-step group, and one of the most powerful moments came when the members and newcomers introduced themselves. It is always the same liturgy. They say who they are and name their brokenness — something we almost never do in normal public gatherings.

"I'm Dale. I'm an alcoholic."

Know what everybody says back? "Hi, Dale!" In other words, *We are glad you're here. You're one of us. Hi, Dale!*

Alcohol is not one of my limps — I have enough other ones — but it was very healing to hear everyone, and I felt that I wanted to say, "My name's John, and I'm an alcoholic," simply because the warmth of belonging in that room was so healing. To say, "My name is John, and I'm a Presbyterian pastor" would sound as if I were in denial.

Somehow prisoners, addicts, or those grieving can meet and identify with each other in ways that people in "normal life" forget.

God comes to us in our grief, and because he shares our grief, it begins to mingle ever so slightly with hope.

We cling to each other, and love meets in shared suffering and broken souls like no other kind of love.

As a young woman, Joni Eareckson Tada became paralyzed and has been in a wheelchair for decades. She would tell you every day she wishes she could walk. She would also tell you she has met God and loved people, in ways she couldn't have imagined on her own, because of that chair. She has been used to inspire thousands because of that chair in ways she otherwise never would. That chair is part of the curse. And yet still she thanks God for the chair.

3. *Adversity can change your priorities about what really matters.*

A friend named Bill Dallas has written a book, *Lessons from San Quentin*, in which he talks about how the moment of his greatest suffering became the turning point of his life. He had been living for money, possessions, success, beauty, pleasure, and parties — and doing quite well. But he took a few wrong turns, got involved in financial dealings that were less than transparent, and ended up in the San Quentin prison. There the strangest thing happened.

He met God. Bill found a group of men serving life sentences who had found God, and there he discovered people with a greater sense of peace and a deeper experience of community than people he had known in penthouses and office suites. More and more, they were becoming the best version of themselves.

As with Joseph, the Lord was with Bill in prison. Bill says that if he were to visit one more place before he dies, it wouldn't be the Eiffel Tower or the Great Wall of China or the Taj Mahal. It would be that prison cell where he met God.

It is as if in normal life we step onto a treadmill and begin running after something—money, security, or success—when adversity knocks us off. Suffering enables us to see the folly of chasing after temporal gods, and when people suffer, they often resolve to not return to their old way of life when things normalize. But the key to accomplishing that is taking action before normal life takes over again. We have a finite window of time to make changes; otherwise we will drift back to our old patterns. Bill changed his work, his lifestyle, his friends, his habits, and his God so that when he was released from prison, his life normalized, but his values and trajectory had been transformed.

> Danish philosopher Søren Kierkegaard said, "Affliction is able to drown out every earthly voice... but the voice of eternity deep in the soul it cannot drown."

As always with the Spirit, a response to his work is needed on our part. If you merely say, "I'm going to remember this new perspective that I've learned," when your life returns to normal, you will get back on the treadmill. But if you have courage to make changes in your life, something can happen in your soul. The Spirit will bring the courage if you keep asking while the experience of adversity is fresh. Ultimately, adversity can produce hope because of a reality much larger than you and I.

That reality is that God is a redemptive God.

4. *Adversity points us to the Hope beyond ourselves.*

What do you think was the largest single publication in the 1960s? What book, magazine, or print product do you think outstripped everything else? It was actually a catalog—and it was not produced by Sears Roebuck or Montgomery Ward.

It was produced by a company called Sperry and Hutchinson, better known as S&H. Ever hear of S&H Green Stamps? No?

At their height, S&H printed three times more stamps than the United States government. They published enough catalogs to more than circle the earth. If you saved enough of their stamps, you could get ... a toaster. Or another appliance. One school in Erie, Pennsylvania, saved 5.4 million green stamps and bought two gorillas for a local zoo.

You would take these stamps to a place called a redemption center to be exchanged. Redeemed. The company is still around, online, and offers what are called greenpoints. Amazingly enough, they are still accepting stamps. If you find any in the attic, you can still turn them in. It's not too late.

With endless patience, at infinite cost to himself, God had been waiting since the beginning of history—watching, suffering, loving—until in the fullness of time he sent his only begotten Son to a redemption center on a hill called Calvary. What does he want to redeem? *Everything.* All creation is groaning for redemption, Paul says. God wants to redeem you.

When circumstances look bleak, when the stock market is down, or when your morale is sinking or your assets are shrinking or your health is collapsing, you may wonder, *Is* anything *going up?*

Yes.

The chance to trust God when trusting isn't easy is wide open. The prospect for modeling hope for a hope-needy world is trending upward. And the possibility of cultivating a storm-proof faith is always going up. This is so because certain truths remain unchanged: God remains sovereign, grace beats sin, prayers get heard, the Bible endures, heaven's mercies spring up new every morning, the cross still testifies to the power of sacrificial love, the tomb is still empty, and the kingdom that Jesus announced is still expanding without needing to be bailed out by human efforts.

God is still in the business of redemption, specializing in bringing something very, very good out of something very, very bad. Julian of Norwich was a woman who could attest to that, living as she did during the Black Plague-infested fourteenth century. She was a great hoper, who sang a song of hope from the depths of the trials of her day:

But all shall be well,
And all shall be well,
And all manner of things shall be well...
He did not say, "You shall know no storms, no travails, no disease,"
He said, "You shall not be overcome."

PART SEVEN
flowing from here on out
»

Chapter 22

Ask for a Mountain

Everyone is looking for just the right logo. Companies spend millions of dollars to find a little icon that will communicate what they offer in a memorable and compelling way. Nike's logo is a little checkmark-looking symbol we call a swoosh. It is actually a stylized version of the wing from the Greek statute "Winged Victory," and the word *Nike* itself comes from the Greek word for victory. Their logo is a swoosh; their brand is *success*.

Apple's logo is, well, an apple. There is a story on the Internet that it was derived from the biblical tree of knowledge, but that may be urban myth. The logo, however, has come to represent the meeting of technology and intelligence at our fingertips. Their icon is an apple; their brand is *smart*.

McDonald's logo is so well known that as bad as I am at art, this is the one that always gets recognized even when *I* draw it. The Golden Arches. On every continent they mean joy and gratification—the Happy Meal. Their logo is a pair of arches; their brand is *pleasure*.

Mercedes-Benz's logo is a three-pointed star inside a circle. Inevitably, when I draw this one, people think it is the peace sign, but nobody is selling peace. The company chose a three-pointed star to express their engines' dominion in land, sky, and sea. Their logo is a star-in-a-circle; their brand is *power*.

If you were to choose a logo for your life, what would it be?

All four logos are known around the planet, but none of them is the *most* famous logo in the world, the one symbol that has been around for centuries. You see it on tombstones and T-shirts, chapels and necklaces; it is the single most famous logo the world has ever seen.

A cross.

Because it has been around so long, people often look at the cross without thinking what it means. There is a story about a woman who walks into a jewelry store and asks for a cross. The clerk replies, "Do you want an empty one, or one with a little man on it?"

The cross was not empty.

Crosses were a way of killing people. Devised by the Persians and popularized by Alexander the Great, the cross was perfected by the Romans as a means of deterring rebellion. It was intended to be both painful and humiliating; the English word "excruciating" comes from the Latin word for crucifixion.

Jesus himself said, "Whoever would come after me must deny themselves, take up their cross, and follow me." It was this image that came to represent the movement associated with Jesus.

Think about how strange this is: In its beginnings, this little movement called Christianity struggled under persecution, trying to attract people to become part of their cause, and the symbol they used to represent their message was not an icon of success, knowledge, pleasure, or power. They chose a symbol universally understood to represent scandal, failure, and death.

Who would choose a means of execution as their company logo? Imagine the electric company hiring a marketing consultant who advises them to make their primary image a little electric chair, with the catchy little slogan underneath, "The power is on."

When Jesus invited his followers to "take up their cross," it was not a call to annihilation. It was a call to spiritual greatness in the divine conspiracy of sacrificial love. Human beings were offered a cause worth living for, dying for, and being resurrected for. God was reconciling all things to himself, and evil, sin, death, and guilt were about to receive their eviction notice.

The cross was not empty. There was a man on it.

Now you and I have something worth living for, dying for, and being resurrected for—something more than success, smarts, pleasure, or power. The God of the cross is renewing and creating all things to flourish through the power of sacrificial love.

And we get to be a part.

» Ask God for a Glorious Burden

We sometimes yearn for a problem-free life, but that would be death by boredom. It is in working to solve problems and overcome challenges that we become the person God wants us to be. Every problem is an invitation from the Spirit, and when we say yes, we are in the flow.

So don't ask for comfort. Don't ask for ease. Don't ask for manageability. Ask to be given a burden for a challenge bigger than yourself—one that can make a difference in the world, one that will require the best you have to give it and then leave some space for God besides. Ask for a task that will keep you learning and growing and uncomfortable and hungry.

There can be no learning without novelty. There can be no novelty without risk. We cannot grow unless there has been a challenge to what is familiar and comfortable. The Spirit leads us into adventure. The Spirit leads us into a dangerous world. To ask for the Spirit is to ask for risk.

A friend of our family decided to change his name. Actually, he was leaving his first and last name alone, but he wanted to add a middle name: *Danger.* Seriously! (This is a true story—I have seen the paperwork.) He felt he had always been a compliant, middle-of-the-road, play-it-safe kind of person, and he wanted to do something to stake out a new identity.

It requires a lot of legal work to get your name changed, and this friend had to go to court multiple times. On the day of his final court appearance he was last on the docket. One of the cases before him involved two parties suing each other, who got so aggressive they had to be escorted out of the courtroom.

Everything finally went according to plan, and the judge granted my friend's request. As he was walking out the door, however, the bailiff stopped him. "Be careful. Those two men who got kicked out have started fighting in the parking lot. It's dangerous out there."

My friend knew this was a once-in-a-lifetime opportunity, and he showed the bailiff his paperwork. "It's okay," he said. "*Danger* is my middle name."

The Spirit wants to make you a dangerous person. The Spirit wants to make you threatening to all the forces of injustice and apathy and complacency that keep our world from flourishing. The Spirit wants to make you dangerously noncompliant in a broken world.

Ask God for a mountain.

» Finding Your Challenge

Caleb was one of twelve scouts sent to explore the Promised Land when Israel had left Egypt. When the scouts returned, ten of them said that the assignment was impossible and they should return to slavery in Egypt. Only Caleb and Joshua trusted God and said, "We can certainly do it."

Because of Israel's unbelief, Caleb had to spend forty years of his life wandering through the wilderness. By the time the Israelites crossed the Jordan River, he was eighty years old. Then another five years passed beyond that before the various tribes of Israel were assigned land to occupy. As Caleb described it years later,

> "I was forty years old when Moses ... sent me from Kadesh Barnea to explore the land. And I brought him back a report according to my convictions, but the others who went up with me made the hearts of the people melt with fear. I, however, followed the LORD my God wholeheartedly."

If you have a negative attitude and a small faith when you are forty, there is a good chance you will not have a negative attitude and a small faith when you are eighty-five, because there's a good chance you won't ever make it to eighty-five. Psychologist Martin Seligman studied several hundred people in a religious community and divided them into quartiles from most to least optimistic and faith-filled. He found that 90 percent of the most optimistic, faith-filled people were still alive at the age of eighty-five. But only 34 percent of the most negative, pessimistic people made it to that age.

Another study, the largest of its kind, tracked over 2,000 adults over the age of sixty-five in the southwestern United States. Optimistic people — faith-filled people — had better health habits, lower blood pressure, and feistier immune systems and were half as likely to die in the next year as negative people. If you have a positive attitude, you are likely to live a decade longer than people with a negative attitude. Are you happy to hear that? If not, you could be in serious trouble.

Twelve spies went out, but only Joshua and Caleb had faith. *We can do it!* they said. *Let's go do it.* The other ten, however, said, *It cannot be done. Let's go back and be slaves in Egypt.* Forty-five years later, Caleb was as feisty as ever. Want to guess what happened to the other ten by then? They were all dead. None of them made it to Caleb's age.

Faith is an amazing life-giver.

A friend of mine named Mark married a woman named Pauline Brand. Her father was Paul Brand, a great doctor who wrote a book with author Philip Yancey. Brand was also a brilliant doctor who devoted his life to serving many of the poorest of the poor. Yancey says he admires Paul Brand more than any other man he's known.

But maybe even more amazing than Paul's life was the life of his mother, Evelyn Brand. When she was a young woman she felt called by God to go to India. As a single woman in 1909, a calling like that required a truckload of faith and an equal amount of determination. She married a young man named Jessie and together they began a ministry to people in rural India, bringing education and medical supplies, and building roads to reduce the isolation of the poor.

Early in their ministry they went seven years without a single convert, but then a priest of a local tribal religion developed a fever and grew deathly ill. Nobody else would go near him, but Evelyn and Jessie nursed him as he was dying. He said, *This God, Jesus, must be the true God because only Jessie and Evelyn will care for me in my dying.*

The priest gave his children to them to care for after he died—and that became a spiritual turning point in that part of the world. People began to examine the life and teachings of Jesus, and in increasing numbers began to follow him. Evelyn and Jessie had thirteen years of productive service, then Jessie died. By this time, Evelyn was fifty years old, and everyone expected her to return to her home in England. But she would not do it. She was as feisty as Caleb.

She was known and loved for miles around as "Granny Brand," and she stayed another twenty years under the mission board she had served so faithfully. Her son, Paul, came over when she was seventy years old, and this is what he said about his mom: "This is how to grow old. Allow everything else to fall away until those around you see only love."

» Do Something Difficult

Caleb's desire for challenge was both God's gift to him and his gift to God. As he prepared to enter the Promised Land, this is what he said:

So here I am today, eighty-five years old! I am still as strong today as the day Moses sent me out; I'm just as vigorous to go out to battle now as I was then. Now, give me this hill country that the LORD promised me that day. You yourself heard then that the Anakites were there and their cities were large and fortified, but, the Lord helping me, I will drive them out just as he said.

Hill country is much more difficult to occupy than flat ground, but that is exactly what Caleb asked for—the hardest challenge. He had to face the Anakites, Israel's most formidable opponents, the ones talked about in Numbers 13 of whom the people said, "We saw the descendants of Anakites there. We seem like grasshoppers next to them."

Caleb asked for the hardest enemies—in the most dangerous territory.

Caleb was eighty-five years old, so you would think he was going to ask for a nice condo at Shalom Acres. But what he wanted was the privilege of a really hard assignment. He chose another battle before he checked out. *God, just give me the hill country.*

» "Give Me the Hill Country, God"

God has wired us so that our bodies, minds, and spirits require challenge, and we flourish especially when we face challenges for a cause greater than ourselves. We experience the flow of the Spirit most deeply when we focus on challenges that enrich the community and when we cease to be preoccupied with our own advancement.

When Joshua—like Caleb, one of the two faithful scouts—became the new leader when Moses departed, Caleb could have withdrawn or sulked. Instead, Caleb's engagement in life just kept growing. He immersed himself among the people around him. As his generation all died out he had to develop a whole new circle of friends as an older man. He became mentor, guide, and cheerleader for an entirely new generation, and he did it to such an extent that they all said they wanted eighty-five-year-old Caleb to lead them when they went to the hill country.

Challenges undertaken for the greater good bind us to people. The pursuit of comfort, however, leads to isolation—and isolation is terminal.

Dr. Marian Diamond, a researcher on aging at the University of California at Berkeley and one of the world's leading neuroanatomists, found that deliberately induced challenges are required to keep our brains healthy and developing. In one experiment, a group of rats was given food directly, while another group had obstacles placed in front of their food dish. Rats that had to overcome obstacles developed a thicker cortex and more dendrites, were able to navigate other mazes more quickly, and were able to solve problems more proficiently than the comfortable rats. The fewer problems that a rat had, the faster its brain went downhill. If you love a rat, give it problems.

Dr. Diamond also wanted to explore the effects of isolation on aging. She found that if twelve rats were in a cage together—a little community of rats—and given challenges, their brains developed more and had a thicker cortex than if they were given a challenge in complete isolation. Then she wanted to see how this worked with older rats, so she took rats that were six hundred days or older, the equivalent of a sixty-year-old human being. Same results.

She was invited to present her findings in Germany, and she found that the rats they were working with there lived to be eight hundred days old. This troubled her, because her rats started dying up to two hundred days earlier. So she told her researchers that there was one item they had not given their rats, and that they were going to start: They decided to give those rats love. The rats would face the same challenges as before, but after each challenge the researchers would pick up the rat and hold it in their hands, press it against their lab coats, pet it, and speak kindly to it. They would say, "You are one sweet rat," or whatever it is you say to affirm a rodent.

When they started loving those rats, those critters did more than break the eight-hundred-day barrier. At 904 days they were not only still alive, but still developing thicker cortexes. They had more developed brains under challenging conditions because facing challenges in community gives life and isolation destroys it.

> "Listen to me, house of Jacob.... Even to your old age and gray hairs I am he, I am he who will sustain you. I have made you and I will carry you; I will sustain you and I will rescue you." (Isaiah 46:3–4)

Life is not about comfort. It is about saying, "God, give me another mountain." It might look like Granny Brand. It might look like Caleb. It might be a story that gets told—or it might not. No one may know about your story but you and God. It doesn't matter.

Living the adventure God planned, becoming the person God created you to be, is not one pursuit among many. It is why you were born.

It is worth wanting above all else.

» Knowing Your Mountain

How will you recognize your mountain? There is no formula. Just as in every other area of your growth, your mountain will not look exactly like anyone else's. But often you will recognize it because it lies at the intersection of the tasks that tap into your greatest strengths and the needs that tap into your deepest passions. Yet know this for sure: *God has a mountain with your name on it.*

When Rich Stearns became engaged as a young man and new Christian, his fiancée wanted to register for china. But he said to her, "As long as there are children starving in the world, we will not own china, crystal, or silver." Then, as he entered the corporate world and started climbing the ladder, he discovered his remarkable gifts of leadership. He loved strategic thinking, team-building, and mission achievement. Twenty years later he became the CEO of Lennox, the top producer of luxury tableware — fine china — in the country.

One day he received a phone call from an organization called World Vision, asking if he would consider getting involved with them. So Rich went to Rakai, Uganda, an area considered ground zero for the AIDS pandemic. In that village he sat in a thatched hut with a thirteen-year-old boy with the same first name — Richard. One pile of stones outside the door marked where they had buried the boy's father, who had died of AIDS, and another pile of stones marked where they buried his mother, who also died of AIDS. That kind of thing happens every day in Africa.

Rich talked for a while with the boy — now the head of the household trying to raise his two younger brothers — and asked him at one point, "Do you have a Bible?"

Yes, the boy said, and he went into the other room and brought back the one book in their house.

"Are you able to read it?" Rich asked, and at that the boy's face lit up.

"I love to read the gospel of John because it says Jesus loves children," the boy said.

Indeed, as the song goes, Jesus loves "all the children of the world." There has never been anybody like Jesus to bring good news to a thirteen-year-old boy in a thatched hut, with a pile of stones where a mom and a dad ought to be.

Richard left his job and his house and his title and asked God for one more hill.

The logo of World Vision consists of its name with a little field of color and a shining star next to it. The star brings to mind the apostle Paul's call to people to "shine like stars" in an often-dark world. It is also reminiscent of the star that announced the presence of God to the world at Bethlehem. Even *World Vision* is only a little part of a larger and more wonderful vision we find at the beginning of John's Gospel: "In the beginning was the Word, and the Word was with God, and the Word was God … and the Word became flesh, and dwelt among us."

What we translate in English as "word" comes from the Greek word *logos*. It is where we get our word "logo."

Jesus is God's logo.

It is as if God has said, "I want my icon, my character, my representation, my will, my symbol to be wrapped up in one single expression. It is Jesus. He is it."

Jesus is God's logo. If you want to know what a life can look like when it is lived with the Spirit flowing from the belly, look at Jesus. On a mountain called Calvary, on a splintered cross, the sin that needed to be cleansed, the price that needed to be paid, was finally and fully paid by Jesus.

At the end of the day, we do not have a program, plan, platform, or product to help the world. We have a Savior. We do not point to success, knowledge, pleasure, or power. We point to a cross.

What is *your* logo?

We saw earlier part of the story about Evelyn Brand. Here is the rest of her story.

Toward the end of her life, everyone called her "Granny Brand." She had spent her life in India, including twenty years of widowhood, and at age seventy she received word from her home mission office in England that they were not going to give her another five-year term. They felt that she was simply getting too old.

But she was also stubborn.

A party was held to celebrate her time in India, and everyone there cheered her on. "Have a good trip back home," they all said.

"I'll tell you a little secret," she announced. "I'm not going back home. I'm staying in India."

Evelyn had had a little shack built with some resources that she had smuggled in. Then she bought a pony to get around the mountains, and this septuagenarian would ride from village to village on horseback to tell people about Jesus. She did that for five years on her own. One day, at seventy-five years old, she fell off and broke her hip. Her son, Paul Brand, the eminent doctor, said to her, "Mom, you had a great run. God's used you. It's time to turn it over now. You go on back home."

"I am not going back home," she said. *God, give me the mountain!* She spent another eighteen years traveling from one village to another on horseback. Falls, concussions, sicknesses, and aging could not stop her. Finally, when she hit ninety-three years old, she could not ride horseback any more. So the men in these villages — because they loved Granny Brand so much — put her on a stretcher and carried her from one village to another. She lived two more years and gave those years as a gift, carried on a stretcher, to help the poorest of the poor. She died, but she never retired. She just graduated.

If Granny Brand had a logo, it would not point toward success, smarts, pleasure, or power. It would be the stretcher on which she was carried up and down the mountains to pour out the end of her life in sacrificial love.

What a remarkable logo!

Your deepest longing should be to be alive with God, to become the person God made you to be, and to be used to help God's world flourish.

That is the life available to you every moment. It is the life found in Jesus, the man on the cross, who mastered sin in his death and mastered death in a tomb and who now dispenses life with unrivaled authority. It is available to you in this very moment, no matter what your situation. God is at work in this hour, and his purpose is to shape you to be not only his servant, but his friend. Out of your belly shall flow rivers of living water. Blessed are you.

Ask for a mountain.

sources

Chapter 1: Learn Why God Made You

14: "For we are God's handiwork": Ephesians 2:10.

16: "Know that the Lord Himself": Psalm 100:3 NASB.

16: "If anyone is in Christ": 2 Corinthians 5:17.

18: "Don't let anyone look down": 1 Timothy 4:12.

19: "I saw the Holy City": Revelation 21:2.

20: "The Spirit and the bride": Revelation 22:17.

Chapter 2: The Me I Don't Want to Be

22: Henri Nouwen, *Can You Drink This Cup?* Notre Dame, IN: Ave Maria Press, 1996, 89.

27: "We know that in all things": Romans 8:28.

28: "Rule-keeping does not": Galatians 3:12 *The Message*.

28: "I have come that you": John 10:10 paraphrased.

30: "When I came to die": From *Walden*. Quoted in William Irvine, *On Desire*. New York: Oxford University Press, 2006, 267.

30: Gordan MacKenzie, *Orbiting the Giant Hairball: A Corporate Fool's Guide to Surviving with Grace*. New York: Viking Press, 1998, 19.

30: A vision of languishing: Ezekiel 37.

30: "Grows and builds itself up": Ephesians 4:16.

31: "I have come that they": John 10:10.

31: Irenaeus, *Adversus Haereses*.

32: "With God, all things are possible": Mark 10:27 paraphrased.

32: "Today you will be with me": Luke 23:43.

Chapter 3: Discover the Flow

36: "Let anyone who is thirsty": John 7:37–39.

36: "You will receive power": Acts 1:8.

37: "Though you have not seen him": 1 Peter 1:8.

37: "Take my yoke upon you": Matthew 11:29.

40: "Breath of life": Genesis 2:7.

40: "As the deer pants for streams": Psalm 42:1.

41: "Whoever is thirsty": John 7:37 paraphrased.

41: "Then the angel showed me": Revelation 22:1–2.

42: "Love, joy, peace": Galatians 5:22–23.

43: "Do not quench the Spirit": 1 Thessalonians 5:19 NASB.

43: "Since we live by the Spirit": Galatians 5:25–26.

45: "There is a way that seemeth right": Prov. 14:12; 16:25 KJV.

Chapter 4: Find Out How *You* Grow

47: "Head and shoulders": 1 Samuel 9:2 NRSV.

47: "Tried walking around": 1 Samuel 17:39.

47: "I cannot go in these": 1 Samuel 17:39.

47: "Go, and the LORD be with you": 1 Samuel 17:37.

48: "Put on the full armor of God": Ephesians 6:11.

48: "Where the Spirit of the Lord is": 2 Corinthians 3:17.

50: C. S. Lewis, *Surprised by Joy.* New York: Harcourt Brace, 1955.

51: "Father, may they be one with you": John 17:21 paraphrased.

58: Saint Benedict: Quoted in Will Derske, *The Rule of St. Benedict for Beginners.* Collegeville, MN: Liturgical Press, 2003, 47.

58: "Indulge the sinful nature": Galatians 5:13.

59: "Don't give up meeting together": Hebrews 10:25 paraphrased.

Chapter 5: Surrender: The One Decision That Always Helps

60: "The fool has said in his heart": Psalm 14:1; 53:1 NASB.

60: "Will be like God": Genesis 3:5.

60: "Out of our bellies can flow": John 7:38 paraphrased.

60: John Calvin, *Institutes of the Christian Religion*, Book III, Chapter 7, Section 1: Quoted in Dallas Willard, *Renovation of the Heart.* Colorado Springs: NavPress, 2002, 143.

64: Alcoholics Anonymous, *The Big Book*, 4th Edition. New York: Alcoholics Anonymous World Services, 2002, 24.

65. Roy Baumeister: M. T. Gailliot, N. L. Mead, and R. F. Baumeister, "Self-Regulation." In *Handbook of Personality: Theory and Research,* 3rd edition. Edited by O. P. John et al. New York: Guilford Press, 2008, 472-91.

66: "Offer your bodies as a living sacrifice": Romans 12:2.

67: "I don't condemn you": John 8:11 paraphrased.

68: "Let this cup pass from me": Matthew 26:39 KJV.

68: "For you died, and your life": Colossians 3:3–4.

68: "Now show me your glory": Exodus 33:18.

69: "I will cause all my goodness": Exodus 33:19 MLB.

Chapter 6: Try Softer

72: Richard Rohr, *Everything Belongs: The Life of Contemplative Prayer.* New York: Crossroad, 2003, 143.

72: "Suppose one of you had a servant": Luke 17:7–10 NIV.

72: Prodigal son: Luke 15:11–32.

74: William Lang: Source unknown.

74: Jesus talked about a Pharisee: Luke 18:9–14.

75: Philip P. Hallie, *Lest Innocent Blood Be Shed: The Story of the Village of Le Chambon and How Goodness Happened There.* New York: Harper Perennial, 1994.

Chapter 7: Let Your Desires Lead You to God

79: "So Jacob served seven years": Genesis 29:20.

80: Who found a treasure: Matthew 13:44.

80: Who found a pearl: Matthew 13:45–46.

80: Jonathan Haidt, *The Happiness Hypothesis: Finding Modern Truth in Ancient Wisdom.* New York: Basic Books, 2005.

82: "Taste and see that the LORD": Psalm 34:8.

82: Lewis Smedes, *How Can It Be All Right When Everything Is All Wrong?* San Francisco: HarperSanFrancisco, 1992, 20.

82: "You open your hand": Psalm 145:16 NIV.

82: "One flesh" with Eve: Genesis 2:24.

83: *Book of Common Prayer,* Evening Prayers, Collect for Peace.

83: "Whoever wants to be my disciple": Mark 8:34.

83: "Every good and perfect gift": James 1:17.

83: "Hope deferred makes the heart sick": Proverbs 13:12.

84: Lydia: Acts 16:11–15.

85: "I have fought the good fight": 2 Timothy 4:7.

85: "Whatever your hand finds to do": Ecclesiastes 9:10.

85: Jonathan and David: 1 Samuel 20.

87: "Like a gold ring in a pig's snout": Proverbs 11:22.

87: Delilah: Judges 16.

Chapter 8: Think Great Thoughts

90: Elijah and Jezebel: 1 Kings 19: 1–18.

91: "Search me, God": Psalm 139:23.

91: "The mind controlled": Romans 8:6.

92: Kept in perfect peace: See Isaiah 26:3 KJV.

94: Like Adam and Eve: Genesis 3:8.

96: John Milton, *Paradise Lost,* Book One, lines 254–55.

98: Jeffrey Schwartz, *The Mind and the Brain: Neoplasticity and the Power of Mental Force.* New York: Harper Perennial, 2003, 325.

99: Joshua Bell: See www.boncherry.com/blog/2009/03/04/a-violinist-in-the-metro-subway/

100: "To what can I compare": Matthew 11:16–17 NIV.

Chapter 9: Feed Your Mind with Excellence

102: "Blessed are those": Psalm 1:1–3.

104: "Whatever is true": Philippians 4:8.

105: Jonathan Haidt, *The Happiness Hypothesis: Finding Modern Truth in Ancient Wisdom.* New York: Basic Books, 2005. See also http://www.virginia.edu/insideuva/2001/26/haidt.html and http://psycnet.apa.org/?fa=main.doiLanding&doi=10.1037/1522–3736.3.1.33c (accessed 3 September 2009).

105: Eugene Peterson, *Eat This Book: A Conversation in the Art of Spiritual Reading.* Grand Rapids: Eerdmans, 2006: quoted in Richard Foster, *Life With God: Reading the Bible for Spiritual Transformation.* New York: HarperOne, 2007, 1.

106: "These were the chiefs": Gen 36:15.

106: "The LORD is my shepherd": Psalm 23:1 KJV.

107: John Dewey: Quoted in David Marcum and Steven Smith, *Egonomics: What Makes Ego Our Greatest Asset (or Most Expensive Liability).* New York: Simon & Schuster/Fireside, 2008, 168.

110: Ellen Langer, *Mindfulness.* New York: Da Capo Press, 1990, ch. 1.

111: Eva Hermann, "In Prison—Yet Free." Philadelphia: Tract Association of Friends, 1984. www.tractassociation.org/InPrisonYetFree.html (accessed 3 September 2009).

111: "God is light": 1 John 1:5.

112: Mark Twain: See www.inspirationalstories.com/1/181.html

112: "Therefore everyone who hears": Matthew 7:24–25.

113: "Love one another": John 13:34.

Chapter 10: Never Worry Alone

115: "Peace, be still": Mark 4:39 KJV.

116: "For the Spirit God gave us": 2 Timothy 1:7.

116: "In this world you have tribulation": John 16:33 NASB.

116: Everett Ferguson, *Backgrounds of Early Christianity*, 3rd Edition. Grand Rapids: Eerdmans, 2003.

117: "My peace I give you": John 14:27.

117: Daniel Goleman, *Emotional Intelligence: Why It Can Matter More Than IQ.* New York: Bantam Books, 1994.

118: Edward M. Hallowell, *Worry: Hope and Help for a Common Condition.* New York: Ballantine Books, 1998.

119: "There is no fear in love": 1 John 4:18.

122: "Is anyone afraid or faint-hearted?": Deuteronomy 20:8.

123: "Which transcends all understanding": Philippians 4:7.

124: "Instead of worrying, pray": Philippians 4:6–7 *The Message.*

125: "Out of your bellies will flow": John 7:38 paraphrased.

Chapter 11: Let Your Talking Flow into Praying

132: Richard Foster, *Prayer.* New York: HarperOne, 1992, xi.

133: Mark Twain: Quoted in *Homiletics* 19, no. 1, January–February 2007, 50.

133: "Where can I go from your Spirit?": Psalm 139:7–8.

134: "Looking up to pray": John 11:41 paraphrased.

134: "Father, I thank you that you have heard me": John 11:41.

135: "Go on up, you baldhead!": 2 Kings 2:23 NIV.

136: "In everything": Philippians 4:6 NIV.

136: Shel Silverstein, *A Light in the Attic*. New York: HarperCollins, 1981.

136: "Nevertheless, not my will but yours be done": Mark 14:36 paraphrased.

Chapter 12: Temptation: How Not to Get Hooked

138: "No temptation has seized": 1 Corinthians 10:13 NIV.

138: Potiphar's wife: Genesis 39.

139: "Do not quench the Spirit": 1 Thessalonians 5:19 NASB.

139: "Committing adultery": See Matthew 5:28.

140: "I made a covenant with my eyes": Job 31:1 NIV.

141: "The joy of the Lord is your strength": Nehemiah 8:10.

141: "Rejoice in the Lord always": Philippians 4:4 NASB.

142: "Deliver us from evil": Matthew 6:13 KJV, NASB.

Chapter 13: Recognize Your Primary Flow-Blocker

143: *USA Today*: From a series of articles published in February 2003.

144: Study on incompetence: Source unknown.

145: Cornelius Plantinga, *Not the Way It's Supposed to Be: A Breviary of Sin*. Grand Rapids: Eerdmans, 1995, 2–3.

145: Eddie Izzard: Standup routine, date unknown.

146: Augustine and Pelagius: See further, for example, in Earle E. Cairns, *Christianity through the Centuries: A History of the Christian Church*, 3rd Edition. Grand Rapids: Zondervan, 1996, 130–31.

146: Richard Lovelace, *Dynamics of Spiritual Life: An Evangelical Theology of Renewal*. Downers Grove, IL: InterVarsity Press, 1979, 99ff.

147: Michael Mangis, *Signature Sins: Taming Our Wayward Hearts*. Downers Grove, IL: InterVarsity Press, 2008.

148: Sherlock Holmes: See the novels by Sir Arthur Conan Doyle.

148: Richard Rohr, *The Enneagram: A Christian Perspective*. New York: Crossroad, 2001.

149: "He must increase": John 3:30 KJV.

149: Simon Magnus: Acts 8:9–25.

150: Parable about the three servants: Matthew 25:14–30.

151: Winston Churchill, on Clement Atlee: Quoted in Alec Douglas-Home, *The Way the Wind Blows*. New York: Fontana, 1976.

151: Winston Churchill, on Lady Astor: Quoted in Consuelo Vanderbilt Balsan, *The Glitter and the Gold*. Maidstone, Kent, UK: George Mann Books, 1953.

151: "How good and pleasant it is": Psalm 133:1.

155: Jesus warned about people: Luke 6:41–42.

Chapter 14: When You Find Yourself Out of the Flow, Jump Back In

156: Carol Tavris and Elliot Aronson, *Mistakes Were Made (But Not by Me): Why We Justify Foolish Beliefs*. Wilmington, MA: Houghton Mifflin/Mariner, 2008.

157: David Marcum and Steven Smith, *Egonomics: What Makes Ego Our Greatest Asset (or Most Expensive Liability)*. New York: Simon & Schuster/Fireside, 2008, 41.

159: "Who can discern their own errors?": Psalm 19:12.

160: "Did not know that the LORD": Judges 16:20.

161: "Call evil good and good evil": Isaiah 5:20.

161: Madame Guyon: Quoted in Richard Foster, *Prayer: Finding the Heart's True Home*. New York: HarperOne, 1992, 30.

165: "You are the man!": 2 Samuel 12:7.

166: "If someone is caught in a sin": Galatians 6:1.

166: Frank Laubach: Cited by Dallas Willard in personal communication.

Chapter 15: Try Going Off the Deep End with God

172: "When you pray, go into your room": Matthew 6:6.

172: Abraham Kuyper: Cited by Richard Mouw in a public address.

174: "Bless the LORD, O my soul": Psalm 103:1 KJV.

174: "Why are you downcast": Psalms 42:5, 11; 43:5.

174: "As he was praying, the heavens opened": Luke 3:21 TLB.

174: "The news about him spread": Luke 5:15–16.

174: "One of those days Jesus went out": Luke 6:12.

174: "When Jesus heard what had happened": Matthew 14:13.

174: "While it was still dark, Jesus got up": Mark 1:35, 38.

175: "Satan has asked to sift all of you": Luke 22:31.

175: "Jesus went out as usual": Luke 22:39–42.

175: "As he was praying": Luke 9:29.

175: "God's Spirit is right alongside us": Romans 8:26–27 *The Message*.

176: Will Derske, *The Rule of St. Benedict for Beginners*. Collegeville, MN: Liturgical Press, 2003.

177: "Eat their own filth": 2 Kings 18:27 NIV.

177: "O LORD Almighty, God of Israel": Isaiah 37:14–17.

177: "I can do all things through Him": Philippians 4:13 NASB.

179: "The LORD bless you": Numbers 6:24–26 NRSV.

180: "Abba, Father": Romans 8:15; Galatians 4:6.

Chapter 16: Make Life-Giving Relationships a Top Priority

182: "The fellowship of the Spirit": See, for example, 2 Corinthians 6:14; 13:14; Philippians 2:1; 1 John 1:6.

183: Robert Putnam, *Bowling Alone: The Collapse and Revival of American Community*. New York: Simon & Schuster, 2000, 332.

183: "It isn't good for man": Genesis 2:18 TLB.

183: "Being rooted and established": Ephesians 3:17.

183: Donald Winnicott, *The Maturational Processes and the Facilitating Environment*. London: Hogarth Press, 1960.

186: "The only exercise I get": Source unknown. Also attributed to nineteenth-century U.S. Senator Chauncey Depew.

186: "Anyone who does not love": 1 John 3:14.

187: "You, my brothers and sisters": Galatians 5:13.

187: "Let us consider how we may": Hebrew 10:24–25.

188: Putnam, *Bowling Alone*.

190: "Satisfy us in the morning": Psalm 90:14.

190: "The joy of the Lord is your strength": Nehemiah 8:10.

190: "A twenty-year study of more than 4,700 people": "Infected with Happiness," *San Francisco Chronicle*, 5 December 2008, A1, 14.

192: Teilhard de Chardin: Quoted in Alan Loy McGinnis, *The Friendship Factor: How to Get Closer to the People You Care For*. Minneapolis: Augsburg Press, 1979, 192.

Chapter 17: Be Human

195: "A man after his own heart": 1 Samuel 13:14.

195: Anne Lamott, *Traveling Mercies: Some Thoughts on Faith*. New York: Doubleday/Pantheon, 1999.

197: "With glad and sincere hearts": Acts 2:46.

197: "Accept one another, then": Romans 15:7.

198: Henri J. M. Nouwen, *The Road to Daybreak: A Spiritual Journey*. New York: Doubleday/Image Books, 1990.

199: "Confess your sins to one another": James 5:16 NASB.

199: "Bridegroom of blood": Exodus 4:26.

199: "Curse God and die!": Job 2:9.

200: "When the disciple Peter": See Matthew 14:28–31; John 18:10; John 13:36–38 and 18:15–18; Matthew 16:22–23.

201: M. Scott Peck, *Further Along the Road Less Traveled: The Unending Journey Toward Spiritual Growth*. New York: Simon & Schuster/Touchstone, 1993, 211.

202: "Just as I am, without one plea": Words by Charlotte Elliott; tune by William B. Bradbury.

Chapter 18: Find a Few Difficult People to Help You Grow

203: George Bernard Shaw: Source unknown.

204: "You're familiar with the old written law": Matthew 5:43–48 *The Message*.

205: Jill Taylor, *My Stroke of Insight: A Brain Scientist's Personal Journey.* New York: Viking Press, 2008, 74.

206: "When someone gives you a hard time": Matthew 5:44–45 *The Message.*

207: "Do not grieve the Holy Spirit": Ephesians 4:30–31.

208: "Life-giving quarter-second": Daniel Goleman, *Emotional Intelligence: Why It Can Matter More Than IQ.* New York: Bantam Books, 1994.

208: "In your anger do not sin": Ephesians 4:26–27.

209: "You have heard that it is said": Matthew 5:38–39.

210: "If anyone forces you to go with them": Matthew 5:41.

211: Charles Lamb: Source unknown.

212: "But Benjamin is so young": Genesis 44:30–34 paraphrased.

Chapter 19: Let God Flow in Your Work

218: Dennis Bakke, Joy at Work: *A Revolutionary Approach to Fun on the Job.* Seattle: PVG, 2006.

218: Eugene H. Peterson, *Working the Angles: The Shape of Pastoral Integrity.* Grand Rapids: Eerdmans, 1987, 67.

219: "Six days you shall labor": Exodus 20:9, 11.

219: "See, I have chosen Bezalel": Exodus 31:2–5.

220: Marcus Buckingham: See Marcus Buckingham and Donald O. Clifton, *Now Discover Your Strengths.* New York: Simon & Schuster/Free Press, 2001.

220: "From strength to strength": Psalm 84:7.

220: Dorothy Sayers, *Creed or Chaos: Why Christians Must Choose Either Dogma or Disaster (Or, Why It Really Does Matter What You Believe).* New York: Harcourt, Brace & Jovanovich, 1949, 53.

222: "Rule" and "dominion" over the earth: Genesis 1:26, 28 TNIV, KJV.

222: "Unless the LORD builds the house": Psalm 127:1 NRSV.

223: Marcus Aurelius: Quoted in Will Derske, *The Rule of Benedict for Beginners.* Collegeville, MN: Liturgical Press, 2003, 17.

Chapter 20: Let Your Work Honor God

224: William Zinsser, *On Writing Well: An Informal Guide to Writing Non-fiction,* 2nd Edition. New York: HarperCollins, 1980, 176.

225: Andy Chan: Personal communication.

225: "Don't just do the minimum": Colossians 3:22–25 *The Message.*

225: "Whatever your hand finds to do": Ecclesiastes 9:10.

225: "Now old and well advanced": Genesis 24:1 NIV.

227: N. T. Wright: Lecture at InterVarsity Conference on Human Flourishing, December 2008. See http://thesuburbanchristian.blogspot.com/2008/12/tom-wright-on-human-flourishing.html (accessed 21 September 2009).

228: Robert Bellah, *Habits of the Heart.* Berkeley: University of California Press, 1985.

229: "When a farmer plows for planting": Isaiah 28:24–26, 29 NIV.

229: Miroslav Volf, *Work in the Spirit: Toward a Theology of Work*. Eugene, OR: Wipf & Stock, 2001, 114.

230: "The Son of Man did not come": Matthew 20:28; Mark 10:45.

230: "Went and traded with them": Matthew 25:16 NASB.

231: Martin Luther: Quoted in Leland Ryken, *Work and Leisure in Christian Perpsective*. Portland, OR: Multnomah, 1987, 130.

Chapter 21: You Have to Go through Exile before You Come Back Home

232: Jonathan Haidt, *The Happiness Hypothesis: Finding Modern Truth in Ancient Wisdom*. New York: Basic Books, 2005.

233: Robert C. Roberts, *Spiritual Emotions: A Psychology of Christian Virtues*. Grand Rapids: Eerdmans, 2007, 148ff.

235: Ernest Hemingway: Source unknown.

236: Meng Tzu: Quoted in Haidt, *The Happiness Hypothesis*, 135.

237: "The LORD was with Joseph": Genesis 39:2.

237: "We know that in all things": Romans 8:28.

237: No temptation is given to people: See 1 Corinthians 10:13.

237: They could command a mountain: See Mark 11:23.

238: Thomas Merton, *Seeds of Contemplation*. Boston: Shambala, 2003, 74.

239: "Mourn with those who mourn": Romans 12:15.

240: Joni Eareckson Tada: See, for example, *Joni: An Unforgettable Story* (Grand Rapids: Zondervan, 1976) and *A Lifetime of Wisdom: Filled with God's Precious Rubie*s (Grand Rapids: Zondervan, 2009).

240: Bill Dallas, *Lessons from San Quentin: Everything I Needed to Know about Life I Learned in Prison*. Wheaton, IL: Tyndale, 2009.

241: Søren Kierkegaard, *Christian Discourses*, translated by Walter Lowrie. 1941; reprint, Princeton: Princeton University Press, 1971.

242: All creation is groaning for redemption: See Romans 8:22.

242: Julian of Norwich, *Revelations of Divine Love*, ch. 27, Revelation 13.

Chapter 22: Ask for a Mountain

246: "Whoever would come after me": Matthew 16:24; Mark 8:34; Luke 9:23.

248: When the scouts returned: See Numbers 14:3–4.

248: "We can certainly do it": Numbers 13:30.

248: "I was forty years old when Moses": Joshua 14:7–8.

248: Martin Seligman, *Learned Optimism: How to Change Your Mind and Your Life*. New York: Simon & Schuster/Free Press, 1998, 7ff.

248: "Faith-filled people": Seligman, *Learned Optimism*, ch. 1.

249: Paul W. Brand and Philip Yancey, *Fearfully and Wonderfully Made*. Grand Rapids: Zondervan, 1980.

250: "So here I am today, eighty-five years old!": Joshua 14:10–12.

250: "We saw the descendants of Anakites there": Numbers 13:33 paraphrased.

250: Joshua became the new leader: See Deuteronomy 34:9; Joshua 1:1–3.

250: Marian Diamond, "Optimism about the Aging Brain," *Aging Today*, May-June 1998. See http://www.asaging.org/default/files/files/booklet_2001.pdf (accessed 21 September 2009).

252: Rich Stearns, *The Hole in Our Gospel: What Does God Expect of Us? The Answer That Changed My Life and Might Just Change the World.* Nashville: Thomas Nelson, 2009.

252: "All the children of the world": From "Jesus Loves the Little Children." Words by C. Herbert Woolston; tune by George F. Root.

252: "Shine like stars": Philippians 2:15 NIV.

253: "In the beginning was the Word": John 1:1, 14 KJV.

Soul Keeping
Study Guide and DVD

Caring for the Most
Important Part of You

Bestselling Author John Ortberg

In this six-session, video-based small group Bible study, Ortberg shows that caring for your soul is necessary for your Christian life. John shows participants what your soul is, why it is important, how to assess your soul's health, and how to care for it so that we can have a meaningful and beautiful life with God and others. When you nurture your soul, your life in this world will come to make sense again; you can find your way back to God from hopelessness, depression, relationship struggles, and a lack of fulfillment. Your soul's resting place is in God, and John Ortberg wants to take participants to that home.

This study guide with DVD includes a DVD with six video teaching sessions from John Ortberg and a study guide with discussion questions, video notes, and in-between studies.

Sessions include:

1. What Is the Soul?
2. The Struggle of the Soul
3. What the Soul Needs
4. The Practice of Grace
5. The Practice of Gratitude
6. The Practice of Growth

Available in stores and online!

The Me I Want to Be DVD Group Study

Becoming God's Best Version of You

John Ortberg

If God has a perfect vision for your life, why does spiritual growth seem so difficult? Pastor and bestselling author John Ortberg has some intriguing answers to that question, and he has organized his thoughts and God's words into a straightforward and timely guide for living your best life in *The Me I Want to Be*.

This DVD group study will show how God's perfect vision for you starts with a powerful promise. All those who trust in God "will be like a tree planted by the water that sends out its roots by the stream. The tree does not fear when heat comes; its leaves are always green. It has no worries in a year of drought and never fails to bear fruit" (Jeremiah 17:7-8).

John Ortberg urges you to recognize your brokenness, understand that God is the project manager, and follow God's directions. He also helps you gauge your spiritual health and measure the gap between where you are now and where God intends you to be.

Learn to be a thriving and flourishing Christ-follower as you study these five sessions.

The Me I Want to Be sessions include:

1. Discovering the Spirit
2. Renewing My Mind
3. Redeeming My Time
4. Deepening My Relationships
5. Transforming My Experience

Available in stores and online!

Who Is This Man?

Bestselling Author John Ortberg

Jesus's impact on our world is highly unlikely, widely inescapable, largely unknown, and decidedly double-edged. It is unlikely in light of the severe limitations of his earthly life; it is inescapable because of the range of impact; it is unknown because history doesn't connect dots; and it is doubled-edged because his followers have wreaked so much havoc, often in his name. He is history's most familiar figure, yet he is the man no one knows. His impact on the world is immense and non-accidental. From the Dark Ages to Post-Modernity he is the Man who won't go away. And yet ... you can miss him in historical lists for many reasons, maybe the most obvious being the way he lived his life. He did not loudly and demonstrably defend his movement in the spirit of a rising political or military leader. He did not lay out a case that history would judge his brand of belief superior in all future books. His life and teaching simply drew people to follow him. He made history by starting in a humble place, in a spirit of love and acceptance, and allowing each person space to respond. His vision of life continues to haunt and challenge humanity. His influence has swept over history bringing inspiration to what has happened in art, science, government, medicine, and education; he has taught humans about dignity, compassion, forgiveness, and hope.

Who Is This Man? DVD

Bestselling Author John Ortberg

In this five-session DVD-based small group bible study, *Who Is This Man?* John Ortberg reveals how Jesus made an inescapable influence on our world and you will learn how you can make one too.

Sessions include:

1. *The Man Who Won't Go Away*
2. *A Revolution of Humanity*
3. *The Power of Forgiveness*
4. *Why It's a Small World After All*
5. *Three Days That Changed the World*

The Life You've Always Wanted

Spiritual Disciples for Ordinary People

John Ortberg

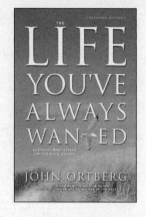

What does true spiritual life really look like? What keeps you from living such a life? What can you do to pursue it? If you're tired of the status quo — if you suspect that there is more to Christianity than what you've experienced — John Ortberg points to a road of transformation and spiritual vigor that anyone can take. It is the road that leads to *The Life You've Always Wanted*.

The Christian life is about more than being forgiven, more even than making it to heaven. John Ortberg calls us back to the dynamic heart of Christianity — God's power to bring change and growth — and shows us how we can attain it ...and why we should attain it. *The Life You've Always Wanted* offers modern perspectives on the ancient path of the spiritual disciplines. Ortberg shows us that Christianity isn't a matter of externals, of outer form that gets the church stamp of approval, but of Christ's character becoming etched with ever-increasing depth into our own character.

As with a marathon runner, the secret lies not in trying harder, but in training consistently. Hence the spiritual disciplines. They're neither taskmasters nor an end in themselves. They're exercises that strengthen our endurance race down the road of growth. As we continue down that road, we'll see the signposts of joy, peace, and kindness, and all the hallmarks of a faith that's vital, real, and growing.

Paved with humor and sparkling anecdotes, *The Life You've Always Wanted* is an encouraging and challenging approach to a Christian life that's worth living. Life on the edge that fills our ordinary world with new meaning, hope, change, and a joyous, growing closeness to Christ.

When the Game Is Over, It All Goes Back in the Box

John Ortberg

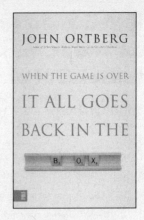

Remember the thrill of winning at checkers or Parcheesi? You become the Master of the Board – the victor over everyone else. But what happens after that? asks bestselling author John Ortberg. You know the answer: It all goes back in the box. You don't get to keep one token, one chip, one game card. In the end, the spoils of the game add up to nothing.

Using popular games as a metaphor for our temporal lives, *When the Game Is Over, It All Goes Back in the Box* neatly sorts out what's fleeting and what's permanent in God's kingdom. Being Master of the Board is not the point; being rich toward God is. Winning the game of life on Earth is a temporary victory; loving God and other people with all our hearts is an eternal one. Using humor, terrific stories, and a focus on winning "the right trophies," Ortberg paints a vivid picture of the priorities that all Christians will want to embrace.

When the Game Is Over, It All Goes Back in the Box

Six Sessions on Living Life in the Light of Eternity

John Ortberg with Stephen and Amanda Sorenson

In the six sessions you will learn how to:

- Live passionately and boldly
- Learn how to be active players in the game that pleases God
- Find your true mission and offer your best
- Fill each square on the board with what matters most
- Seek the richness of being instead of the richness of having

If You Want to Walk on Water, You've Got to Get Out of the Boat

John Ortberg

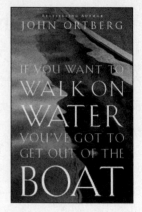

Deep within you lies the same faith and longing that sent Peter walking across the wind-swept Sea of Galilee toward Jesus.

John Ortberg invites you to consider the incredible potential that awaits you outside your comfort zone. Out on the risky waters of faith, Jesus is waiting to meet you in ways that will change you forever, deepening your character and your trust in God. The experience is terrifying. It's thrilling beyond belief. It's everything you'd expect of someone worthy to be called Lord.

The choice is yours to know him as only a water-walker can, aligning yourself with God's purpose for your life in the process. There's just one requirement: *If You Want to Walk on Water, You've Got to Get Out of the Boat.*

Everybody's Normal Till You Get to Know Them

John Ortberg

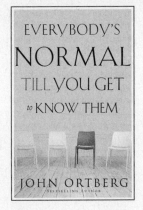

Not you, that's for sure! No one you've ever met, either. None of us are normal according to God's definition, and the closer we get to each other, the plainer that becomes.

Yet for all our quirks, sins, and jagged edges, we need each other. Community is more than just a word—it is one of our most fundamental requirements. So how do flawed, abnormal people such as ourselves master the forces that can drive us apart and come together in the life-changing relationships God designed us for?

In *Everybody's Normal Till You Get to Know Them*, teacher and bestselling author John Ortberg zooms in on the things that make community tick. You'll get a thought-provoking look at God's heart, at others, and at yourself. Even better, you'll gain wisdom and tools for drawing closer to others in powerful, impactful ways. With humor, insight, and a gift for storytelling, Ortberg shows how community pays tremendous dividends in happiness, health, support, and growth. It's where all of us weird, unwieldy people encounter God's love in tangible ways and discover the transforming power of being loved, accepted, and valued just the way we are.

God Is Closer Than You Think

This Can Be the Greatest Moment of Your Life Because This Moment Is the Place Where You Can Meet God

John Ortberg

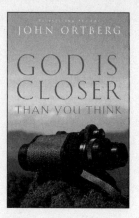

Intimacy with God can happen right now if you want it. A closeness you can feel, a goodness you can taste, a reality you can experience for yourself. That's what the Bible promises, so why settle for less? God is closer than you think, and connecting with him isn't for monks and ascetics. It's for business people, high school students, busy moms, single men, single women ... and most important, it's for YOU.

God Is Closer Than You Think shows how you can enjoy a vibrant, moment-by-moment relationship with your heavenly Father. Bestselling author John Ortberg reveals the face of God waiting to be discovered in the complex mosaic of your life. He shows you God's hand stretching toward you. And, with his gift for storytelling, Ortberg illustrates the ways you can reach toward God and complete the connection — to your joy and his.

Available in stores and online!